Everyday Wonders

Also by Barry Evans

The Wrong-Way Comet and Other Mysteries of Our Solar System,
TAB/McGraw Hill, 1992

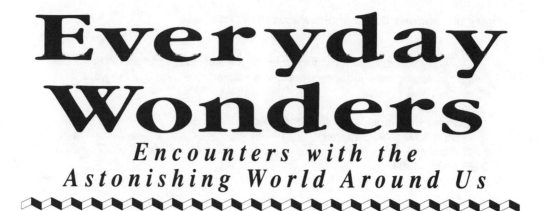

Everyday Wonders

Encounters with the
Astonishing World Around Us

B a r r y   E v a n s

CONTEMPORARY
BOOKS

CHICAGO

Library of Congress Cataloging-in-Publication Data

Evans, Barry.
    Everyday wonders : encounters with the astonishing world around us / Barry
Evans : including contributions from Linus Pauling, Stephen Jay Gould, Diane
Ackerman, and others.
        p.   cm.
    Includes bibliographical references and index.
    ISBN 0-8092-3798-9 (paper)
    1. Science—Popular works.   I. Pauling, Linus, 1901–   II. Title.
Q162.E88   1993
500—dc20   93-1949
                                                                  CIP

Interior illustrations by Andrew Toos.

Published by Contemporary Books, Inc.
Two Prudential Plaza, Chicago, Illinois 60601-6790
Manufactured in the United States of America
International Standard Book Number: 0-8092-3798-9
10   9   8   7   6   5   4   3   2   1

Dedicated to Martin Gardner,
whose "Mathematical Games" column was always
the first thing I read in Scientific American.
And I wasn't the only one.

Nothing is too wonderful to be true.

—Michael Faraday

Contents

Saturday: Day of Saturn

Sunday: Day of the Sun

Appendixes

Acknowledgments

*T*his book was a turning point for me: in my own eyes I graduated from "someone who writes" to "a writer." No such profound transformation occurs in a vacuum. I'm grateful to a whole community of "midwives."

For technical help, I thank Dr. Scott ("Walking Encyclopedia") Sandborn of NASA-Ames, who was always available and invaluable; Dr. Scott Hildreth of Chabot College, who reviewed the manuscript with a loving eye; Dr. Dennis Bazylinski of Virginia Tech and Dr. Albert Van Helden of Rice University; and my seven graceful guest contributors.

Illustrations came from all over. Special thanks to Nina Adelman (SLAC), Penny Ahlstrand (California Academy of Sciences), Gaynor Barber, Brian Day, Dr. Tom Eisner, Pete Hamilton, Dr. Bill Hartmann, Ramona Heimlich, Dewitt Jones, Pat Linse, Mike Moore (USGS), Paul Mortfield, Patricia Napoli (Serono Laboratories), Dr. Eric Newman, Dr. Eugene Stanley, Gérard Therin, Dr. Mervin Tuttle (Bat Conservation International), Laurie Vogel, Roger von Oech, and Dr. James Watson.

Location, they say in real estate, is everything. For providing me with cozy places to write I thank my Mum, Osha Reader, and my fellow Gondolynians.

I also appreciate exceptional support from Richard Bauhaus, Richard Beal, Mark Conover, Harvey Plotnick, and Tom Rogers. For emotional and editorial sustenance, I thank my buddy and wife, Louisa Rogers.

Everyday Wonders

Introduction

That Was Then. This Is Now.

Life is not a problem to be solved but a reality to be experienced.
—Søren Kierkegaard

Nothing evades our attention so persistently as that which is taken for granted. . . . Obvious facts tend to remain invisible.
—Gustav Ichheiser,
Appearances and Realities

*I*n the fall of 1978 I had just returned to North America after a yearlong round-the-world odyssey. It had been a time full of rich experiences and new friendships, but light on personal insight, which is really what I'd been seeking on my wanderings. To remedy that minor omission, I enrolled in a nine-day Buddhist retreat held on the beautiful, ocean-bounded grounds of a Catholic seminary on Cape Cod, Massachusetts.

The retreat was intense, involving about eight hours of meditation each day. It was also silent. We dressed silently, ate silently, showered silently, and walked silently, so as not to disturb the inner rhythm of concentration. The only exception to the rule of silence was a half-hour period after lunch each day, when we could approach our 81-year-old master, a Cambodian monk living in the United States, and ask for help with our contemplation. I decided at the outset that, as a matter of personal pride, I wouldn't take advantage of this respite. By the third day, I'd repented.

"Bhante," I said, "I'm having so much trouble with my meditation. My mind is constantly distracted and I never seem to stay centered for more than a few seconds at a time. What's really frustrating is that I've been meditating on and off for about 10 years, and this is even worse than all those other times in the past when I couldn't maintain my concentration. Can you help me?"

Bhante Dharmawara, 1979. (Barry Evans)

He looked at me with his ageless, jolly, baby-blue eyes. "That was then. This is now," he said. That was it. He didn't add or expound on these words. I finally nodded, thanked him, and he rose, bowed, and left me sitting there.

"That was then. This is now." Those six words have stayed with me for 14 years. When I find myself worrying about the future or feeling remorse about the past, the words come back. They foreshadow one of my purposes in writing this book: to celebrate the present.

Bhante's words are here now, an immediate mental response to any regrets I have about the past. All my "coulda, shoulda, woulda's" ("I coulda done this," "I shoulda done that") are transmuted into "That was then. This is now." Bhante's words echoed, with remarkable brevity, the pragmatism of Edward Fitzgerald's "Rubáiyát of Omar Khayyám":

> *The moving finger writes, and having writ*
> *Moves on; nor all your piety nor wit*
> *Shall lure it back to cancel half a line*
> *Nor all thy tears wash out a word of it.*

If the past is immutably frozen, the future is a fluid vision that may or may not come to be. Even the next few hours are uncertain, no matter how clear our plans. Days, weeks, and months ahead blur into uncertainties. I suppose Bhante would say about the future: "That will be. This is now."

Which brings us, by a not-too-subtle process of elimination, to the present. This book is about the present, because it's about awareness: noticing, stopping, looking, heeding, remarking, observing, beholding, discerning, perceiving, asking, examining, probing, considering, pondering, weighing, appraising, studying . . . right now. It's about wonder.

Wonder as Innocence

"Children enter school as question marks and leave as periods," wrote author and educator Neil Postman. I believe that what I've termed curiosity-wonder is innate to children, but that as adults we sometimes need to be reminded of it. Does the 5-year-old child who is full of questions lose his or her innocence and become the 18-year-old full of answers, as Postman implies?

For me, the answer is a qualified "yes." How about you? At the age of 5, you were probably a little mobile questioning machine, brimful of curiosity, noticing and wanting to know the answers about everything. And a few years later, your sense of curiosity may have been dampened, your questions having become less important than the answers (which determined whether you got a B+ or a B−). If your sense of curiosity remained undiminished through school, you're indeed blessed. Later in this book, we'll meet some remarkable people who have managed to keep their sense of wonder intact and lively throughout their lives.

It's instructive and awe-inspiring to watch and listen to the innocent spontaneity of humans during the first 1,500 or so days of their lives, up to age 4 or 5. Every other utterance is a question about something and everything in their environment:

> How high is up?
> Is the sea alive?
> What shape is red?
> When will I grow up?
> Where is heaven?
> What are the birds singing?
> Why does ice cream taste happy?

I believe that most children are later taught to come up with answers, not to wide-sky, open-ended questions like these, but to those cold-as-steel problems that demand just one answer, the right one:

> What's the capital of Cambodia?
> Who shot Lincoln?
> When was the Battle of Hastings?
> How many acres are in a square mile?
> What's the square root of 729?
> Who wrote *The Tempest*?

In this book, we'll try to recapture some of our childhood sense of wonder. Now, however, that sense will be accompanied by our adult capacity for reasoning to help us understand: "He who has imagination without learning has wings and no feet," said French essayist Joseph Joubert.

Wonder as Appreciation

In one of Gary Larson's whimsical "The Far Side" cartoons, two cows sit cross-legged across from one another. One, sporting a monk's robe (just like Bhante's!), counsels the other: "And, as you travel life's highway, don't forget to stop and eat the roses."

In this book, we'll not only stop and eat the roses; we'll also see what they're made of and why they taste so good!

Wonder as Awe and Curiosity

Thirteen hundred years ago, *wonder* was only a noun, synonymous with "miracle" or "marvel." *Beowulf*, written around A.D. 720, contains some of the oldest English prose ever written. In stanza XIII, we encounter the word for the first time:

> *Then, so I've heard, there were many warriors*
> *Round the gift-hall that fine morning;*
> *Chieftains came from near and far,*
> *Long distances, to look at the marvel, the monster's tracks.*

In the Old English verse, the last line reads, "geond wid-wegas wondor sceawian, lathes lastas." There it is, *wondor*, translated here as "marvel."

Today, *wonder*, both as a noun and verb, has many meanings (the *Oxford English Dictionary* lists a total of 43!). I'll be using two of its basic meanings as verbs in this book: "curiosity-wonder" (to think or speculate curiously, to meditate, ponder, or question) and "awe-wonder" (to be filled with admiration, amazement, or awe).

Suppose natives of a distant country were shown a beautiful clock for the first time. If they were filled with curiosity-wonder, they might try to figure out how it worked, what mechanism was hidden behind the face that caused the hands to move and the chimes to sound. If overtaken by awe-wonder, they'd be more likely to prostrate themselves in front of the clock and worship it, or mount it in a place of honor. The first, curiosity-wonder, implies an active response on the part of the onlooker, while awe-wonder results in more of a passive acceptance.

Each has a place in our lives. Let me give you an example. I'm an amateur astronomer, so much of my time stargazing is spent looking through my telescope, comparing the brightness and color of stars, noting the differences in the appearance of Jupiter's bands, or trying to see detail in faint galaxies and nebulae. At those times, I'm in my curiosity-wonder mode, wanting to know more, analyzing and trying to figure things out. For the most part, this book is about curiosity-wonder. It's about stopping and noticing phenomena in the world around us—air, water, light, gravity, breath, dolphins, rocks, wind, and heartbeats—and appreciating them more for understanding them a little.

Other times when stargazing, I walk away from my telescope and just breathe. That's when I experience long moments of awe-wonder, awe-full, precious, profound times. I know of no words to better express such moments than these: ". . . like lying on one's back as we did in Spain when we slept out looking up between the fig-branches into the star-corridors, the great seas and oceans of stars. Knowing what it was to be in the universe."[1]

That's awe-wonder. It's wonder-full, too.

Wonder as Discovery and Creativity

The best scientists and artists are those possessing the greatest sense of wonder. I can't prove that, any more than I can prove that the most beautiful people are those with the highest sense of self-worth. It's just

---

1. John Fowles, *The Collector*.

something I take for granted. I'm convinced strong links connect wonder, creativity, and discovery. Whether we're talking curiosity-wonder or awe-wonder, wonder presupposes innocence.

For the artist and scientist alike, wonder implies an openness to look at life, the environment, or the universe as if for the first time, without preconceptions. It calls for an unshackling from the past. ("This is now. That was then.") It's a willingness to make the question more important than the answer. Biochemist Albert Szent-Györgyi said, "Discovery consists of seeing what everybody has seen and thinking what nobody has thought." Pablo Picasso pointed out, "Computers are useless. They only give you answers."

In this book we'll look at the process of discovery and creativity through the eyes of those who have shown an unusual capacity for creativity and discovery. And we'll see how, time and again, innocent wonder was a vital ingredient in the lives of those who made the greatest contributions.

Wonder as the "Purloined Letter Syndrome"

"The fish is the last to see the water," said Ruth Benedict. Our lives are filled with obvious phenomena that sit right in front of our noses (sometimes literally), yet we often miss seeing them at all. I call it the purloined letter syndrome,[2] after Edgar Allan Poe's short story "The Purloined Letter."

Synopsis: If the letter in question becomes public, tragic consequences could result for the French royal family. The letter is known to have been stolen by a government minister and is believed to be in his home. The police can't accuse him, for fear the letter would be published, so they've made secret searches of his residence, looking in every conceivable hiding place: hollow chair legs, secret panels, the linings of books. It seems everything and everywhere has been checked, without success. Where *is* the letter? The story ends with the detective pointing out that the best hiding place is in full view. Sure enough, that's where he finds the letter, where every visitor could have seen it: hanging from the mantelpiece over the fireplace, as obvious as obvious could be.

Similarly, obvious, unnoticed facts abound in our everyday lives.

---

2. This idea originated with a blurb on the back of Eviatar Zerubavel's book *The Seven Day Circle*, to which I refer later. David Landes wrote, "[Zerubavel] is the master detective of society's purloined letter—those aspects that are so ubiquitous and familiar that nobody notices them."

Living with them on a day-to-day basis, we may never question them. For example:

♦ Gravity is a constant force in our lives (notice it now, between your derrière and the chair you're sitting on), yet we rarely give it a second thought. See Chapter 5, "Crisis on the Scales."

♦ Much of the stuff that constitutes our bodies originated billions of years ago in the fiery hearts of stars. See Chapter 9, "From Whence We Came."

♦ Most faucets turn on counter-clockwise. Would it be different if civilization had arisen in the Southern Hemisphere? Would clocks go the other way? See Chapter 6, "Hemicentrism."

♦ The act of putting our hands in water flowing from a faucet links us to the world. See Chapter 17, "Politics of a Supermolecule."

♦ Every breath links us with everyone who died more than 100 years ago. See Chapter 3, "Cleopatra's Last Breath."

♦ Our lives are paced in 7-day cycles called "weeks"—except in countries and cultures in which the week is anything from 4 to 19 days. See Chapter 8, "For the Week-Hearted."

♦ The image we have of ourselves is the opposite of how others see us. We normally view ourselves in mirrors, in a right-left inverted view. Is there a difference? See Chapter 15, "The Right (and Left) Stuff."

These examples appear in this book because I know of no more direct route to wonder than to notice that which is in front of my nose, seeing it as if for the first time. The child who asks, "Why do we have colors?" is our door to the world of the unseen obvious.

Our Tools

The tools offered you in this book are various, including:

♦ Essays on all the above and more, everything from elements to evolution and from time to turtle navigation.

♦ Puzzles (with hints, in case you're a puzzle-phobe) to remind you there's usually more than one way of looking at anything. You'll have ample opportunity to flex your "wonder muscles."

♦ Conversations with some remarkable scientists and science writers.

♦ Quotations, for fun and insight.

The book is structured into seven sections, each representing one day of the week. If you like, you can read Monday's section on a Monday. But don't worry about it: it's just a way of organizing the book into manageable chunks (for the reader's ease and the author's sanity alike!). The book isn't meant to be read sequentially. If you want to open it up at random, go ahead. It's waiting for you.

Time to Go Play

Come play with your childhood sense of wonder. Prepare to be astonished, to learn. And while you're at it, stop and eat the roses.

If I had influence with the good fairy who is supposed to preside over the christening of all children, I should ask that her gift to each child in the world be a sense of wonder so indestructible that it would last a lifetime, as an unfailing antidote against the boredom and disenchantments of later years, the sterile preoccupation with things that are artificial, the alienation from the sources of our strength.

—Rachel Carson, *The Sense of Wonder*

Monday

Day of the Moon

Welcome to Monday, the moon's day. And the first day of the week.

Or is it the second day of the week? There appears to be some confusion about it. Most calendars show the week starting on Sunday and ending on Saturday—except for desk calendars. They show the first day of the week as Monday, and collectively, Saturday and Sunday are known as the weekend, of course. This ambiguity is the result of the Christian assignment of the Lord's Day to the day after the Jewish Sabbath (see Chapter 8, "For the Week-Hearted").

While some people dread returning to work on Mondays, many others psychologically restart their lives, heralding it as a day of renewal and bright beginnings. Welcome to the first day of a week of everyday wonders.

One

The 12-Second Life

When one subtracts from life infancy (which is vegetation), sleep, eating and swilling—buttoning and unbuttoning—how much remains of a downright existence?—the summer of a dormouse.

—Byron, *Diary*, December 1813

*O*ur lives last for two or three billion seconds.

The universe is 15 billion years old.

Looking at those two sentences on the computer screen in front of me, I feel slightly giddy. I have a faint whiff of what the first statement means, and very little understanding of the second. The exercise that follows has helped me to glimpse "all of time." That's the period that has elapsed since the Big Bang, the moment that defines "time zero," when time started. Most physicists agree that talking about what happened "before" the Big Bang is meaningless, since the universe was infinitely small at the moment of the Big Bang (that is, it had no size at all!), and any meaningful concept of time depends on measurable space.

One problem with getting a handle on time is that a relatively "short" period, such as the span of my life, feels arbitrary. I have nothing in my day-to-day experience with which to compare it. Looking back, some years seem fleeting and empty, others rich and drawn out. I can viscerally experience a single minute simply by looking at my watch or counting my pulse. But much more than that and the feeling is lost to

11

mere words. Do we live long lives or short lives? I don't know, and I doubt if I'll know on my deathbed. The problem with trying to grasp time is that we're too much *in* time.

Distance, at least up to a global scale, is different. Tell me something is 100 miles away, and I can imagine driving there. One hundred miles is a concrete, readily accessible concept. I can compare that 100 miles with other known distances: New York to Philadelphia, four marathons, whatever. Unlike time, it's tangible.

The purpose of this exercise is to compare three very different lengths of time: 12 seconds of the immediate present, your lifetime, and the age of the universe. In order to do this, we're going to pretend that your entire life lasts only 12 seconds. Here's how it works: in a 12-second period, you're going to imagine viewing your entire life, from birth to death, in 12 images. Each image represents a six-year segment of your life. To make the arithmetic work smoothly, your death will occur at age 72. (If you're over 72 now, you can wonder at the impertinence of such thought experiments!) Run through this 12-second journey with me, in which each second is equivalent to six years.

In the first second, you're born, you learn to talk, and you start kindergarten. By the end of your third second, you're thinking about college or a job. A couple of seconds later, you're probably married, having kids, and paying off the mortgage. At ten seconds, you're retiring, and at the end of 12 seconds, you breathe your last breath. Close your eyes and try to visualize it, counting slowly up to 12. If visualization isn't your strong suit, divide a sheet of paper into 12 frames, as I've done, and draw significant events from your life for each of those time periods. You'll have to anticipate the periods beyond your present age, of course, so that you end up with 12 pictures.

When I did this, for instance, I picked a memorable moment when I stood at the summit of an icy volcano in New Zealand for my "24-to-30-year" picture frame. That adventure left a powerful impression on me, so it's easy to use it to encompass those six years in 1 second. For age 60 to 66, I decided I'd like to do some sailing in the Caribbean, so that image becomes my 1-second snapshot to sum up those six years.

When you've got your pictures, either mentally or on paper in front of you, get used to living your entire life in 12 seconds. Count "one" and look at the first frame, at "two" move on to the second, and so on. At the end of "twelve," picture yourself gracefully (or defiantly, your choice) expiring. When you feel comfortable with the idea of a 12-second life, make this mental comparison: *There are roughly as many of those 12-*

Second 1 = Birth to age 6
Second 2 = Age 6 to 12
Second 3 = Age 12 to 18
Second 4 = Age 18 to 24
Second 5 = Age 24 to 30
Second 6 = Age 30 to 36
Second 7 = Age 36 to 42
Second 8 = Age 42 to 48
Second 9 = Age 48 to 54
Second 10 = Age 54 to 60
Second 11 = Age 60 to 66
Second 12 = Age 66 to 72

My "12-second life," with each panel representing six years. Try this yourself, drawing a significant event for each panel. You'll have to imagine panels beyond your present age. To simplify the arithmetic, you're scheduled to die at age 72. (If you're 80 now, your imagination may be severely challenged!)

second lifetimes in a span of 72 years as there are spans of 72 years in the age of the universe.

Got it? If you can glimpse how a full lifetime of learning and talking, sleeping and eating, laughing and crying, stacks up against that 12-second life, you'll be able to get some feel for the age of the universe by comparison with your actual life.

Just a Second!

Of course, to some creatures, 12 seconds is a long time. We must appear like sleepwalkers to a fly, which has a reaction time of one-hundredth of a second (ever wonder why it's so hard to swat one?), or to an adult mayfly, for whom 12 seconds represents a significant portion of its one-day active life. Let's take a closer look at the shortest time interval we normally use, the second.

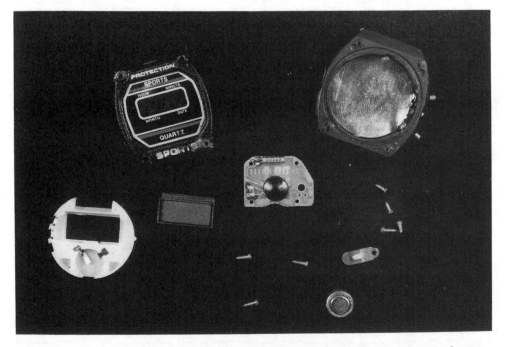

In one second, the quartz crystal inside a digital watch (even this one, bought for 75 cents in a street market in Peru) vibrates 32,768 times. The quartz crystal is inside the round cylinder, which you can see above the round housing on the printed circuit board in the center of the photo. (Barry Evans)

There went one. And another. And another. They keep on escaping, running through my fingers like there's no tomorrow. Come to think of it, there isn't, tomorrow never comes (curious, that).

Yesterday's a different story. It came, all right, and went. All 86,400 seconds of it. When I'm up against a deadline, I remind myself that there are over half a million seconds in a week, lots of time to get things done. (Counting in seconds, you celebrate your 1 billionth birthday a few months before your "actual" 32nd birthday.)

In any one average second:

♦ Five members of our species are born and two die.
♦ The sun radiates 13 million times the annual U.S. energy consumption.
♦ A man's testicles manufacture over 2,000 sperm, each carrying his entire genetic code: about the same amount of information as that stored on a compact disc.[1]
♦ Eight million blood cells in a normal, healthy human body die.
♦ Worldwide, about $32,000 is spent on the military (of which the U.S. accounts for nearly one-third).
♦ The U.S. accrues $7,000 interest on its national debt.
♦ The quartz crystal in your wristwatch vibrates 32,768 times.
♦ The U.S. Postal Service delivers 200 pieces of junk mail.
♦ Light travels three-quarters of the distance from the moon to the Earth.

Half a Million Trillion Seconds

Let's go to the other extreme, the age of the universe. Surprising things can happen in great stretches of time. For instance, a tongue-in-cheek (but accurate!) definition of hydrogen is, "A light colorless gas that, given enough time, turns into people." This refers to the fact that the early

---

1. The human genome consists of approximately three billion pairs of nucleotide bases, each of which can assume one of four possibilities (G-C, C-G, T-A, A-T) so the information in the genome is equivalent to six billion bits or 750 megabytes. A compact disc holds about 600 megabytes. Harvard molecular biologist Walter Gilbert envisages taking this analogy into the real world: he foresees the not-too-distant day when you'll take your ultimate "personal CD," that is, your entire genetic code on a compact disc, with you when you visit your doctor. (*Omni*, February 1992.)

Light travels three-quarters of the way from the moon to Earth in one second. The moon is 1¹/₃ light-seconds away, while the sun is eight minutes away. Amateur astronomers may do a doubletake looking at this photograph: it's a composite of the quarter and three-quarters moon. The sun is shining from the right for the right-hand half of the photo and from the left for the left-hand half. (Lick Observatory, copyright © UC Regents, photo #L9)

universe consisted mostly of hydrogen,[2] and 15 billion years (or half a million trillion seconds[3]) later, here we are.

The immense age of the universe gave astrophysicist Robert Dicke an opportunity to counter the fuzziness many of us feel when we try to fathom the immense size and age of the universe. The universe, he claims, isn't much use without something being aware of it. (Does a falling tree make a sound if nothing or nobody hears it?) For awareness, you need life and mind. For life and mind, we think you need carbon, oxygen, silicon, and iron—that is, elements heavier than hydrogen and helium. To create these heavier elements, you need thermonuclear combustion, which requires billions of years of "cooking time" in a star (see Chapter 9, "From Whence We Came"). And for that, according to Einstein's general relativity, you need a universe several billion light-years of space in size. So the universe has to be as large and as old as it is in order for us to be asking questions about how large and old it is!

This is essentially a statement of the so-called weak anthropic principle. Another way of stating it is, "What we see is limited by our presence as observers." Dicke is saying that we can't see a universe much younger than 15 billion years because the universe needs that much time to create observers. The strong anthropic principle says, "The universe must be such as to admit the creation of observers within it at some state."[4]

The Cosmos in D.C.

In my book *The Wrong-Way Comet and Other Mysteries of Our Solar System*, I offer one way to picture the enormous age of the universe with

---

2. Soon after the Big Bang, the universe consisted of about three parts hydrogen to one part helium-4, with traces of helium-3, deuterium (isotopes of helium and hydrogen, respectively), and lithium-7, an isotope of lithium. (The suffix numbers refer to "isotopes" of an element. See Glossary.)

3. Huge numbers are difficult to comprehend. Once, in an effort to illustrate what a trillion really means (a huge galaxy containing an estimated trillion stars had been found), I pointed out in my syndicated astronomy column that the human brain contained about one-hundredth that many neurons. A concerned reader wrote, "Dear Barry, I counted the neurons in my brain and there weren't nearly as many as you said. It makes me wonder if the rest of your information is right."

4. If this intrigues you, I recommend *The Anthropic Cosmological Principle* by John D. Barrow and Frank J. Tipler. It's important to understand that neither of these anthropic principles is a scientific hypothesis, since they can't be proven wrong. (Thus, the existence of God isn't a scientific hypothesis, while general relativity is.)

Top of postage stamp = NOW

Bottom of postage stamp = 8,000 B.C.

1 BILLION
YEARS AGO

555' 5⅛" = 15 BILLION YEARS

BIG BANG

"All of time," as represented by the height of the Washington Monument. The thickness of a postage stamp placed on the apex represents the last 10,000 years of time, that is, all of recorded history. (The monument is actually capped by a nine-inch-high, six-pound aluminum pyramid. When it was made in 1884, it was the largest and costliest block of aluminum ever cast.)

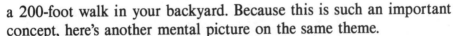

a 200-foot walk in your backyard. Because this is such an important concept, here's another mental picture on the same theme.

Picture the Washington Monument, all 555 feet, 5⅛ inches of it. Scramble up the side and balance a postage stamp on its very apex. Got that? Great, now come on down and stand back to admire your handiwork. The height of the monument represents the age of the universe, about 15 billion years, so the entire history of the cosmos is represented in the monument. On this scale, the thickness of your stamp on top represents the last 10,000 years. All of history, from the misty origins of agriculture and the very first cities (such as Jericho, arguably the oldest settlement in the world, dating back to about 8,000 B.C.) to the present time is depicted in the thickness of your stamp!

OK, analogy over. You can go get your stamp back now.

TWO

Blind Luck

Statistically, the probability of any one of us being here is so small that you'd think the mere fact of existing would keep us all in a contented dazzlement of surprise.

—Lewis Thomas, *The Lives of a Cell*

Extinction is such a barrier to dialogue.

—Ian Shoales

*H*ere we are.

It's impossible to overemphasize the role of luck in those three words. So many instances of pure, blind, zillion-to-one chancy luck allow you to sit there reading this book just as I now sit here writing in front of my computer. Five examples, out of many:

♦ Blind luck led to the start of life on Earth about four billion years ago. Through a series of uncountable permutations and combinations, the precursor molecules of life somehow fashioned themselves into an arrangement that automatically reproduced itself. This fluke may have happened more than once. Some investigators now believe it took many attempts to start the four-billion-year chain, since all but the final version were wiped out by the then-frequent bombardments of huge comets and asteroids.

The moment of conception. In size, the human egg overwhelms spermatozoa seeking to enter. Normally, only one out of five million gene-carrying spermatozoa penetrates the egg, which immediately seals itself against other intruders. Who would "you" be if some sperm other than the one from which you were conceived had entered first? (Serono Laboratories, Inc.)

◆ Untold numbers of reproductions over four billion years (first by mitosis, i.e., self-reproduction, and later by sexual interweaving of genetic material) resulted in the humans you know as Mom and Dad. If any one of those reproductions had misfired, you wouldn't be reading this.

◆ For that matter, what were the odds of your parents not meeting? Imagine how easily they might not have.

◆ Taking this to its logical conclusion, of some five million spermatozoa, it was blind luck that the one that gave rise to the entity you recognize as "you" won the race to your mother's egg. Congratulations!

◆ Yet only 65 million years ago (just a moment of geological time) an asteroid perhaps the size of Manhattan Island collided at high speed with our planet, causing global devastation. The collision is referred to as the "KT" impact, so named because it occurred at the boundary of the Cretaceous (from the Latin *kreta*, meaning chalk) and Tertiary geological periods. Its casualties included every dinosaur then alive. Mammals, which until then had been small and generally nocturnal, not only survived, they thrived in the vacant ecological niches left by the dinosaurs. Eventually they branched out into hundreds of new species, including Homo sapiens—you and me. Had that asteroid missed, none of us would be here (as we shall soon see).

I hope you'll agree that the odds of you or me being alive are infinitesimally small (while the odds of you *and* me being alive are smaller still!). In the face of all this blind luck, I find it impossible not to feel blessed. Of course, I could take the other tack and say, "The fact that I am here proves that the odds of it happening are 100 percent." But late at night, when the house is quiet, wonder takes over from pragmatism, Lewis Thomas's "contented dazzlement of surprise" hits, and gratitude floods in.

Dinosaurs and Mammals: The Bad News

Let's take a closer look at the last example. Twenty years ago, almost no one had connected dinosaur extinction with asteroid impact. Now the most frequently asked question isn't "Did it happen?" but "Where was the impact?"

"Dinosaurs" is the name we give to two extraordinarily successful orders of land reptiles, Saurichians (reptilelike hip) and Ornithischians (birdlike hip). They came on the scene about the same time mammals did, around 200 million years ago. For over 100 million years, dinosaurs were the lords of the Earth as they evolved into our cornflakes-box heroes: tyrannosaurus, apatosaurus (aka brontosaurus), triceratops, and all the rest. Over the past two decades, their status has been elevated from slow, dim-witted, and clumsy brutes into fast-moving, relatively bright, and dexterous creatures.

Today, controversy abounds regarding the role of the asteroid in causing their extinction. Those who believe that dinosaurs might have become extinct anyway, asteroid or no asteroid, point to their already dwindling number of species (from 61 species six million years before the impact to 18 species two million years before). Other experts point out that some of the last species of dinosaurs, like triceratops, were flourishing just before the impact. They may have been the best-designed dinosaurs, and maybe they would have evolved into even faster, brighter, and more agile animals.[5] If only that asteroid hadn't hit . . .

---

5. For an educated guess, read *The New Dinosaurs: An Alternative Evolution* by Dougal Dixon, in which he fantasizes about what might have happened if the asteroid had missed. Great fun!

Triceratops, 20 feet long and 8 feet high, one of the last and most successful of the Ornithischian group of dinosaurs. Despite its three horns (after which it's named) and fierce armor, it was a herbivore. It appears to have become extinct right at the time of the KT impact, so it was in all likelihood a victim of a chance asteroid collision. This fossilized skeleton comes from a formation a little more than 65 million years old. (Copyright © Smithsonian Institution)

British Museum reconstruction of a triceratops. (Barry Evans)

Artist's impressions of the impact that is believed to have caused the extinction of the dinosaurs 65 million years ago. A six-mile-diameter meteorite, heated to incandescence as it plummeted through the atmosphere, probably impacted the Earth near Mérida, in Mexico's north Yucatán Peninsula. The 150-mile-diameter crater is now thought to be buried beneath over half a mile of sediments. (Copyright © William K. Hartmann, from *The History of the Earth*)

But it did. Most scientists are quite certain that a six-mile-diameter asteroid[6] caused devastation to the entire biosphere when it struck our planet 65 million years ago. Many now think it hit what is now Mexico's Yucatán Peninsula, near the city of Mérida. At that time the area was a

---

6. Or nucleus of a comet. Most investigators favor an asteroid, but some are attracted to a comet on the following grounds: Some evidence exists for periodic mass extinctions at about 26-million-year intervals. One possible mechanism to explain this (if there is anything to be explained, which many investigators doubt) is that the sun has a companion star. Nicknamed "Nemesis" after the Greek goddess of retribution, it would have to be in a highly elliptical orbit so that it approaches the sun once about every 26 million years. At perihelion it would disturb the Oort Cloud, a vast "shell" of comets a thousand times farther out from the sun than Earth, causing a "rain" of comets to fall in toward the sun. Some would eventually impact Earth over a period of a few thousand years. Nemesis, if it exists, would be small, faint, and hard to find. A few astronomers (notably UC Berkeley's Richard Muller) are looking, though.

shallow sea, and the resultant tidal wave (three miles high, according to one researcher) was only one local cause of destruction. Other effects, which caused deaths and extinctions on a global scale:

♦ Worldwide darkness, resulting from dust in the atmosphere, caused photosynthesis to virtually cease.

♦ Cold, because not just sunlight, but the sun's heat, was cut off by the dust, resulted in worldwide freezing temperatures lasting many months.

♦ Fire storms, triggered by incandescent material hurled from the impact site, devastated forests in North and South America.

♦ Acid rain, from "shock heating" of the atmosphere by the asteroid as it plunged to Earth, wreaked havoc on marine animals and plants.

♦ Following the cold spell, "greenhouse effect" warming resulted from the vast quantities of water vapor and carbon dioxide that were expelled from the sea and from pulverized limestone into the atmosphere.

The global devastation resulted in Earth losing about two-thirds of all its species, including every dinosaur and all land animals weighing over 50 pounds. In the ocean, 90 percent of all marine invertebrates, including ammonites, became extinct.

The Good News

The good news is that mammals survived. While dinosaurs were evolving into huge, efficient, and powerful creatures, mammals never progressed beyond a few inches in size. They differed from dinosaurs in many other ways, too, which helped them survive the crisis. They were generally smaller than dinosaurs, so they required less food to stay alive; furry and warm-blooded, making them more adaptable than dinosaurs to drastic changes in temperature; and night-loving (possibly an adaptation to protect them from carnivorous species of dinosaurs), so they could survive in low-light conditions.

The immediate postimpact environment was inhospitable to dinosaurs. With little available vegetation, cold temperatures, and darkness, dinosaurs died while mammals somehow made it through. Our devastated world belonged to them, and they were soon able to take advantage of ecological niches left vacant by the dinosaurs. Within 3 or 4 million years the first modern carnivores, ancestors of lions and bears, appeared. By 55 million years ago, rodents, bats, dog-sized protohorses, and protomonkeys emerged. By 20 million years ago, some of those early tree-living monkeys had evolved into tailless apes. As recently as 5 or 6 million years ago, our ancestors split from the main primate line—and here we are.

None of the above would have happened if the asteroid had missed. As paleontologist Stephen Jay Gould remarks, "In an entirely literal sense, we owe our existence . . . to our lucky stars."

Three

Cleopatra's Last Breath

To an asp, which she applies to her breast. (Stage direction.)

—William Shakespeare, *Antony and Cleopatra*

*T*ake a deep breath. Did you notice? Did you catch a whiff of Shakespeare, a dash of Socrates, a trace of Cleopatra? No? They were there, just the same. You just inhaled millions of molecules that each of *them* once exhaled.

Let's take a look at just one historic breath: Cleopatra's last. This came, if we're to believe Shakespeare, moments after his second-most-interesting stage direction, quoted above.[7] You just inhaled about 20 molecules from her dying exhale. You may have heard such a claim previously and wondered if it was true. I'd certainly dismissed it as pure hokum, but I was wrong. A few minutes with reference books and a calculator showed that, in very round numbers, Earth's atmosphere contains 1.6×10^{44} atoms, and each breath we take contains 8×10^{22} atoms.[8] To get some sense of that number, if each of those 8×10^{22}

---

7. The *most* interesting, in my view, being, "Exit, pursued by a bear."
8. Very large numbers are usually handled by using powers of 10. The superscripted numbers (i.e., 44 and 22) indicate that 10 is to be multiplied by itself that many times. For instance, 10^2 means $10 \times 10 = 100$, and $10^5 = 10 \times 10 \times 10 \times 10 \times 10 = 100,000$. So 8×10^{22} means 8 times 10 multiplied by itself 22 times—that is, 8 followed by 22 zeros, or 80,000,000,000,000,000,000,000.

atoms was a grain of sand, you could cover the entire United States to the depth of an eight-story building with each breath you exhaled!

Dividing the number of atoms in the atmosphere as a whole by the number in any one breath, we can show that 1 in every 2×10^{21} atoms we breathe in the air right now is from Cleopatra's dying breath (assuming, reasonably enough, that winds over two millennia have done a thorough worldwide mixing job). This, in turn, means that each of us inhales about 40 atoms—say 20 molecules—from her last gasp with every breath we take.[9]

In fact, it's probably safe to say that each breath you take includes air that passed out of the lungs of everyone who has ever lived, at least up to a hundred or so years ago (to allow time for their breath to be sufficiently well mixed in the atmosphere). For someone who died more recently, say Elvis, the mixing process probably hasn't been thorough enough (sorry). But it's a safe bet that your last inhale did include molecules from Plato, Pontius Pilate, Charlemagne, Michelangelo, and Marie Antoinette.

Breathing the Astrodome

Human beings are significant movers of air. Every day we breathe in and out 500 cubic feet of the stuff. If I live to be 80, I'll have taken over 200 million breaths, moving nearly 600 tons of air in the process (more than the weight of a fully laden Boeing 747). On average, each of us will breathe 15 million cubic feet of air in our lifetimes. Four of us together will breathe a volume of air equivalent to that enclosed by the Houston Astrodome!

From our first natal inhale to our parting exhale, breath happens, regularly and dependably, nonstop. It takes place in two distinct phases. When we inhale, we suck comparatively cold, oxygen-rich air in through our noses and, when we're gasping, our mouths. After barely a moment's

---

9. Still not convinced? Earth's atmosphere weighs 5,000 trillion tons, and one ounce of air contains 1,000 billion trillion atoms. Hence, there are about 1.6×10^{44} atoms in the atmosphere. Every day you breathe 500 cubic feet of air (mostly nitrogen), which weighs 1.25 grams/liter (0.078 pounds per cubic foot). Hence, with each breath you inhale about 0.08 ounces, i.e., 8.0×10^{22} atoms per breath. So on average, one in every 2.0×10^{21} atoms is from Cleopatra's last gasp. But you breathe in about 8.0×10^{22} atoms each breath. So you inhale about 40 atoms (say, 20 molecules) from Cleo's last breath every time you breathe. Even if you lose a few due to uneven mixing, photodissociation, etc., you're still left with a significant number.

Four of us in our lifetimes inhale a volume of air equivalent to that enclosed by the Houston Astrodome. (Greater Houston Convention and Visitors Bureau)

pause, we exhale, having warmed the air and traded some of its "fresh" oxygen for some "stale" carbon dioxide. (I put the words *fresh* and *stale* in quotation marks because they're relative terms, as any self-respecting plant will tell you. Plants work in reverse: carbon dioxide in, oxygen out.) For adult humans, the whole process typically lasts 12 seconds, the time it takes us to read 20 or 30 words. Waking or sleeping, fighting or making love, riding a bike or knitting a sweater, breathing stays with us from birth to death.

This automatic process is regulated by a deceptively simple feedback mechanism. When carbon dioxide in our bloodstream builds up to a critical level (which it does every few seconds) we inhale. It's a finely tuned process: an increase of only three parts in a thousand of carbon dioxide automatically causes our finely tuned feedback mechanisms to double the volume of air we move in and out of our lungs.

The whole procedure is so effortless and mindless that it takes willpower to interrupt the cycle and fight the body's natural instincts. When we were young, my sister and I would compete in breath-holding competitions, staring and straining, trying to block out our bodies' demand for oxygen. Just a few more seconds . . . then we'd gulp and wheeze and accuse the other of cheating. That was 40 years ago. Even

today, I secretly play the same game if I'm in
a meeting or at a lecture and bored.
Now anything over two minutes wins my
personal gold medal. That's no big deal:
"free" divers regularly stay down
for three minutes, while the
underwater record is over
six minutes.

My Talisman

For many years, I carried a smooth stone in my pocket wherever I went.
It was my talisman, an ever-present reminder that my life was richer
than I usually felt it to be. In Walt Whitman's words, "I am larger, better
than I thought / I did not know I held so much goodness."

Now, breath is my talisman. When I'm tense—driving in heavy
traffic, giving a speech, feeling defensive in an argument—conscious
breathing reminds me, "It's OK. Relax and slow down. Nothing really
matters. You're larger and better than you think!" My breath is like a
childhood teddy bear, always there, comforting, nonjudgmental, safe, and
dependable.

Pay attention to your own breath now. Be aware of its subtle
nuances, how much warmer your exhale feels in your nostrils than your
inhale, the progressive rise from belly to chest, the smoothness with
which your body reverses the cycle, from in to out and from out to in.
Now breathe through your mouth. Notice, again, the temperature
difference, more pronounced on the wetness of your tongue and throat.
Imagine the zillions of impurities inhaled into your lungs and resume
breathing through your nose, with gratitude for the complex filtering/
warming/moistening system between your nostrils and throat.

Try inhaling and swallowing simultaneously, then give thanks for
that little flap of elastic cartilage in your throat, your epiglottis, that
immediately cuts off the air. It's there to prevent food and liquid from
entering your lungs. You're usually only aware of it when it has a
momentary glitch and you choke.

Breathing awareness is an ancient centering device for meditators. I
remember Dr. Richard Alpert, aka Baba Ram Dass, talking about his
initiation into a form of *vipassana* (mindfulness) meditation. He arrived

at a Buddhist monastery in Thailand, where a monk instructed him to sit quietly in his room and count his breaths. "What else?" he asked. "Nothing else. That's it!" he was told. (If you've never tried this, do so now. Close your eyes and count your breaths. It's unusual for someone who doesn't meditate regularly to get much beyond ten breaths without losing concentration.) From time to time, another monk would come to the room and repeat the instruction: "Keep counting your breath." If the novices stuck it out, after days or weeks or months of practice in this form of meditation, they would begin to appreciate the sublime behind every breath. And that, according to Baba Ram Dass, was when the real work of self-understanding and mastery of their emotions began.

Your work can begin right now, with your next breath. You can enjoy the company of the rich and famous, from Cleopatra to Napoleon. Best of all, it's free!

A Conversation with
Linus Pauling

————

One way for me to have a new idea is to set my unconscious to work on a problem. This is probably what the philosopher Avicenna, a thousand years ago, also did when he was unable to solve a problem. He would go to the mosque and pray for his understanding to be opened and his difficulties to be smoothed away; he probably had fixed the problem in his mind before going to the mosque, and his nature was such that his unconscious could then set to work on it. . . .

— Linus Pauling, 1969

*L*inus Pauling was born in 1901 in Portland, Oregon. He received his Ph.D. from Cal Tech in 1925 and was professor of chemistry there from 1931 to 1963. He's only recently resigned as head of the Linus Pauling Institute of Science and Medicine in Palo Alto, California, and lives nearby on the coast at Big Sur. Pauling is the only person to have received two unshared Nobel Prizes: the 1954 chemistry prize and the 1962 peace prize.

One hundred years ago, "chemistry" consisted of several quite separate fields, including inorganic chemistry, organic chemistry, and analytical chemistry. Many consider that Pauling's greatest contribution

Linus Pauling. (Barry Evans)

to science as a whole has been to unify these disciplines into one: physical chemistry, which now incorporates quantum physics. He's been called "the first molecular biologist."

The day the 1962 peace prize was announced, October 10, 1963, was (not coincidentally) the day the ban on U.S.–U.S.S.R. atmospheric nuclear testing came into effect. Pauling, who had been an ardent and active opponent of nuclear-bomb testing (citing the damaging effects of radioactive fallout on human genes), said then that he valued the peace prize more than the chemistry prize.

For the last 10 years, Pauling has been the subject of fierce controversy on the value of taking megadoses of vitamin C. His book *How to Live Longer and Feel Better* advocates taking up to 18,000 milligrams of vitamin C daily to ward off colds and flu and help prevent cancer, arthritis, rheumatism, and heart disease. That's 300 times the U.S. recommended daily allowance!

Pauling is a walking advertisement for his dietary and vitamin recommendations. He is tall, lithe, and lean, with piercing blue eyes and a phenomenal memory. When he talked to me in early 1991, he appeared to have more in common with a 5-year-old about to see the ocean for the first time than with an 89-year-old who has seen—and participated in—several scientific revolutions.

Barry Evans   Can you tell me something about the state of knowledge in chemistry and physics when you were a boy?

Linus Pauling   Major scientific revolutions had taken place just before I was born, in 1901. In particular, the period from 1895 to 1900 saw vast improvements in our understanding.

Take physics. In a short period that began in 1895, the electron was discovered, x-rays and radioactivity discovered, spectroscopy had begun in earnest, and quantum theory discovered, most of this between 1895 and 1900. What became clear was that Newtonian physics and electromagnetic theory didn't answer all of the questions, and it didn't apply to many phenomena. Around the same time, too, relativity was discovered and the Michelson-Morley experiment[10] was carried out.

In chemistry, there had been great developments, since Lavoisier had founded what was called modern chemistry 150 years earlier. Lavoisier recognized the difference between elements and compounds. Then Dalton came along with quantitative ideas about molecules, and the chemical bond was invented, in about 1850. So much information about the chemical structure of molecules had been formulated, but there were still many questions that couldn't be answered in 1900. What is the chemical bond? For example, if each carbon atom forms four bonds with other atoms, just what does that mean? Especially after the discovery of electrons and nuclei of atoms.

Or take the old quantum theory, which had originated in 1900 with Max Planck. By 1920 it was pretty well developed and answered some of these questions, in that you obtained a theoretical result that agreed with experiment and was different from what classical theory would give. But sometimes it didn't work. It gave the wrong answer, and people began fiddling with it to see what else was there.

So, especially up to the time when quantum mechanics was discovered, there were a great many questions that one could ask and not find the answer to. I think a student might ask his teacher, "Why is it that such and such an observation is made?" And the teacher might have to answer, "Well, nobody really knows. That's something we don't understand." There was a tremendous amount of uncertainty in these sciences. Now and especially since 1926, when quantum mechanics was developed, a science teacher can answer almost all questions a student might ask.

Today, there are still many basic questions that we don't know the answer to, but not nearly so many as there were 50 or 80 years ago.

B. E. Do you think the fact that so much is now known inhibits curiosity?

---

10. In 1887, A. A. Michelson and E. W. Morley paved the way for Einstein's special relativity by demonstrating that light travels at the same velocity parallel to Earth's direction of motion around the sun as at right angles to it. This appeared to show that there is no fixed frame of reference, or "ether."

L. P.   I am sure there are many young people who are not at all put off by the fact that we know many answers that weren't known 60 or 70 years ago. There's still a great deal that isn't known. I certainly continue to look for phenomena that I don't understand.

For instance, this morning, before breakfast, I was making an effort to develop a theory of Trouton's rule, which involves the thermodynamic properties of what happens when a liquid is boiled into a gas.[11] Nobody really knows why it works, but I'm certainly closer now to understanding it than I was when I wrote my freshman chemistry textbook in 1960.

B. E.   How did you come to be thinking about this before breakfast?

L. P.   A few days ago I read in *Nature* an article which discussed Trouton's rule, and I thought, "This isn't a very good job. I did a better job in my book written 30 years ago!" The author had essentially restated the problem without explaining why. So I decided it was high time that I developed a new theory, and for two or three days I've been thinking about it. I got out a copy of my book and made some calculations, and this morning I was still thinking, and I'm quite optimistic that I may be able to formulate a theory to explain the rule.

B. E.   Is this a typical process with you, to carry a problem around in your head for a while?

L. P.   Oh yes. One time, it took me seven years before the answer came to me. I'd heard a lecture on the theory of general anesthesiology in 1952. At that time no one really had any idea why certain agents acted as anesthetics. What caught my attention at the lecture was the fact that the noble gas xenon was a good—but expensive—anesthetic. I thought about it for several days, then went on to other things.

Seven years later, I read a manuscript about the crystal structure of a particular compound, a hydrate, nothing to do with anesthetics. As I was reading it, I suddenly said to myself, "I understand anesthesia!"

---

11. Trouton's rule states that for almost all liquids, with a few well-known exceptions like water, the entropy of vaporization is the same. Take two very different elements: the noble gas neon boils at 20 degrees above absolute zero, while the metal gold boils at 3,000 degrees above absolute zero. In effect, Trouton's rule says that for both neon and gold, the heat of vaporization is proportional to the absolute temperature at which the substance boils.

What had happened was that I saw a similarity in this crystal hydrate with the structure of xenon hydrate. I already knew the structure of xenon hydrate—it had been determined two years earlier by a young associate of mine, but that apparently wasn't enough to make me conscious of the fact that *that* had something to do with xenon's being an anesthetic agent. But this new crystal structure was the last piece of the puzzle I'd been carrying around for seven years, and I saw immediately how certain hydrates, including that of xenon, could trap ions and interfere with electrical oscillations in the brain, in other words, acting as anesthetics.

It was a very exciting moment! It took a few months to confirm and publish the result, but I was quite sure then and there that I had the right answer.

B. E.   How do you explain your knack for making discoveries?

L. P.   I think I was born with an exceptional memory, and I have acquired a tremendous background knowledge of chemistry and related subjects. I was fortunate when I was a boy in having good teachers who didn't put me off learning, so that my curiosity was not quenched, and I was not given the impression that there were any limits to my understanding.

I think that people who say, "I have no gift for mathematics," really just had the bad luck of falling behind in the study of mathematics, which is such a logical subject, built up from basic parts to the more advanced parts. If you fall behind because there's something you haven't understood, then you're not going to understand anything which follows from that something.

I've said that the passing grade in mathematics should be 100 percent. Suppose it's 70 percent, then you go on to the next year, and again you only understand 70 percent, so this time you only understand 70 percent of the 70 percent that you did understand, or 49 percent. The following year, you understand 70 percent of that, or 35 percent, and so on. So the student gives up and says, "I'm just incapable of understanding!"

I was fortunate that this didn't happen to me. In fact, I had the feeling that I could understand everything! And I continue to be astonished at the discoveries that scientists and others continue to make about the nature of the world.

I've retained this feeling that if I try hard enough, I can understand something. When I read *Nature*, here's somebody reporting something, and if it fits into my picture of the universe, OK, I won't think any more about it. But if it doesn't fit in, then I ask, "Can I find out something new by seeing why it doesn't fit in?"

B. E.   Have you always felt that way?

L. P.   I think so, yes. When I was a boy, I began formulating a picture of the universe, and there were parts of the universe I didn't understand and didn't make any effort to understand. But there were also parts of the universe that I tried to understand. And I think I was observant even then.

I remember I was in Portland, perhaps 10 or 11 years old. I was walking along in the rain with an umbrella over my head, and there was a streetlight ahead—it was an arc lamp in those days. So there was this point of light up ahead, but what I noticed was that not only could I see this point of light, but also I saw eight symmetrical little rainbow patterns, spectra of light. I wondered why, and wondered long enough so that I still remembered this episode years later when I learned about the diffraction of light by a ruled grating. Of course, the threads in the umbrella acted as a cross grating, producing the diffraction pattern that I noticed.

I didn't understand it at the time because I didn't know about the wave nature of light and diffraction phenomena, but some years later in college I did understand. So I was interested, even then, in building up a consistent, rational picture of the universe, and after I got reasonably mature, I had developed a picture, which included things I didn't understand.

B. E.   You have a reputation for knowing a lot in many different fields of knowledge.

L. P.   I think it's valid, yes. For instance, many of my discoveries have been the result of applying quantum mechanics to chemical problems. This is how it is: There are many theoretical physicists who are smarter than I am and who know more about theoretical physics than I know. There are a good number of chemists who know what I know, or knew in 1927, say. But there is no one else, probably, who combined these two. The theoretical physicists could have solved the problems, but they didn't know what the problems were. The chemists knew what the problems were, but didn't know how to solve them. I knew what the problems were and knew how to solve them.

B. E.   Is a theoretical understanding of some phenomenon a complete understanding?

L. P.   Not always. Let me give you an example. It's well known that the number of neutrons in an atomic nucleus determines its shape. Below 90, the nucleus is always spherical, and above, it's always elongated.

This is a fact, it's observed, and it's predicted by the wave equations of quantum mechanics. But it's not explaining it. I discussed this many years ago with Aage Bohr [Niels Bohr's son], who insisted that there was nothing to explain because mathematics showed it to be so. Now that didn't satisfy me. I wanted to know why it happened, not what the equations predicted!

I thought about this and other aspects of nuclear structure year after year. In the meantime, the nuclear physics people had been carrying out experiments and gathering a great body of information about the nuclei. All of this was done after quantum mechanics had been discovered, so the nuclear theoretical physicists would say, "Let's see if the Schrödinger wave equation agrees with the observations." Of course, it does, but they didn't ask the question *why*. Why do you get these differences from one nucleus to another?

There are 10 million chemical substances, or molecules, described in the literature, but only 1,500 different chemical nuclei, a pretty minor matter in comparison.[12] Nevertheless, I'm interested in these 1,500 different nuclei. Why does one differ from another? Why does a certain property change from one nucleus to the adjacent nucleus?

This is the difference between the way I think and the way many theorists think: I can make predictions about a property, such as the energy level of a nucleus, based not on mathematics, but on a picture that I've formed in my mind. Sometimes I think I can do a better job [than many theorists] in some cases, by reducing the complexity of the problem.

B. E.   Are you able to actually visualize the structure of whole molecular structures in your mind? For instance, the alpha helix, which you discovered in 1948 and which started a revolution that led to the discovery of the structure of DNA?

---

12. The actual composition of a nucleus of an element depends on two numbers: (1) the number of protons present, called the atomic number, which determines what the element is, and (2) the number of neutrons for that element, which refers to the different isotopes. Each element has, on average, 10 to 15 known isotopes.

L. P.   Oh yes. Starting in 1927, I started determining very complicated crystal structures by saying that I wasn't satisfied with just interpreting the x-ray data in a straightforward manner. I said, I'll take all of the information that I have that has a bearing on possible structures for this particular crystal, and I'll combine this information with the x-ray data. It was essentially saying, I'll take some guidance from the simpler conclusions I can reach from the x-ray experiments, and then I'll ask myself, "If I were this substance, and constrained by these pieces of information, what structure would I assume?" And so I would predict a structure and then calculate the x-ray intensities to see if they agreed. And if they agreed, I said, well, I've got the right structure.

B. E.   When did you first start thinking about the problem of the polypeptide chains, which led to the alpha-helix breakthrough?

L. P.   In 1937, but without success, and I decided then that I didn't have enough data. I thought that there must be something unusual about proteins that I didn't know, so I initiated a program of investigation on proteinlike substances. By 1948, we knew a lot more about these structures, and one day I sat down to think about this. I was sure that by now, after 11 years of research, something unusual would have turned up, yet it hadn't. In fact, we had nothing in 1948 that I didn't know in 1937. I realized I had all the data I needed back in 1937, and I just hadn't thought it out enough.

    So I stopped asking the question I'd been asking all along, which was, "What would a polypeptide chain look like if it satisfied a requirement that is indicated by the x-ray diffraction pattern?" Now I asked the question, "How would I fold if I were a polypeptide chain?" Two hours later I had the answer! It was very satisfying.

B. E.   Over 40 years ago you said, "If you want to get a good idea, you've got to have a lot of ideas, and throw away the bad ones." Does your reputation as a maverick come from putting out a lot of ideas to the world, knowing that some of them will probably be wrong?

L. P.   Well, I have a lot of ideas that the world never hears about! When I said that, I didn't go on to say how you know which are the bad ones! Sometimes I follow up an idea year after year without talking about it. In one case I worked on an idea for 30 years, from

1922 to 1952. Finally a student of mine got the answer, so I stopped working on it.

B. E. Is scientific education as good now as it was when you were at college?

L. P. Well, there is one aspect of graduate work that bothers me. I've pestered some of my grandchildren with respect to this. When I went to graduate school, I got there the 28th of September, say. By the 28th of December I had written my first experimental paper with my teacher, and I had learned x-ray crystallography in its simpler forms reasonably well in these three months, not to mention a heavy course load in mathematics and physics and 25 hours a week doing research. In another three months I had sent off another paper (this time by myself). So every few months I would send off some new results for publication. Now my grandchildren would go three years without having published! I said to them, "You have to find some field of investigation where you can answer questions reasonably fast!"

B. E. Most people know you through your books espousing the value of vitamin C. How did you get into that?

L. P. In 1965, I received the Virchow Medal in medicine. At the medal ceremony in New York, I talked about the marvelous discoveries that scientists had made during the previous 25 years and said that I hoped I could live another 25 years, so I could enjoy and appreciate the marvelous studies that I was sure scientists would be making during that time.

Irwin Stone, a biochemist, was present at the ceremony. He wrote to me after, saying, "If you take 3 grams of vitamin C a day, you'll live for another 50 years!" That started me taking high doses of vitamin C. I now take 18 grams a day.

B. E. It's obvious that you still get enormous pleasure from your work.

L. P. Oh yes, I get great enjoyment from reading the scientific literature, seeing what other scientists have discovered. And of course I get great pleasure when I think I've discovered something, or found the answer to some question that's been puzzling me. That pleases me very much.

Monday's Puzzles

Yoga for the Brain

I believe my objection to the notion of "problem" is due to my deep conviction that the moment one labels something as a "problem," that's when the real problem starts.

—Raymond Smullyan,
What Is the Name of This Book?

*B*rainteasers are to your mind what yoga is to your body. Both promote flexibility and the ability to stretch beyond previous limitations, mental or physical.

Over 100 years ago, U.S. psychologist Edward Thorndike tried to learn something about how chimpanzees think by presenting them with a puzzle and observing how they solved it. For instance, on the floor of the chimp's cage was a stick, and just out of reach beyond the bars was a banana. After getting frustrated trying to reach the banana, the animal would usually sit down and apparently ponder. Then it would suddenly jump up, seize the stick, and use it as an extension of its arm to get the fruit.

More recently, when behaviorist Konrad Lorenz set similar tasks, he got similar results. (This time, the banana was in the cage hanging out of the chimpanzee's reach, and there was a box in another part of the cage.) "The matter gave him no peace, and he returned to it again. Then, suddenly—there is no other way to describe it—his previously gloomy face lit up. The next moment he somersaulted over to the box in sheer high spirits. Completely assured of his success, he pushed the box below the banana and climbed up on it. No one watching him could doubt the existence of a genuine 'aha!' experience in anthropoid apes."

According to Thorndike, "A problem exists when the goal that is sought is not directly attainable by the performance of a simple act available in the animal's repertory; the solution calls for either a novel action or a new integration of available actions."[13]

Since thoughts generally precede actions, the purpose (in case you need to justify having fun!) of puzzle solving is clear: to help the mind to either think in a novel way or to combine old ways of thinking. What's the difference? When, 6,000 years ago in what is now the Ukraine, someone first mounted a horse, that person was thinking in a new way. Similarly when the first cart was made, a new way of thinking was invoked. But when a horse was first hitched to a cart, old ways of thinking were combined in a novel way.

Nothing's quite that simple, of course. In the first experiment, it might appear that the chimpanzee had found a novel way of using a stick. But suppose it had been carefully observing the cage being swept using a broom on the end of a broomhandle. You could then make the case that it was combining two ways of thinking: if a stick can be used to reach detritus on the cage floor, then it can also be used to reach a banana outside the cage. The solution to many puzzles seem to have this same gray quality.

Most of the teasers that follow (immediately, and throughout the book) are akin to Lorenz's "aha!" puzzles: they are simple when you know how. If you persevere and solve them yourself (without looking at the answers at the back of the book), you will experience that happy "aha!" rush of pleasure when you "get it."

More than that, your brain will be jogged a little, so that perhaps you'll see more solutions to life's day-to-day problems. A friend once assured me that there were at least four solutions to every problem.[14] I think he might have been a little extreme, but just going from one to two is often great progress!

13. See Martin Scheerer, "Problem-solving," *Scientific American*, April 1963, page 118.

14. Robert Maidment said, "There are three ways to get to the top of a tree: (1) climb it; (2) sit on an acorn; (3) make friends with a big bird." Quoted in *A Whack on the Side of the Head* by Roger von Oech.

Please note: Many people experience puzzles negatively. If that describes you, I want you to enjoy the "aha!" anyway, so I've given one or more hints after each puzzle. These should help you if you're really stuck. *Don't automatically read the first hint: use it only after you've had a shot at the answer. Some questions have more than one hint, graded in order of helpfulness. Read the other hints only if you have to, and cover them all up if your eyes have a tendency to stroll.*[15]

Unless you've seen these puzzles before (most are unoriginal), they invite you to venture into uncharted terrain! Oh yes: you don't have to be a math whiz to solve any of these.

Here are five puzzles for Monday. Remember, the hints are graded. Cover them up, and then reveal them *one at a time* if you absolutely can't solve the puzzle without them.

1. You have a drawer containing black and white socks. It's nighttime and the power is off. How many socks do you have to remove to ensure you have a matching pair?

  Hint 1: How many do you need to not *make a pair?*
  Hint 2: Put some socks in a drawer and try it!

2. What's the next symbol in this series?

  Hint 1: This puzzle asks that you see something very familiar in what, at first glance, appears incomprehensible. Ask yourself, what is common about each of the symbols?
  Hint 2: Whatever it is that's common is shared (approximately) by your face: symmetry.
  Hint 3: Go on to puzzle 3, to which this is related. Then come back to this one.

---

15. That innocent aside took on a new dimension when I read, "We should start taking a good look at how our brains function. It seems, for instance, that when we view a printed page our brains see and busily process far more than the few lines we are consciously engaged in reading. How else explain how a misleading headline, or even a minor typo in a fine-print ad, will draw the eye across the width of the page as to a mystery to be solved?" Edgar R. Jones, letter to *Science News*, July 25, 1992.

3. What's the next letter in this series? O T T F F S S

> *Hint 1: If you solved puzzle 2, this should be a cinch! If you didn't, think of the first series you ever encountered.*
>
> *Hint 2: If that was A B C, think of the second series you ever encountered!*
>
> *Hint 3: In France, the series would be U D T Q C S S.*
>
> *Hint 4: Even if you don't speak French, why should it be different from one language to another?*
>
> *Hint 5: It's as simple as 1, 2, 3.*

4. "Brothers and sisters have I none, But that man's father is my father's son." Who am I talking about?

> *Hint 1: This isn't a trick. It only requires clear thinking, yet it's surprising how many people get it wrong. Take it one step at a time.*
>
> *Hint 2: Who is "my father's son"?*

5. Two people were born on the same day of the same year. They share the same father and same mother, yet they're not twins. Explain.

> *Hint 1: Like the chimpanzee trying to get the banana, this may require you to go and sit in a corner, metaphorically, and ponder. It's not a trick question, but it needs a willingness to stand back from the problem.*
>
> *Hint 2: Do humans have only one or two babies at a time?*

Puzzle answers are at the back of the book.

Monday's Quotations

Wonder and Creativity

Genius is an African who dreams of snow.

—Vladimir Nabokov

The strokes of genius are but the outcome of a continuous habit of inquiry that grasps clearly and distinctly all that is involved in the simple things that anyone can understand.

—Bernard J. F. Lonergan

It was [Amy] Lowell who said she used to "drop" her ideas into her subconscious "much as one drops a letter into the mailbox. Six months later, the words of the poem began to come into my head. . . . The words seemed to be pronounced in my head, but with nobody speaking them."

—Diane Ackerman

Creativity has an unlimited future.

—James Adams

The creative process cannot be summoned at will or even cajoled by sacrificial offering. Indeed, it seems to occur most readily when the mind is relaxed and the imagination roaming freely.

—Morris Kline

Having made a discovery, I shall never see the world again as before. My eyes have become different; I have made myself into a person seeing and thinking differently. I have crossed a gap, the heuristic gap which lies between problem and discovery.

—Michael Polanyi

People differ from other animals because they have curiosity, and they look at the stars with wonder. We might try to teach dolphins and chimpanzees to speak, and sometimes we're successful, but they're sure not going to look at the sky and imagine constellations. This is the way that people, or at least little children, differ from animals. Children are curious. My kids ask me, "Where does the sun go at night?" and "How come I can suck a soda up through a straw?" Later in life they are trained not to ask questions of this kind. Not all of them. Some of them maintain this primordial quality of curiosity. Some of them become artists. Some become composers. Some become physicists. Some become astronomers. These people in a sense have kept the faith. They really want to know what's going on.

—Sheldon Glashow

Men love to wonder, and that is the seed of science.

—Ralph Waldo Emerson

Just as knowing how a magic trick is done spoils all its wonder, so let us be grateful that wherever science and reason turn they plunge finally into stygian darkness.

—Martin Gardner

We all have a genetic, God-given capacity for wonder that's being starved, and that's what I'm interested in exploring.

—**Norman Lear**

The sense of wonder is the mark of the philosopher.

—**Plato**

The larger the island of knowledge, the longer the shoreline of wonder.

—**Ralph Sockman**

Everything of importance has already been seen by someone who did not discover it.

—**Alfred North Whitehead**

How can life be so beautiful, providing such sublime rewards for mediocrity?

—**Umberto Eco**

I realize that Being is surrounded east, south, north and west, above and below, by wonder. Within that frame, like a little house in strange, cold, vast and beautiful scenery, is life upon this planet, of which life I am a temporary speck and impression. There is interest beyond measure within that house. . . . Nevertheless at times one finds an urgency to go out and gaze at those enigmatical immensities.

—**H. G. Wells**

They are ill discoverers that think there is no land when they can see nothing but sea.

—**Francis Bacon**

Tuesday
Day of Mars

*T*uesday has traditionally been associated with war. Tyr was the Nordic god of war, and he was associated with the Italian war god Mars (who in turn is identified with Greek Ares). The astrological-astronomical symbol for Mars, a shield with a spear, also represents an entire gender: mine.

In popular culture, the view of Mars, the planet, has often paralleled the belligerency of Mars, the warrior god. From H. G. Wells's 1898 *The War of the Worlds* (successfully revived by Orson Welles as a radio play 40 years later for a war-jittery United States) to Gustav

Holst's hypnotic "Mars" in his *The Planets* suite, the Red Planet has more than lived up to its militant origins. Yet our image of Mars deserves better. Not only haven't the Martians invaded, they may not even have been there in the first place. Despite some ambiguous results from soil analysis carried out by the two Viking landers, most scientists concede that there's little chance of finding any life, even microorganisms, on Mars today. However dissimilar the two planets are today, *early* Mars was quite similar to *early* Earth, so perhaps future missions to Mars will unearth (unmars?) four-billion-year-old fossils of tiny critters.

Four

Animal Magnetism

Ask where's the North? At York, 'tis on the Tweed;
In Scotland, at the Orcades; and there,
At Greenland, Zembla, or the Lord knows where.

—Alexander Pope, "An Essay on Man"

*Q*uickly, point in the general direction of the North Pole with one arm. With your other arm, point to the South Pole. What's the angle between your arms?

Most people stand looking like this.

If you're one of them, take a moment to think about it. And if you're still thinking about it, peek at the figure on the next page.

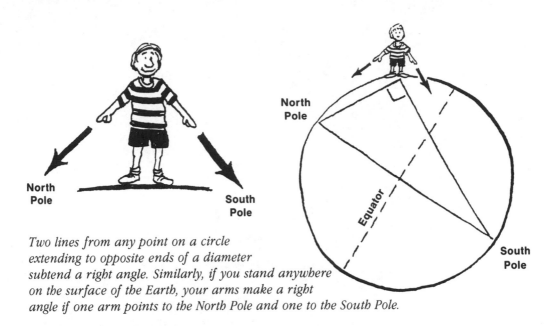

*Two lines from any point on a circle
extending to opposite ends of a diameter
subtend a right angle. Similarly, if you stand anywhere
on the surface of the Earth, your arms make a right
angle if one arm points to the North Pole and one to the South Pole.*

Since we're used to pointing in the direction of north or south, sticking our arms straight out seems perfectly natural. But I think there's another reason why many people instinctively point straight out to the poles: despite 2,500 years of knowledge about the shape and size of our planet, we still have a built-in tendency to think of it as flat! Look outside, what do you see? A flat Earth. Look at a map, any map (other than a globe, of course) and it subtly reinforces our sense of living on flatness. I'm not suggesting that anyone is a genuine flat-earther today. I'm saying that it wasn't *that* silly for countless generations of intelligent people who lived before the ancient Greeks to believe that the Earth was flat.

By the way, contrary to popular myth (promulgated by Washington Irving), no one really thought Columbus would fall off the edge of the world. Although none have survived, globes are described in Greek texts dating back to several hundred years B.C. A round Earth was a tenet of Pythagorean teachings, circa 500 B.C.

No matter where you are (with a couple of exceptions), when you point to the two poles your arms will form a right angle: any point on the circumference of a circle makes a right angle with the ends of any diameter. (What are the two exceptions?[1]) The North Pole is always down, below your horizon, as is the South Pole. The poles are at the ends of one of the Earth's diameters, its axis.

---

1. The poles.

Downward-Bound Bacteria

Most species of animals are so tiny that gravity has a negligible effect on them compared to other influences. Their vast ratio of surface area to mass (unlike humans, for instance) means that their lives are dominated by forces of which we larger creatures are virtually unaware. Here's how Scottish biologist D'Arcy Thompson put it in a classic text 75 years ago:

> *Life has a range of magnitude narrow indeed compared to that with which physical science deals; but it is wide enough to include three such discrepant conditions as those in which a man, an insect and a bacillus have their being and play their several roles. Man is ruled by gravitation, and rests on mother earth. A water-beetle finds the surface of a pool a matter of life and death, a perilous entanglement or an indispensable support. In a third world, where the bacillus lives, gravitation is forgotten, and the viscosity of the liquid, the resistance defined by Stoke's law, the molecular shocks of the Brownian movement . . . make up the physical environment and have their potent and immediate influence upon the organism. The predominant factors are no longer those of our scale; we have come to the edge of a world of which we have no experience, and where all our preconceptions must be recast.[2]*

What's this got to do with Earth's poles? Very roughly, if you point directly to the North Pole from temperate latitudes in the Northern Hemisphere, your arm is parallel to Earth's magnetic field. What you may have forgotten when you pointed to the North Pole, that it's angled downward compared with your local frame of reference, is probably "known" to certain bacteria that incorporate one or more strings of tiny cubes of magnetite in their bodies. Each cube is a tiny magnet, and strings of them make the bacterium act as a minuscule bar magnet. In scientific parlance, they are magnetotactic, that is, magnetic-field orienting.

In 1974, such bacteria were found in a freshwater swamp near Woods Hole, Massachusetts. Bacteria are so small that they live in Thompson's "third world." Why on Earth would bacteria (which move no more than a few inches in their brief lifetimes under their own motive power) want to know which direction is north? Exactly that, because they are on Earth. It's not that they want to know north the *horizontal*

---

2. *On Growth and Form.*

direction, as we think of it. They want to know north the *vertical* direction. As we'll see, they want to know which way is *down*.

As Thompson pointed out, they have no means of telling "down" by appealing, as we do, to gravity, because that force is quite irrelevant in their lives. But by knowing north, by orienting themselves to Earth's

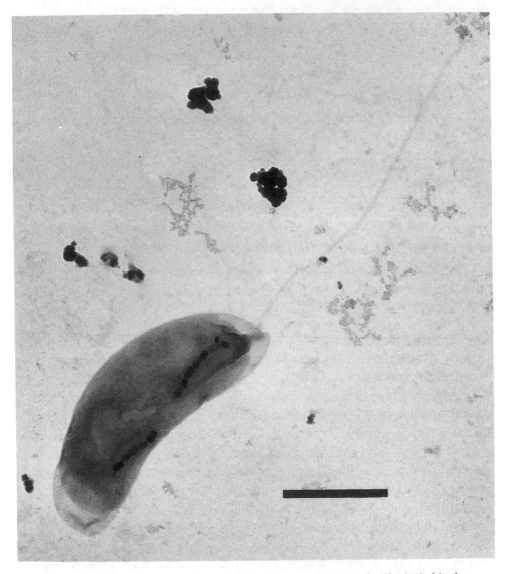

Magnetotactic bacterium, in a transmission electron micrograph. The little black squares are cubes of magnetite, Fe_3O_4, which is opaque to the electron beam. The bar represents a distance of 0.5 microns (millionths of a meter), so you could lay about 100 of these critters end to end across the thickness of a human hair. (Dennis Bazylinski)

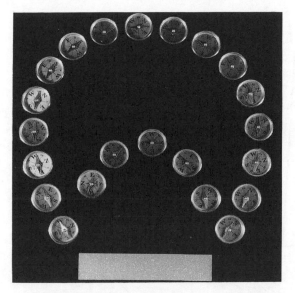

A bunch (crowd? camp?) of compasses surrounding a bar magnet simulates Earth's magnetic lines of force. Each compass is placed head to toe with the needle of the previous one, so the needles follow a line of force (two such lines of force are outlined by the "arches" of compasses shown here). You may remember doing the same sort of experiment with iron filings.

magnetic lines of force, they know in which direction down is.[3] Actually, it's easier than that: all they do is swim, and nature does the rest (which is quite useful, because they have no brains). As they move, the magnetite in their bodies causes a torque (twisting force), which automatically orients them along the Earth's magnetic field. If the field is heading down, the bacteria go down.

Why is the direction of down important to these tiny critters? Biologists believe it's healthier. Atmospheric levels of oxygen are toxic to them, so they need to go deeper to survive: in a word, down means life. You may have already anticipated a neat test for this theory: what happens to bacteria living in the Southern Hemisphere, where the magnetic force lines are headed upward? If magnetotactic bacteria living near Woods Hole were transported to, say, New Zealand, they'd swim up (to extinction), not down (to survival).

Don't worry, evolution has taken care of everything. Similar bacteria do, in fact, live in New Zealand. When they were examined, sure enough their polarity was *opposite* to that of their northern cousins. They too automatically swim downward. How deliciously humbling to realize that magnets, which huge-brained humans have figured out only over the last 2,000 years, were bestowed by nature long ago on one of its smallest creations.

---

3. The tendency of a compass needle to point down, as well as north, has been known since Georg Hartmann and Robert Norman (working independently) discovered magnetic dip in the middle of the sixteenth century.

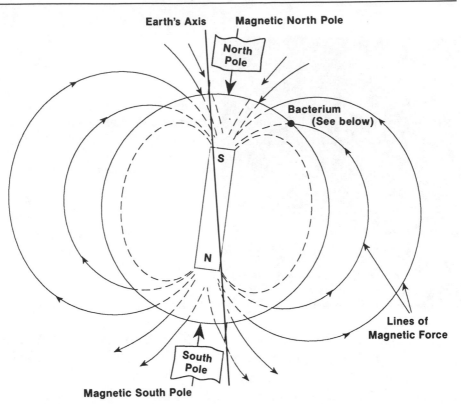

A cross section through the Earth, showing lines of magnetic force. Visualize a huge bar magnet inside our planet to see how it works. (In fact, Earth's magnetic field derives from molten iron in the outer core churning around the solid inner core, creating a dynamo. See the illustration on p. 274.) Earth's magnetic north and south poles are located a few hundred miles from their counterparts on Earth's spin axis. Note that Earth's so-called magnetic north pole is actually a north-seeking pole, so it's really a south pole.

A magnetotactic bacterium in Massachusetts acts like a tiny bar magnet, with the north pole at its "head." Opposites attract: as it swims, it passively follows Earth's magnetic lines of force, heading down as it does so. From the point of view of the bacterium, down is healthier. Similar bacteria in the Southern Hemisphere have magnetic north poles at their tail ends, so they also swim down.

Think Globally . . .

I'd now like you to get a model of the Earth, that is, a globe, and orient it in space. To orient a map (as you may remember, especially if you were a Girl or Boy Scout), you rotate the map so north on the map is in the same direction as north on the ground. It's the same with a globe, except now you have to do it in three dimensions. Ready? First find the spot on the globe where you live and bring that to the top, so it's horizontal. Now, keeping your home uppermost, rotate the globe until north on the globe is in the same direction as north on the ground, just as you do with a map. The globe is now oriented in all three directions.

Notice where the poles are relative to your home. Check that lines from them to you are indeed at right angles to each other, as we've discussed. Imagine having a hole-boring machine parked in your backyard. Locate where you were born, or find some faraway place (with a strange-sounding name) that intrigues you, and see yourself jumping into your machine, aiming it in carefully, and going straight there. None of this "great circle" stuff that guides airplane routes across the Earth's surface. (To find the great circle route from New York to Cape Town, for instance, just stretch a string tightly between them on the globe.)

Notice where you'd end up if you were to drill a vertical hole to your "antipodal" spot precisely opposite you, that is, at the lowest point

Orienting a globe.
With your location on top (here, northern California is uppermost), rotate it until north on the globe is in the same direction as north on the ground. Louisa's right hand is pointing north. When you try this, note that if you drilled a hole straight down, you'd come out at the lowest point of your globe. (Barry Evans)

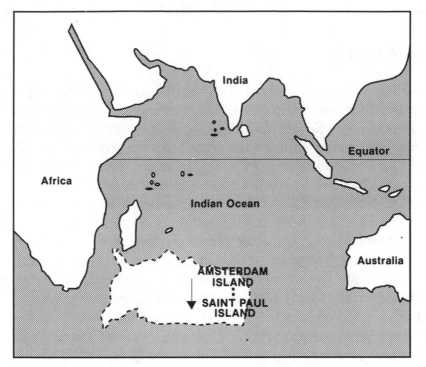

The United States superimposed on its antipodes, the Indian Ocean. Every point lies over the point you'd reach if you drilled straight through the center of the Earth. Two tiny islands provide the only alternative to ending up at the bottom of the ocean, but you have to start from one of two precise locations southeast of Denver, Colorado.

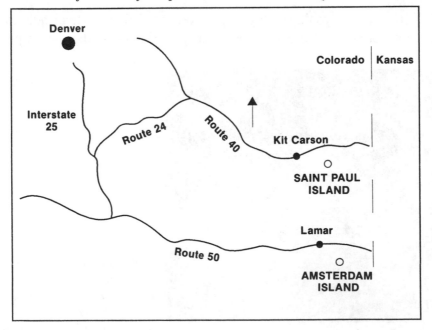

The dry spots antipodal to the United States are Amsterdam Island (latitude 37°55′S, longitude 77°40′E) and Saint Paul Island (latitude 38°44′S, longitude 77°30′E).

on your globe. With two exceptions, anyone heading straight down from the United States would experience a watery climax when they reached the bed of the Indian Ocean at the end of the upward leg of their journey.

Those exceptions result from the fact that two tiny French islands in the middle of the Indian Ocean are antipodal to, or directly opposite, two locations southeast of Denver, Colorado. Drill 8,000 miles straight down from a point 15 miles east of Kit Carson, Colorado, and you'll emerge, dry, from below Amsterdam Island, while a vertical hole starting 20 miles southeast of Lamar, Colorado, will land you on Saint Paul Island. These are the only two places in the contiguous United States antipodal to dry land.

Growing up in England, I was told that if you dug a hole straight down, you'd come out in China. It was quite a shock to learn, on coming to the United States, that children here believe the same thing. The real question then became, of course, where do Chinese kids think they'll end up? Actually, to get to Beijing, you'd have to start off from near Buenos Aires, Argentina.

Taking the Tube

I remember a physics examination problem that concerned a futuristic means of transport, the tube. Not the London underground railway, you understand, but a system of dead-straight tunnels connecting the major cities of the world. You'd hop aboard a train that would whiz down an evacuated (vacuum) tube under the influence of gravity to the halfway point. Its momentum would then keep it going to its destination without any need for external power, just as an idealized, friction-free pendulum swings down and up to the exact level from which it started.

Ignoring a couple of minor engineering details (such as coping with iron-melting temperatures and pressures in the Earth's core), the idea didn't seem that farfetched. The exam problem was to estimate how long it would take to travel from any point to any other point, making several approximations. The answer, surprisingly, was always about 40 minutes, no matter how far your journey. The reason is spelled out in Appendix 2.

Of course, you can't ignore friction, so the trick's impossible. Or can you? Suppose you drill right through the Earth's center, on a diameter. Now it's just a straight drop down to the center, from where you'd keep

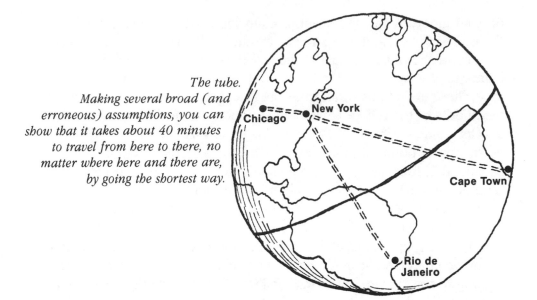

The tube.
Making several broad (and
erroneous) assumptions, you can
show that it takes about 40 minutes
to travel from here to there, no
matter where here and there are,
by going the shortest way.

going to the surface at the other end. The tube's been evacuated, so you don't have to worry about air resistance.

It turns out that air resistance is the least of our problems with a straight-through tube. The planet spins! You wouldn't drop straight down, you'd rub against the inside of the tube all the way as your vehicle tried to follow a complicated, spiraling path. Wait a moment, though. There's one, and only one, diameter of the Earth where a tube wouldn't be subject to the problem of the Earth's spin: from pole to pole, on the axis of rotation.

Now we're on to something. This is the perfect solution for researchers who specialize in investigating the polar regions. They could spend a six-month summer spell at the North Pole, wait until the sun was setting, jump into the tube (why bother with a vehicle?), and free-fall all the way through, coming out at the other end (the South Pole) 42 minutes later, to see the sun rising. (They have to remember to hang onto the edge of the hole when they arrive, or they'll drop down and end up, 84 minutes after starting, right back where they came from.) All right! Now we've got a convincing reason to build an axial tube, so what are we waiting for? Let's go get a government grant![4]

One final point. As one of our intrepid tubers jumps in, she waves goodbye to her boyfriend, who happens, at that very moment, to be

4. In *A Journey into Gravity and Spacetime*, John Archibald Wheeler proposes another reason for at least imagining such a tube: as a brilliant way to comprehend gravity and curved spacetime according to Einstein.

passing overhead in a satellite in a very low polar orbit around the Earth. So as she arrives at the South Pole, guess who's passing overhead? It's possible to show that the period (84 minutes) of a low-orbit spacecraft to complete one revolution around the Earth is the same as the time our intrepid tube-travelers would take to go through the Earth and back again, so tuber and orbiter take the same time to travel from pole to pole. You can get a feel for why this is so by imagining that the circular orbit is "squashed" into a straight line. The math is shown in Appendix 2.

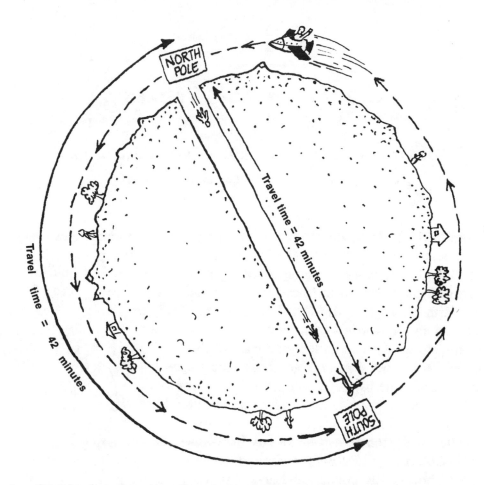

Just the ticket for polar researchers: the North Pole to South Pole tube, unaffected by the rotation of the Earth. The trip through takes 42 minutes, exactly the time for a low-orbit satellite to make the journey from one pole to another.

Five

Crisis on the Scales

Thou art weighed in the balances, and art found wanting.

—The Book of Daniel

*F*rom birth to death, gravity dominates our physical lives and rules every movement.[5]

Imagine going to bed tonight feeling fine, your normal self. In the morning you wake and feel heavier. When you reach up to turn off the alarm clock, your arm feels like lead. Your body is deeper into the mattress than normal, and when you try to get out of bed, you feel like you weigh a ton. A ton? Well, not quite. Let's go check. You stagger or crawl into the bathroom and get on the bathroom scale. (Note the singular: these aren't scales, plural, on which you balance weights. This is a spring-operated scale, the kind you can buy in K-Mart for $12.99 or so.) Last night before you went to bed, it showed 120 pounds, and now it shows 132. That's a 10 percent increase overnight. Yikes! What happened?

Your bathroom spring scale reads 132 pounds.

5. With the exception of swimming, the one sport that would feel roughly the same on the moon as here.

Possibility 1: You really are heavier. You got up in the middle of the night and indulged in an unconscionably wild orgy of eating (although 12 pounds does sound slightly excessive for one sleepwalking meal). Fortunately your doctor's office is next door. You hustle over there as fast as you can and stand on the scales (which don't depend on springs).

Now that's strange: they show that you weigh your regular 120 pounds. And there's a line of people behind you with the same concern: they feel heavier, their bathroom scales tell them they're heavier, yet the doctor's scales tell them they haven't changed since last night. Just what is going on here?

You look more closely at the doctor's scales and notice that they work by comparison: you find your weight by sliding a lump of iron along a lever arm until you and the iron (multiplied by its leveraging factor) are in balance. So, you reason, if you feel heavier and these scales say that you're at your normal 120, whatever is affecting you is *also* affecting the sliding mass of iron. You haven't changed, but something else, external to you

Your doctor's balance scales read your usual 120 pounds.

and the doctor's scales, has. (Again, your bathroom scale doesn't compare masses. It determines your weight by the compression of a spring.) An awful thought comes to you. . . .

Possibility 2: The Earth is heavier. Suppose that sometime in the night, the wily Klangons (a breed of aliens noisier and less fixated than Klingons) injected a huge amount of mass into the center of our Earth! (Seems they'd just rented the movie *2010*, in which the aliens did just that to Jupiter to turn it into a sun.)

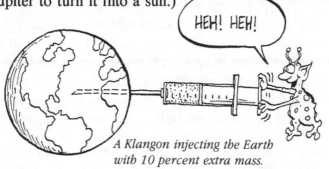

HEH! HEH!

A Klangon injecting the Earth with 10 percent extra mass.

Our planet, while still the same size, now has 10 percent more mass than when you went to bed. Instead of *you* putting on 12 pounds, *Earth* put on 1.3 trillion trillion pounds. (OK, I know that's a lot, but you're allowed to do this in thought experiments. Einstein traveled at the speed of light in his!) Either way, whether the mass of you or the Earth increased by 10 percent, it feels the same.

How can you know for sure if that's what happened? You can't literally put the Earth on a balance in order to compare it with another known mass (like on a doctor's scales). We can, however, find Earth's mass by comparing it with another convenient known mass, that of the moon. The moon's distance and orbital velocity tells us exactly what Earth's mass is.

Fortunately, some lasting legacies of the Apollo missions are several laser reflectors left on the moon's surface. We use the latest laser distance-ranging equipment to check the moon's position and velocity and find, to our bewilderment, that everything is as it was last night, so the mass of the Earth hasn't changed. And your doctor's scales tell you that your mass has not changed. This gets more complicated. Can it be that those fiendish Klangons used another, even subtler method to confuse us?

A Klangon shrinking the Earth to 95 percent of its present radius.

Possibility 3: Honey, they shrunk the planet! Suppose the Klangons made the Earth shrink! That means we're closer to the center of the Earth—and therefore the Earth's center of gravity—than we were last night. For you to weigh 10 percent more, with neither you nor the Earth changing mass, they'd have had to shrink the Earth to about 95 percent of its former radius.[6] If last night your distance from the Earth's center

---

6. Gravitational attraction is proportional to the reciprocal of the distance between the centers of two bodies squared (see Appendix 1), so for you to weigh 10% more than you did before, Earth's radius (the distance between your center of mass and Earth's center of mass) would need to be reduced to $\sqrt{\frac{1}{1.1}}$, or about 95% of what it was.

was 4,000 miles, and this morning it's only 3,800 miles, you'd feel that 10 percent weight gain. It seems the Klangons used their fiendish Planet Shrinker to make You Consider that you are Heavy and Overweight (PSYCHO). Without making any change in the mass of the Earth, they changed its size, shrinking it to 95 percent of its previous radius. Diabolically cunning![7]

A Real Experiment

In a sense, we've vicariously experienced this last scenario (mercifully, without Klangon intervention) through the twelve Apollo astronauts who walked on the lunar surface over 20 years ago. On the moon, they experienced changes in their weight because the moon (1) has less mass and (2) is smaller than the Earth. These two factors work against each other. Let's take them one at a time.

Everything on the moon weighs about one-sixth what it does on Earth: a 160-pound astronaut on Earth weighs about 26 pounds. Even with suits and life-support back-packs weighing nearly 200 pounds (on Earth), astronauts were able to leap around almost effortlessly on the moon. (NASA, frame P10642)

7. Alert readers may have caught on to a fourth possibility, that the "gravitational constant" isn't. See Thomas C. Van Flandern "Is Gravity Getting Weaker?" *Scientific American*, February 1976, page 44.

If the moon were expanded to the size of the Earth, the astronauts would be farther from the moon's center of gravity, so they would have simply experienced a weight loss proportional to the ratio of masses of the moon and the Earth. The Earth is about 80 times as massive as the moon, so they would have weighed $\frac{1}{80}$ of their Earth weight. An Earthly 160-pound astronaut would weigh a mere 2 pounds on the surface of a moon-mass, Earth-size body.

Suppose instead that the mass of the moon were the same as that of the Earth, but compressed into the moon's size. On this Earth-mass, moon-size body, our 160-pound astronaut would weigh a ton. More precisely, he would weigh about 13.7 times what he weighs on the Earth, because the radius of the Earth is 3.7 times that of the moon, and we need to square that to get the relative weight change.

So what did astronauts actually weigh on the moon? The smaller mass of the moon (compared to Earth) causes an 80-times weight loss, and its smaller size causes a 13-times weight gain. The net result is approximately a 6-times weight loss, that is, 80 divided by 13. On the moon, a 160-pound Earth-weight astronaut weighs less than 30 pounds. That's why they could make those great, effortless leaps.

Weight and Mass

All this melodrama helps to clarify the difference between two very different quantities: your *weight* and your *mass*. Your mass is simply how much stuff you have inside you, essentially the sum total of all the protons and neutrons[8] in your body. Your weight is the force all that stuff experiences as a result of the gravitational attraction of the Earth, the moon, or wherever you happen to be at the time. The greater your mass, and/or the greater the mass of the other body, and/or the closer you are to it, the more you weigh.

So take heart. Next time you're worried about your weight, recognize that it's a function of much more than your mass. Perhaps it's not you that's the problem: maybe the Earth is too small or too massive. You're fine the way you are, you just happen to be living on the wrong planet!

---

8. And, of much lesser significance, electrons and binding energy.

--------------------------- **Waking Up Light** ---------------------------

*T*he incredible scenarios just discussed have all considered waking up heavy. What about the other possibility, waking up *lighter* than you went to bed? Assuming your mass has remained the same, here are some possibilities.

1. You were kidnapped (it used to happen all the time on "The Twilight Zone") and taken to a location closer to the equator. At the poles, there's no centrifugal force, while it's at its maximum at the equator. The force counters gravity to a small extent.[9] Also, the Earth has an equatorial bulge, meaning you're about 30 miles farther away from the center of the Earth at the equator than at the poles, resulting in a further decrease in gravity's effect. The net result is that a person weighing 201 pounds at sea level at the poles weighs about 200 pounds at sea level at the equator.

2. Why specify, "at sea level"? Because, as we've seen, the higher you are, the less the force of gravity (again, because gravity decreases in proportion to the square of your distance from the Earth's center). A 200-pounder at sea level at the equator could lose another pound by simply moving to the top of a 10-mile-high mountain.

3. There's one other direction we can go to lose weight. Let's see, we've tried moving from the poles to the equator, and climbing up, so what's left? Down? But down brings us closer to the center of the Earth, so wouldn't that mean we'd weigh more if, for example, we went down a mine shaft? Think about this for a moment before reading on.

True, you're closer to the Earth's center, but you've also got some of our planet above your head, pulling you up! Where's the one place on the Earth where gravity has no effect on you whatsoever? At the center, where everything cancels out.

So now we know the force of gravity is zero at the center and maximum at the surface. How does it vary between center and surface?

9. Actually, what is popularly called "centrifugal force" doesn't exist. The force you feel if you stand on a spinning disk is due to your inertia. The closer you are to the center of the disk, the slower you are moving, so the less inertia you generate. Similarly, near the poles you are "orbiting" around Earth's axis at a slower speed than at the equator, requiring less gravitational force.

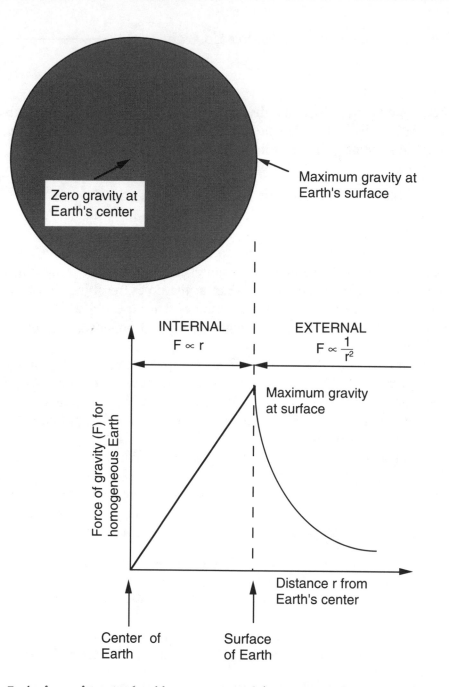

How F, *the force of gravity (and hence your weight) varies according to your distance,* d, *from the Earth's center. We falsely assume that Earth has uniform density for simplicity. As you move out, your weight increases linearly (*$F \propto r$*) from zero at the center to a maximum at the surface. Thereafter it falls off according to Newton's inverse square law (*$F \propto \frac{1}{r^2}$*) as you move out into space. We happen to live at the point on the graph where we weigh the most.*

It's surprisingly simple. If you're at a point inside the Earth, then the mass of the external shell above you, pulling you away from the center, is exactly counterbalanced by the mass of the external shell below you, tugging you toward the center (see Appendix 2). So your gravitational attraction at a point distance r from the center is proportional to (1) the mass of the internal sphere, that is, to r^3 (falsely assuming uniform density), and (2), by the inverse square law, to $\frac{1}{r^2}$, netting you a simple r. Your weight, then, changes linearly as you move outward from the center of the Earth, where it's zero, to the surface, where it's at its maximum. From there, as you head out into space, it falls off in proportion to the square of the distance.

Isn't it a little curious that the surface where we live happens to be the place where we weigh the most? The franchise opportunities are obvious. Set up weight-loss clinics underground, where the loss is guaranteed, without any effort by the participants. Can I sign you up?

Six

Hemicentrism

The Lakota holy man Black Elk once took poet John Neihardt to the top of Harney Peak in the Black Hills to pray. Neihardt asked Black Elk why it was necessary to go to Harney Peak. Black Elk explained that Harney Peak is the center of the world. Neihardt asked Black Elk why he thought Harney Peak was the center of the earth, and how he came to know such a thing. Black Elk chuckled at the white man's innocence and with studied patience explained that on a ball like the earth, every place is the center.[10]

—Roger L. Welsch

*Y*ou do, of course, recognize the pattern at the top of the following page. (You don't? Splendid. You've just absorbed the whole point of this chapter almost without reading a word of it!)

November 1963, Taumarunui, New Zealand. I'd been in the country just a week and was already homesick for England. I'd always found reading to be an effective antidote for the blues, so I found a sunny spot by the window and opened my book on what was to be a memorable spring afternoon. An hour or so later, I looked up and suddenly felt goose bumps rattling down my spine. Something was terribly wrong, but

---

10. "The Infrequent Flier," *Natural History*, October 1992.

I was unable to identify its source. Then I had it: the sun was moving the wrong way.

For 21 years, through 7,000 daily repetitions, my subconscious brain had absorbed one particular lesson about the world of my birth, that is, the sun moves from left to right in the southern sky. But this southern hemispherical sun, in the average direction of north instead of south, moved from right to left. It was not enough that the seasons were topsy-turvy, with November in late spring and summer just round the corner. Now my basic sense of left and right was thrown asunder.

I lived in that upside-down world for four years, not long enough to undo my basic bias about the globe that says our Northern Hemisphere is up here and "right" and their down-under half-world is "wrong." When Copernicus wrote that the Earth goes around the sun, relegating our planet to a regular member of the solar system, he was combating geocentrism. Now, like sexism and all the other irrational prejudices learned in childhood, I was finding that "hemicentrism" was an equally tough puppy to shake.

But Suppose . . .

Civilization, I was taught, arose on five great rivers of the world: the Nile, Hwang ("Yellow"), Indus, and the Tigris and Euphrates (the latter two becoming a single river 50 miles upstream of the Persian Gulf).

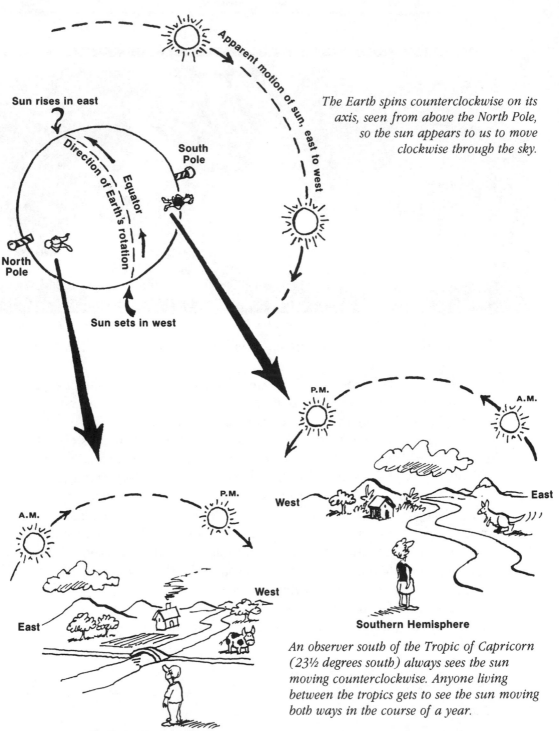

Sun rises in east

South Pole

Direction of Earth's rotation

Equator

North Pole

Sun sets in west

Apparent motion of sun, east to west

The Earth spins counterclockwise on its axis, seen from above the North Pole, so the sun appears to us to move clockwise through the sky.

P.M.

A.M.

West

East

Southern Hemisphere

An observer south of the Tropic of Capricorn (23½ degrees south) always sees the sun moving counterclockwise. Anyone living between the tropics gets to see the sun moving both ways in the course of a year.

A.M.

P.M.

East

West

Northern Hemisphere

An observer living north of the Tropic of Cancer (23½ degrees north) always sees the sun moving clockwise.

Notice anything? They're all in the Northern Hemisphere. Suppose, instead, that 5,000 to 10,000 years ago, some group of southern hemispherites had one day decided to quit all that tedious huntin' and gatherin' and settled down by the banks of, say, the Plate (or Plata, in South America), or Orange (in South Africa). They did all the right things—herded goats, raised corn, baked bricks—and they thrived. Their settlements multiplied in size and sophistication, and almost before you knew it, they'd invented maps and sundials and compasses,[11] long before anyone in the other hemisphere on the far side of the equator had given such things a thought. How would our world today be different if that's the way it had happened?

One o'clock in the afternoon. The movement of the shadow on a sundial led to the direction we think of as clockwise. If the predominant civilization had arisen south of the equator, it's a safe bet that the numbers on a sundial, and hence on clock faces, would run the other way. (Barry Evans)

11. The first known reference to a magnet used as a compass dates to A.D. 83 in China, when Wang Ch'ung wrote *Discourses Weighed in the Balance,* in which he referred to a "south-controlling spoon" made from lodestone that pointed south when placed on a polished bronze plate. It was probably only used for divination at the time. One hundred and fifty years earlier, Lucretius (in *De Rerum Natura*) explained "what law of nature causes iron to be attracted by that stone which the Greeks call from its place of origin *magnet*, because it occurs in the territory of the Magnesians." The magnetic compass didn't come into its own as an aid to navigation until the Middle Ages.

I think it's safe to say that:

- South would be at the top of maps (as shown at the beginning of this chapter, with black and white inverted in a crude attempt to delay your perception).[12]
- The direction "clockwise" would be opposite from how we define it now. Clocks rotate the way they do because our daily celestial timekeeper, the sun, goes "clockwise," as does the shadow on a sundial. In the Southern Hemisphere, the movement of the sun and a sundial's shadow is counterclockwise, as my jarring realization in New Zealand made clear.
- Compass needles would point south instead of north. They do now, of course (i.e., they have two ends), but the convention is to paint the north-pointing end red or some other distinctive color.[13]
- The names of the constellations would be different. Viewed from, say, Australia, Orion the Hunter is standing on his head, while Leo the Lion lies on his back with his paws in the air—hardly heroic or imposing poses.
- Spring, when new buds "spring" from the branches, would be the season from September to December, while fall (as in leaves falling) would be from March to June. The same goes for winter (which is probably cognate with "wet" and "water") and summer (probably related to "sun").

---

12. Or would it? Since the word *south* may be related to "sun," they may have called the direction we call north, south! *West* (related to "evening", as in *vespers*) and *east* (Greek *eos*, "dawn") wouldn't be affected, since the sun sets in the west and rises in the east in both hemispheres.

13. Nothing's as simple as it seems. A magnetized needle aligns itself in the direction of Earth's magnetic field. For instance, where I live in California, it points in a direction about 20 degrees west of the North Pole, toward the magnetic north pole. But which end of the compass points which way? Paradoxically, Earth's so-called magnetic north pole is actually a magnetic south pole! The north pole of your compass needle points north, since north is attracted to south. (Similarly, a weather vane points in the opposite direction to the name of the wind, that is, a wind blowing toward the east is a westerly.)

Of more than semantic interest is the fact that Earth's magnetic field reverses every few 100,000 years. Earth itself doesn't flip over, of course, but you can imagine that the hypothetical bar magnet inside our planet does.

These days, it's easy to find which way the equator is, whether you're north or south of it, without recourse to a compass. Just note which direction all the TV-dish antennae are pointing! TV relay satellites are in geosynchronous orbit 22,000 miles above the equator, so dish antennae in the Northern Hemisphere point south and vice versa.

Star trails recorded by a camera aimed at Polaris (the Pole Star) with the shutter left open for an hour. A huge knitting needle entering Earth at the South Pole and leaving at the North Pole would point toward Polaris, which appears nearly motionless while all other stars appear to revolve around it. (If Polaris were exactly aligned with Earth's axis, its image in the center would appear sharp. Because it's half a degree off, it shows as a short line.) Navigators in the Northern Hemisphere can easily orient themselves with Polaris if the night skies are clear. (Paul Mortfield)

◆ The art of navigation might not have arisen as fast as it did, since there's no equivalent in southern skies to Polaris, the North Star. This star appears to stand almost still in the sky, while the other stars rotate around it, because Polaris is only one-half of a degree (the diameter of the full moon) from the celestial north pole.[14] That's a boon to navigation, since it always lies in the direction of north.

It's trickier navigating in the Southern Hemisphere, where Polaris is below the horizon. The closest star as bright as Polaris to the celestial south pole is Miaplacidus (meaning "placid waters"), but it's a full 20 degrees from the pole.[15] That's nearly the width of the Big Dipper. Lacking a fixed star to give direction at night, long-distance mariners might have been slower to dare to sail out of sight of land than their northern-hemispherical counterparts.

And even if early navigators had figured out celestial navigation, they might not have had the Vikings' or Columbus's luck in reaching the New World as easily as they did. A glance at a globe will confirm that there's a lot more ocean in the Southern Hemisphere than in the Northern Hemisphere. It is, for instance, about half as far again from Cape Town to the mouth of the Plate as Columbus's route across the Atlantic from the Canaries to the West Indies.

You can take this speculation to extremes. Would faucets turn in the opposite direction than we're used to? How about rotary phone dials? Would we drive on the opposite side of the road?[16] Would Republicans veer to the left?

And if we're really going to fantasize about left and right inversions: If civilization had arisen south of the equator, our present 90 percent predilection for right-handedness might be reversed! Perhaps 90 percent

---

14. "I am as constant as the northern star," said Julius Caesar in Shakespeare's drama of that name. Actually, because Earth's axis precesses (that is, it wobbles around, like a top does when it slows down), Polaris was 3 degrees from the celestial north pole in Shakespeare's time and 12 degrees off when Caesar lived. (*Sky and Telescope*, March 1991, page 238.)

15. See footnote 14. Miaplacidus used to be farther from the celestial south pole than it is now.

16. Coming from the U.K., where roundabouts (traffic islands) move traffic clockwise, I still can't quite bring myself to say the "wrong" side of the road.

of the world would be left-handed, while the usual 10 percent minority would be righties (northpaws?).

Isn't that left?

--------------------------- **The Coriolis Effect** ---------------------------

We have acquired confidence in the hypothesis that carefully performed experiments on liquid drainage from a tank will show clockwise rotation, if done in the Southern Hemisphere. [17]

—Investigators at the
University of Sidney

*D*espite popular belief, one thing that doesn't change between the Northern Hemisphere and the Southern Hemisphere is the direction in which your bathwater swirls when you pull the plug. Because the Earth is spinning, it's reasonable to assume that your bathwater spirals counterclockwise when you're north of the equator, and vice versa. After all, winds in the Northern Hemisphere veer to the right, as do artillery shells and ICBMs. They are all at the mercy of the Coriolis effect, which is best understood by imagining what happens to a big vat of water sitting right over the North Pole. The water at the edge of the vat is moving counterclockwise around the pole. If you pull the central plug, water will move from the outside to the center. As it does so, its momentum causes it to drift to the right, resulting in a counterclockwise spin. As you move the vat away from the pole toward the equator, water on the side farthest from the pole is always going to be moving a little faster than water on the side closest to the pole, so you'll end up with a net counterclockwise rotation anywhere in the Northern Hemisphere. In the Southern Hemisphere, the reverse is true.

The trouble with relating this to your bathwater is that you're dealing with a minuscule difference in velocity across the width of your bath, and the tiny Coriolis effect is going to be swamped by you, your breathing, the shape of the drainpipe, previous motion of the water, air

---

17. *Scientific American*, November 1965.

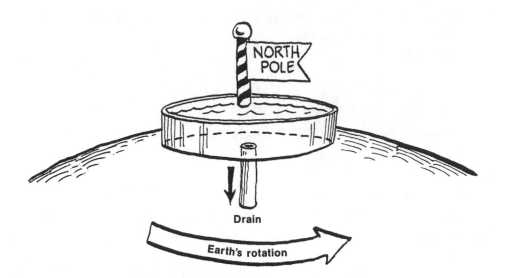

The Coriolis force. As water drains from the central outlet of a tub at the North Pole, momentum causes the fluid to drift to its right, resulting in a counterclockwise spin. Water in a tub anywhere in the Northern Hemisphere always moves a little faster on the side farthest from the North Pole, resulting in a net counterclockwise rotation. Similarly, winds and artillery shells in the Northern Hemisphere drift to the right, and vice versa for the Southern Hemisphere.

blowing over the tub, and so on. It takes carefully controlled conditions to confirm that water going down a drain really does obey Coriolis—such as in two experiments undertaken in the 1960s. Water was allowed to settle for several days in six-foot-diameter circular tubs placed in vibration-free rooms at Massachusetts Institute of Technology, Cambridge, and at the University of Sidney, Australia. When the plugs were pulled (from below, to minimize turbulence), sure enough . . . well, let the dry quotation that heads this section tell the story.

The Coriolis effect is also responsible for an odd demographic phenomenon: the poorer parts of cities in temperate climates are usually to the east of downtown (and smelly industry) while the wealthier sections are to the west. London, Paris, and Dallas, for instance, share this feature. Between about 30 and 60 degrees of latitude, winds mostly blow from the west because cold air, heated at the equator, descends at about 30 degrees of latitude north and south of the equator. If our planet didn't spin, that air would spread out due north and south. What actually happens is that the Coriolis effect causes winds headed north to veer to the right north of the equator, and vice versa south of the equator. The net effect is for winds in temperate climates to mostly blow from the

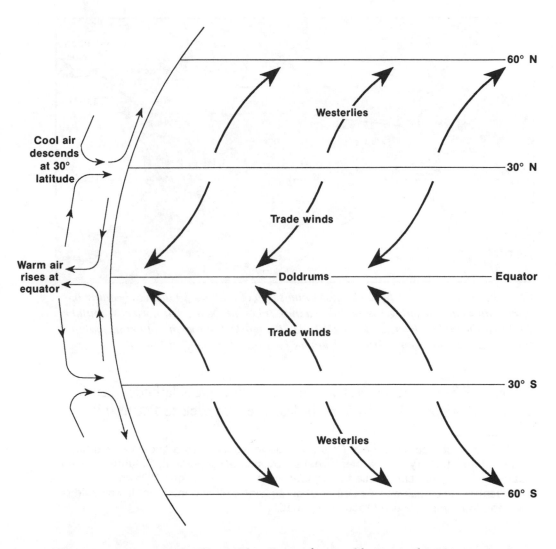

Wind patterns on Earth. The wealthier parts of most old cities in the temperate regions (between 30 and 60 degrees of latitude) are to the west because the Coriolis effect causes winds to blow predominantly from the west (more correctly, from the southwest in the Northern Hemisphere and from the northwest in the Southern Hemisphere).

southwest in the Northern Hemisphere and from the northwest in the Southern Hemisphere.

Being a mariner, Columbus knew this, of course. Heading west on his first transatlantic voyage, he stayed south of latitude 30 degrees (sailing from the Canary Islands to San Salvador in September and October 1492), thereby missing the worst of the westerlies. Returning home between January and March the following year, he started by

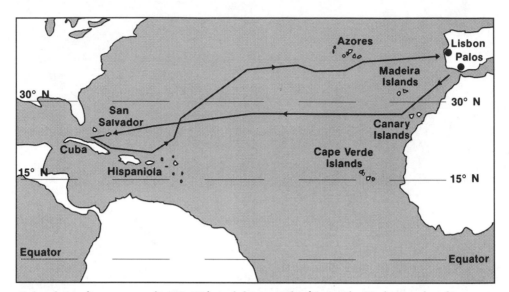

Columbus's first voyage (1492–93) took him south of latitude 30 degrees heading out so he could take advantage of the trade winds. Inbound, he headed northeast until he could run with the westerlies above latitude 30 degrees. I've shown Columbus making landfall at San Salvador, but no one knows for sure where he first landed.

sailing northeast until he was well north of 30 degrees latitude, then he turned half-right and sailed more or less due east back to Portugal.[18]

18. In *The Mysterious History of Columbus*, John Noble Wilford quotes an earlier author, John H. Parry, who wrote, "Whether by luck or judgement, Columbus sailed nearly the best possible course throughout most of the passage." Wilford comments, "Columbus was a mariner of surpassing skill and intuition. It was said of this man that he had 'a wind rose in his head.'"

A Conversation with
Stephen Jay
Gould

——

I could only say with the most fierce resolution, "Not yet Lord, not yet." I could not dent the richness in a hundred lifetimes, but I simply must have a look at a few more of those pretty pebbles.

—Stephen Jay Gould,
considering his own mortality in
The Flamingo's Smile

*D*r. Stephen Jay Gould is a professor of geology at Harvard University. A prolific lecturer and author, his monthly essays in *Natural History* magazine have been republished in books such as *The Panda's Thumb* and *Hens' Teeth and Horses' Toes.* In 1989, his fans were treated to *Wonderful Life: The Burgess Shale and the Nature of History.* In that book, Gould discussed fossils found in a particularly well-preserved layer of shale in the Canadian Rockies, where the soft anatomy of organisms dating back nearly 570 million years has been serendipitously preserved "down to the last filament of a trilobite's gill." Gould made the case that data from the Burgess shale reveal just how lucky we humans and other extant fauna are to be here. Former life-forms—as re-created from their

Stephen Jay Gould.
(Harvard University News Office)

fossil remnants in the shale—are quite different from anything alive today. For no particular reason, said Gould, they died out while others survived. Recently, many of the Burgess re-creations he cited have been challenged as erroneous. However, Gould stands by his conclusion that contingency is pivotal in deciding which species live and which die.

Barry Evans The popular concept of evolution is that it is a directed mechanism, a march of progress which somehow culminates in Homo sapiens. Cartoons frequently show a sequence of figures from an ape on all fours to a human being, generally male, striding into the future—

Stephen Jay Gould I'm probably the world's biggest collector of those figures!

B. E. You've repeatedly stressed that this idea of a march, or ladder, of human progress is an erroneous one. If you could pick just one example from the fossil record which counters it, what would it be?

S. J. G. The vast predominance of the fossils of insects in the current biota. Eighty percent of living animals are species of arthropods,[19] and in those we see no trends towards the increase of neurological complexity. Look at "Burgess shale" arthropods [whose fossils date to about 530 million years ago] and look at modern arthropods: they're much the same sort of thing. They are the most common of all groups over a period of nearly 600 million years, not moving in any canonical direction. Clearly [an increase in complexity] can't be characteristic of the history of life.

B. E. You've frequently discussed the role of what you call contingency in evolution. It seems to relegate Darwin's natural selection to a lesser status than just pure luck.

S. J. G. Darwin's theory is local adaptation *for the moment.* So [the climate] gets colder and the elephant grows hair and becomes a

---

19. The phylum, or category, of creatures that includes insects, arachnids, and crustaceans.

woolly mammoth. That caricature isn't grossly off, but that [adaptation] doesn't accumulate through time to anything, especially if it gets warm again. The point is, whatever determinism you have for the moment is only adaptation to immediate and changing local environments. It doesn't "coagulate" into directional trends [over a long period of] time.

I think contingency allows you to have causality for the moment. But since the vector of environmental change is effectively random, there's no reason why even the processes under the control of natural selection should accumulate towards any patterned increase of general excellence.

B. E. In *Wonderful Life*, you wrote, "This final result [of a sequence of evolutionary steps] is therefore dependent, or contingent, upon everything that came before—the unerasable and determining signature of history." Somehow it's hard to dissociate this idea of contingency with pure, blind luck! Is there really a difference?

S. J. G. Absolutely. Again, natural selection is a mechanism of immediate change. You get your environmental change and you might have a very predictable kind of selected response in organisms, but the question is, what does that translate to through time? There's no predictability or pattern to the panoply of environmental change through time, nor can you predict it. It's not random in the vernacular sense of that term, nor subject to explanation; but it is formally unpredictable.

B. E. There isn't anything predictable in that sense? Could an extraterrestrial paleontologist who visited Earth 66 million years ago have inferred nothing about the future of dinosaurs by looking at the previous hundred million years?

S. J. G. Oh yes. They would have predicted continued success for them. They were doing very well, after all. I think that would have been the best prediction, but it would have been wrong.

B. E. Is there anything about the mammalian record to suggest that we would still be little nocturnal creatures if the KT impact [See Chapter 2, "Blind Luck"] hadn't happened?

S. J. G. Sure—a hundred million years of previous history. What else do you have to go on? For two-thirds of the history of mammals, that's all there were. Why would you have predicted anything else (even though something else happened)?

There were broadly predictable features in evolution, but I don't think they apply much to the history of particular linkages. If you want to ask me whether I'd predict that there would be predators and prey, I'd say yes. Would I predict there would be bilateral symmetry?[20] Yes, as long as things are mobile. But would I predict that arthropods would come to dominate? No. Would I predict that mammals would eventually rule the vertebrate world? Certainly not.

B. E.   Does intelligence run counter to natural selection at some level?

S. J. G.   Not counter to natural selection. It might run counter to our long-term survivability, that remains to be seen; you can't predict it.

B. E.   But isn't survivability the whole point of natural selection?

S. J. G.   No! The whole point of natural selection is to become better adapted *to the moment*. Natural selection has no future prescience. Whatever happens in the future is due to good or bad luck with respect to the reason why natural selection made you that way. Intelligence might have been a great thing a million years ago, and it might do us in. Natural selection can't pay attention to that. It isn't that kind of process. It's a momentary process.

B. E.   The way most scientists think of science is as a *process* to converge on "the truth," whereas many lay people think of science as *content*, a black box of facts. Do you agree?

S. J. G.   It's not erroneous. I would certainly align myself with most colleagues as defining it as the process whereby knowledge is gained and tested. But as far as the public is concerned, the tidbits of knowledge thereby gained are fascinating. I don't mind including this part within the definition of science, that is, the accumulation of the bits themselves. You don't want to define it that way, though, because the bits are always changing, and what we learned as kids is mostly wrong, while the process remains.

B. E.   On the PBS "Nova" show about you, you talked about how your dad took you to see dinosaur skeletons in a museum when you were five years old, and you were inspired then and there to become a paleontologist. What's been the major change in paleontology since then?

---

20. That is, the left side being roughly mirror-imaged by the right side.

S. J. G.   At that time invertebrate paleontology was basically a geologically oriented discipline, with very little evolutionary work. There's a lot more attention now to evolutionary theory and what you can learn from the fossil record about processes of change and the meaning of history. Also, there have been a whole bunch of things that have happened since then: catastrophic impact mass extinction theories and punctuated equilibrium theory,[21] to name just two.

B. E.   Would it be fair to say that paleontology has evolved from a "static" to a "dynamic" science?

S. J. G.   It's certainly become dynamic; I wouldn't say it was totally static. I would say it's evolved to be more a theoretical discipline.

B. E.   Do you believe that qualities like "curiosity" and "wonder" play a role in evolution? Doesn't a strong sense of curiosity have an adaptive advantage?

S. J. G.   The idea that curiosity has an adaptive advantage reflects a caricatured version of evolutionary theory, that is, everything that exists has a direct and immediate adaptive significance in terms of natural selection. Biology is much more complicated. There are massive imperfections, nonadaptations, side consequences, oddities, quirks, changes.

B. E.   Isn't curiosity like intelligence? That is, aren't the more curious species of, say, primates the ones more likely to reproduce?

S. J. G.   I think you're trying to quantify something that doesn't lend itself to quantification. I don't work in the field of speculations about adaptive advantages of things that can't be quantified. There's not an entity called "curiosity." [Even if there were] I don't think natural selection works on it in the direct sense.

B. E.   But curiosity does seem to play a major role in the lives of humans and other primates.

S. J. G.   Sure, most children have intense curiosities about things, and it's very characteristic, at least of mammals, for juveniles to be very

---

21. Dr. Gould is coauthor, with Niles Eldredge, of the 1972 theory of punctuated equilibrium, which postulates that evolution occurred in short periods of rapid change interspersed with long periods of little change. Charles Darwin had assumed that small gradual changes accumulated to ultimately produce large changes.

playful and exploratory. Since people are juveniles all their lives in some important respects, it does seem to be an important component of our makeup, but I don't think it can be measured.

B. E. Does curiosity drop off with age?

S. J. G. Yes, it's very characteristic of mammals, as they become sexually mature, that there's a marked decrease in the amount of time devoted to play and those behaviors that you would call flexible and curious.

B. E. Is it possible to look at our primate cousins and make some conclusions by comparing their curiosity with their adaptability?

S. J. G. As I said, curiosity isn't a quantifiable entity. What we rank as curiosity in primate species, given how different they are from us, is not likely to be the same thing we call curiosity in us. Also, your basic premise behind even posing the question that way is that the right way to look at curiosity is in terms of its adaptive significance under natural selection. That's wrong.

I suspect we're primarily curious because our brains are complex enough to force it on us. The [human] brain got complex perhaps, by natural selection, but not in order that we could be curious. It's probably just the way brains work.

B. E. Do you consciously nurture your own curiosity and wonder?

S. J. G. I think the best way to deal with wonder is to let it work and not get too introspective about it. Let me make an analogy: Can writing be taught? Well, certain things can be taught, grammar and construction of paragraphs. You can teach anyone to be a competent writer, but can you teach them to be a very good writer? Probably not.

I feel the same about this: I don't think you can teach creativity or that you can teach the sense of wonder. All you can do is talk about its value, talk about what you can do with it, how the potential for it is in all of us. And how easy it is for education to suppress it.

Tuesday's Puzzles

Beyond the Assumptions

What is science if not the posing of difficult puzzles
by the universe?

—Martin Gardner, *Aha! Insight*

I like to think that puzzling, whether over a crossword or a murder mystery, frees me from old thinking patterns. Puzzles force my mind into new (or forgotten) territory, and in that sense the process is akin to creativity, but it isn't quite the same. We're talking lateral thinking. Edward de Bono said, "Whereas insight, creativity and humour can only be prayed for, lateral thinking is a more deliberate process. It is as definite a way of using the mind as logical thinking—but in a very different way."[22]

1. Here's an almost absurd example of lateral thinking that occasionally stumps the brightest and best. Take a coffee cup and an $8\frac{1}{2}$-by-11-inch sheet of paper, make a small hole, say, 1 inch in diameter in the center of the paper, and push the cup through the hole.

   Hint 1: Suppose the assignment was to push the cup along the table?
   Hint 2: First, put your finger through the hole, then . . .

---

22. Edward de Bono, *Lateral Thinking: Creativity Step by Step.* De Bono formally defines lateral thinking as "a set of attitudes, idioms, and techniques . . . for cutting across patterns in self-organizing asymmetric patterning systems. It is used to generate new concepts and perceptions."

2. Part 1: Here is a regular chessboard except its opposite corners are missing. Can you cover the board with 31 rectangular blocks, each the size of two squares?

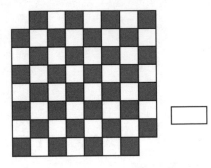

Part 2: Here is a five-by-five-inch chessboard. Starting on the square marked with a dot, can an ant walk through each square once and only once without going outside the heavy line?

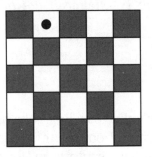

Hint 1: What's common to both problems?
Hint 2: In Part 1, how many black squares have to be covered?
Hint 3: How many white? Are they the same?
Hint 4: In Part 2, what color will the ant end on?

3. How many triangles are in this figure?

Hint: There are more than 30.

4. Speaking of self-imposed boundaries . . . no, that's giving away too much. Here's the puzzle: Take six wooden matches as shown. Assemble them, without breaking, so they form four triangles, each side of which is equal to the length of the matches.

Hint: Like the last puzzle, you may be working within your own self-imposed boundaries. How many dimensions can you work in?

5. Does this next one require you to enter new mental territory? Perhaps not. It does, however, call on you to go beyond the obvious: A jeweler charges one dollar to cut a link of chain and reweld it. You take her four chains of 3 links each, as shown. What's the least it will it cost to make them into a closed loop of 12 rings?

Hint: Suppose the task was to create a 12-link chain out of three chains of three links each plus three loose links?

Puzzle answers are at the back of the book.

Tuesday's Quotations

Surprise and Passion

It is one thing to be amazed at a gorgon or a griffin, creatures which do not exist; but it is quite another and much higher thing to be amazed at a rhinoceros or a giraffe, creatures which do exist and look as if they don't.

—G. K. Chesterton

A day of acquaintance
And then the longer span of custom
But first—
The hour of astonishment.

—Apple Computer HyperCard credits

Is not life a hundred times too short for us to bore ourselves?

—Friedrich Nietzsche

When one door closes, another opens: but we often look so long upon the closed door that we do not see the one which has opened for us.

—Alexander Graham Bell

I travel not to go anywhere, but to go. I travel for travel's sake. The great affair is to move.

—**Robert Louis Stevenson**

The great affair, the love affair with life, is to live as variously as possible, to groom one's curiosity like a high-spirited thoroughbred, climb aboard, and gallop over the thick, sun-struck hills every day. Where there is no risk, the emotional terrain is flat and unyielding, and, despite all its dimensions, valleys, pinnacles, and detours, life will seem to have none of its magnificent geography, only a length. It began in mystery, and it will end in mystery, but what a savage and beautiful country lies in between.

—**Diane Ackerman**

Give me miraculous eyes to see my eyes,
Those rolling mirrors made alive in me,
Terrible crystal more incredible
Than all the things they see.

—**G. K. Chesterton**

As their highnesses travelled, they were always making discoveries, by accident or sagacity, of things they were not in quest of.
—**Horace Walpole (*The Three Princes of Serendip*,**
hence our word *serendipity*. "Serendip" is
present-day Sri Lanka.)

All the arts we practice are apprenticeship. The big art is our life.
—**M. C. Richard**

A pile of rocks ceases to be a pile of rocks when somebody contemplates it with the idea of a cathedral in mind.
—**Antoine de Saint-Exupéry**

*[The reason riders on the London subway look so sad and tired is]
because after they have passed Sloane Square they know that the
next station must be Victoria, and nothing but Victoria. Oh, their
wild rapture! Oh, their eyes like stars and their souls again in
Eden, if the next station were unaccountably Baker Street!*

—**G. K. Chesterton**

Wednesday

Day of Mercury

*A*fter the Roman withdrawal from Britain
early in the fifth century, Germanic raids
devastated with fire "all the neighboring
cities and lands . . . until it burnt nearly
the whole surface of the island, and licked
the western ocean with its red and savage
tongue," according to the British cleric
Gildas. Those tough raiders, soon to
become settlers (and, incidentally, ethnic
ancestors of most Americans), also
brought their language to Britain,
including our words *Tuesday*, *Wednesday*,
Thursday, and *Friday* (see Chapter 8, "For
the Week-Hearted").

Wednesday must have been a day of

great importance to the German tribes, since they named it for their supreme god, Woden. Woden's children Tyr and Thor became Tuesday and Thursday, while his wife, Frigga, gave us the word *Friday*. For most of us, however, Wednesday is the middle of the working week, perhaps the least "interesting" of all our days.

Curiously, of all children, Wednesday's child has been given a bad rap: he or she is, according to the well-known nursery rhyme, "full of woe" (no connection to Woden!). Kids born on other days of the week sound OK, from Monday's "fair of face" to Friday's "loving and giving." Do you know on what day you were born?

Seven

Secret Worlds

I can't see you, but I know you're there.

> —Ex-angel Peter Falk talking to an
> invisible angel in Wim Wenders's
> *Wings of Desire*

*If the eye could see the demons that people the universe,
existence would be impossible.*

> —The Talmud

***P*icture** this: You're walking down the street minding your own business when suddenly there's a little buzz, a faint smell of ozone, a momentary chill, and everything looks different than it did a second earlier. You find yourself standing in a clearing in the middle of a jungle, somewhat dazed but alert. Fortunately, you've seen enough late-night "Twilight Zone" episodes to know exactly what's going on. "I must have walked right into an Einstein anomaly," you calmly say to yourself. "One of those little tears in the fabric of the universe that instantly transports a person from one set of space-time coordinates into another. Oh well, no big deal. Might as well make the best of it."

Turns out you've been shifted in space but not in time, and you've landed in a remote village in New Guinea. The locals gather round, for they've never seen anyone like you. They're particularly curious about that little box you're holding. Did I mention you happened to be carrying a battery-powered shortwave radio? You switch it on and someone's speaking. "Where's the voice coming from?" they ask. (You're a fast language learner.) "From the air," you reply. "We don't see anything," they say. "Radio waves are invisible," you tell them. They look at each other, licking their lips. "Looks like we've got a live one here," they say.

Without a radio to act as a detector, you'd never be aware of radio waves. In fact, right now, your body is being inundated with uncountable waves, forces, sounds, and particles to which your natural detectors—that is, your five senses—are blind. Detectors come in all shapes and sizes: a compass needle is sensitive to lines of magnetic force, a dog hears sounds beyond your range of hearing, a seismograph registers movements in the Earth's crust that you can't feel. In fact, our bodies are constantly flooded with information of which we're unaware because our senses are very limited in what they can detect.

Which is fortunate for our sanity! If our senses did register all the

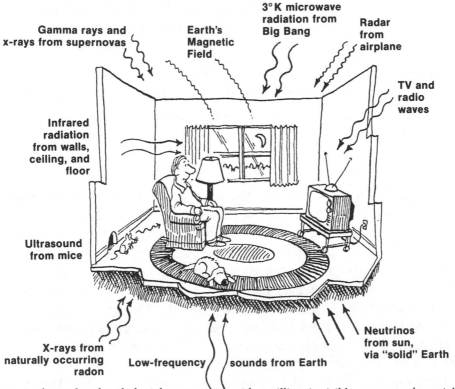

Gamma rays and x-rays from supernovas

Earth's Magnetic Field

3° K microwave radiation from Big Bang

Radar from airplane

TV and radio waves

Infrared radiation from walls, ceiling, and floor

Ultrasound from mice

X-rays from naturally occurring radon

Low-frequency sounds from Earth

Neutrinos from sun, via "solid" Earth

You're being bombarded, right now, with a zillion invisible waves and particles. The dog pricks up its ears, hearing an ultrasonic noise beyond the human range.

activity going on in the world around and inside us they'd be overloaded, and we'd probably lose our minds in minutes. It's been said that if a man's life were so totally informed that every bird and leaf spoke to him, and every happening had meaning, he'd be considered psychotic. There's so much going on around us to which we're oblivious.

Take neutrinos, for example. They are incredibly tiny particles that interact very weakly—if at all—with other particles, having no charge and probably no mass.[1] Day and night, 100 million of these particles, which originated deep in the sun, zip through our bodies every second. (There went another 100 million.) By day they come from above, a straight shot from the sun. By night, they enter us from below, through our feet, having passed through our apparently solid planet with the same ease that they pass through us. If we could feel them, I suppose it would be like standing in a never-ending torrential downpour (or "uppour," at night). Our senses would be literally swamped.

Similarly, if we saw the molecules that jostle in the air around us, if we heard the beat of our hearts, if we smelt not-so-recent cooking odors (which linger in tiny quantities for months), if we felt each atomic mountain on the surface of a page of a book, or if we tasted the glaze on a cup of coffee, we'd be overwhelmed. Our senses are attuned to the merest fraction of the cacophony of sensual activity surrounding us, and of those they can register, a yet-smaller fraction reaches our consciousness. Without the limited detection capabilities of our senses and relentless filtering of our nervous systems, we'd know no peace.

Limited Sensitivity

The human eye-brain structure has the marvelous ability to convert the two upside-down images on our retinas into single, upright, three-dimensional scenes for our comprehension. However, it's also very limited. Consider our restricted response to electromagnetic radiation, for instance. Electromagnetic radiation is a form of energy that comes in different wavelengths.[2] Of all possible wavelengths, our eyes are sensitive

---

1. Recent experimental evidence indicates that the electron neutrino may have a tiny "rest" mass, perhaps 20–30 electron volts.
2. In addition to being responsible for electromagnetic radiation, the electromagnetic force (the mutual attraction of particles having opposite electric or magnetic charges) holds atoms together as molecules, thus giving structure to matter.

to a very limited segment, the so-called visible-light spectrum: red, orange, yellow, green, blue, indigo, and violet. Some of what we don't see, we can feel. And what we can neither see nor feel we can detect with instruments, artificial extensions to our senses.

Beyond red lies, naturally, infrared. Our hands can feel infrared: when we first turn on a heating element on top of an electric stove, our eyes say "black," but our hands say "hot." Beyond the infrared lies the microwave band, and beyond that, radio and TV waves (detectable by, yep, radios and televisions).

At the opposite end of the spectrum, that is, beyond violet, lie shorter, more energetic waves. Just beyond our eyes' sensitivity (but within the range of the eyes of many insects), ultraviolet rays from the sun carry enough energy to give you a sunburn. Beyond ultraviolet, we encounter yet more energetic waves: x-rays and their extremely powerful cousins, gamma rays. The wavelength of gamma rays is so much smaller than individual atoms that they pass through most solids. At the extreme range, they are so strong that we detect them as gamma particles.

What we actually see, then, is but a tiny part of the whole. In the whole range of wavelengths running the gamut from a mile (radio) to the size of an atomic nucleus (gamma rays), our eyes detect only the tiny corridor lying between the infrared and ultraviolet.

With such a wide span of wavelengths available, why do we see in the range that we do? Because we're in thrall to the sun. If you were raised in Rome, you'd automatically speak Italian, since that's the

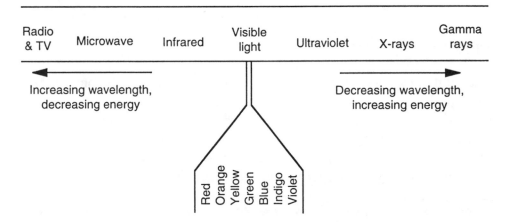

The electromagnetic spectrum. Of nature's entire spectrum, our eyes are sensitive only to the tiny fraction we call "visible light." The (logarithmic) scale is deceptively short: the wavelengths shown actually span a range from a mile to the diameter of an atomic nucleus. We see in wavelengths corresponding to the size of the largest atoms.

language you'd mostly encounter. Similarly, if you evolve near a particular star, you're likely to develop organs sensitive to the predominant wavelength of electromagnetic radiation available, that of your star. In our case, that's the sun.

Imagine being kidnapped (yet again) and taken to a planet in a distant galaxy. When you arrive, the kidnappers realize they forgot to check what sort of star our planet orbits. No problem! They send you to the local Alien Ophthalmologist, who checks your eyes and declares, "This being's visual detectors are sensitive to radiation with a wavelength a little blueward of one micron.[3] That means the being's star must radiate most strongly at that wavelength, so it's probably from a G2 V-type star about halfway through its 10-billion year life." That's our sun the A.O. is talking about.

Limited Awareness

Not only do we have limited detection abilities, but we have limited awareness of what our senses *do* detect. Most of the visible activity registered by our eyes, in the slender visible-light spectrum, is filtered out by our brains before reaching consciousness. Looking at the computer screen in front of me, I can see, but am not normally aware of, the hills through the window on my right, the fax machine on the table on the left, and the mosaic *Earth from Space* on the wall behind the computer. By an effort of will, I can be aware of them without turning my head or eyes, but most of the time I see but don't see. I (whoever that is) am constantly choosing what to be aware of and what to ignore.

It's much more subtle than this brief discussion, of course. I remember sitting on the shore of an island in British Columbia nearly 20 years ago, seeing as if for the first time. It was one of those utterly magical days that comes from time to time, and I was intensely aware that my eyes were picking up details of form and color I'd never noticed before. Two miles away, across the channel, the sun shone brightly on the forested flank of another island, and I saw individual leaves on those trees. Part of my mind rejected this as an outright lie: I assumed it was

---

3. 1 micron = 1 millionth of a meter. Visible light is usually specified in nanometers, billionths of a meter. The human eye is sensitive to light between about 380 (violet) and 750 (deep red) nanometers. The sun radiates most intensely at about 600 nanometers, while our eyes are most sensitive at about 550 nanometers.

impossible to see individual leaves at that distance, no matter how good one's eyesight. As a test, I picked an individual limb on one tree and noted the pattern of leaves. Then I looked away, trying to memorize the pattern. When I looked back, I saw the same pattern. Not too scientific, granted, but a clue, perhaps, to the relationship between what I can see— and, for the most part, filter out—and what I do see and am aware of.[4]

The invisible world swirls all around us. Perhaps we're not so far removed from those New Guineans you amazed when you switched on your radio. Only in the last few decades have we learned to detect energies that would have seemed to be magic, witchcraft, or the work of the devil a few centuries ago. Much is still unknown to us. Can animals sense the very low frequency vibrations that may forewarn of earthquakes? Possibly. Do homing pigeons have built-in magnetic compasses? Almost certainly. The following section gives some examples from the animal world, demonstrating that they can "see" what we can't.

Meanwhile, watch out for those Einstein anomalies!

Animal Sensitivity

It is only with the heart that one can see rightly; what is essential is invisible to the eye.

—Antoine de Saint-Exupéry,
The Little Prince

*E*volution has endowed many species with receptors, sensitive far beyond our own, to meet particular needs in their lives. What follows is a brief look at just one or two examples of animal sensitivity from each of our five senses.

Vision. While most larger animals sense their surroundings in what to us is the visible-light (red through violet) spectrum, many smaller creatures can see what to us is invisible, in the infrared or ultraviolet

---

4. According to *The Guinness Book of Records*, the eye can separate details in an image 3–5 seconds of arc (a measurement of angle) away from each other. That's like making out a silver dollar from a mile. The record goes to a Houston physician who could identify the position of a thin white line within 0.85 seconds of arc. That's equivalent to resolving a pencil a mile away, so my observation is within the bounds of possibility.

Human view of a marsh marigold (Caltha palustris*) in the visible-light spectrum.* (Thomas Eisner)

The same flower photographed in ultra-violet light, making it easily recognizable to a flying insect whose eyes are sensitive to the ultraviolet. (Thomas Eisner)

spectrum (or, in the case of the lowly goldfish, infrared *and* ultraviolet). Many flying insects—bees, for instance—are sensitive to colors deep into the ultraviolet, seeing what we can't: plants advertising their wares of nectar. Where we only see a white blossom, some insects see an advertisement as unmistakable as a neon-lit Coca-Cola sign: "Free food in return for cross-fertilization!" (Incidentally, a human whose lens has been surgically removed in cataract surgery can detect light some distance into the ultraviolet because the slight yellowness of our lenses normally filters out ultraviolet light.)

All snakes at one time burrowed underground, and some have retained their ability to see in what to us is the dark. Some snakes known as pit vipers (including rattlesnakes and copperheads) have retained their ability to "see" in infrared (beyond red) wavelengths. Their name comes from pit organs, deep facial openings on each side of the head between nostril and eye, which can detect infrared stereoscopically.[5] This means they can detect both the direction and distance of nearby warm prey by its temperature, in the same way our two eyes can tell us where and how far away an object is by visible light. (Try closing one eye to see how limited your depth-perception is with single vision.)

5. *Cuatro narices*, that is, "four nostrils," is the name given to pit vipers in parts of Latin America.

A rattlesnake's infrared-sensitive pit organs, located below its eyes, enable the animal to "see" the warm body of its prey. (Eric Newman)

In experiments, rattlesnakes could detect temperature differences as small as a quarter-degree Celsius up to 14 inches away.[6] Speed of detection is vital for a predator: a boa constrictor responds to infrared radiation from a carbon dioxide laser in $\frac{1}{30}$ second, while it takes man-made instruments almost a minute to do the same.[7]

Smell. A dog's world is dominated by smell. Have you ever watched one follow a scent? My friend Mark told me how his German shepherd would follow a fresh trail as if it were visible. While a friend distracted Osa in the car, Mark would run zigzag up a hill and hide at the top, all the while out of the dog's sight. When let out of the car with the exhortation "Go find him!" Osa would bound up the hill, nose to the ground, turning, on cue, exactly where Mark had turned a few minutes earlier, "as if she were seeing a bright yellow ribbon to follow."

The gold medal in smelling sensitivity currently goes to the emperor moth. In an experiment in Germany, male moths could detect the sex

6. Laurence M. Klauber, *Rattlesnakes: Their Habits, Life Histories, and Influence on Mankind*, page 69.
7. Sandra Sinclair, *How Animals See: Other Visions of Our World*, page 85.

attractor of a virgin female moth nearly seven miles upwind. Now that's chemistry! Incidentally, human body odor hasn't always been viewed with the disgust that TV deodorant commercials have taught us should be our natural reaction. Only recently has bathing become socially proper. As Napoleon wrote to Josephine after a battle,"Ne te lave pas. Je reviens."[8]

Touch. "[Touch] is the most basic, the most nonconceptual form of communication that we have. In touch, there are no language barriers; anything that can walk, fly, creep, crawl, or swim already speaks it."[9] Most aquatic animals have a sublime sense of touch. Fish, for instance, know how fast they're moving thanks to a complex organ, the "lateral line," which is acutely sensitive to the rate of flow of water past it. The Mexican cave fish is blind, its eyes having degenerated aeons ago, yet it uses its astounding sense of touch to sense differences in water pressure and navigate unerringly in eternally dark caves.

In addition to being exquisitely sensitive to water pressure, dolphins are masters of echolocation, that is, production of high-pitched bursts of ultrasound that reflect back to them off their prey, much as radar shows

Osa following a scent trail in Baja California. (Mark D. Conover)

8. "Don't bathe. I'm coming."
9. Ina May Gaskin, *Spiritual Midwifery.*

an air-traffic controller the location of airplanes. For 20 years, I've been haunted by the only slightly hyperbolic opening lines of *The Day of the Dolphin*. Actor George C. Scott is showing a movie (within the movie) of some mammalian cousins of ours, dolphins, in action. "Imagine," he says,

"that your life is spent in an environment of total physical sensation. That every one of your senses has been heightened to a level that in a human being might only be described as ecstatic. That you're able to see, to perceive, with every part of your being—sight, hearing, taste, smell—and that every inch of your surface, your skin, is a receptor, a continuous source of perfectly accurate information about the world for miles around."

These two Atlantic bottlenose dolphins helped researchers evaluate the species' echolocation abilities during a two-year stay at the University of California at Santa Cruz's Long Marine Laboratory. They were subsequently released in their home waters in the Gulf of Mexico, where their successful readaptation to the wild was monitored. (Randall Wells)

Hearing. In Bracken Cave, near San Antonio, Texas, the normal population of 20 million Mexican free-tailed bats doubles every March as each female bears her single baby, or pup. (Since males are outnumbered 200 to 1, you can ignore them in the figures!) Twice a night, the mother leaves her offspring and takes to the outside air, flying up to 60 miles in one trip to feed on moths and winged ants. On her return, she faces a problem of insane proportions: how to locate her pup out of 20 million others, in order to feed it. First, she emits high-pitched squeaks inaudible to human ears, which bounce back to her from the cave walls, to find the specific "crèche" region of the cave where she left her pup. We call that sonar echolocation. Then, incredibly, she hones in on squeaks from her own pup, ignoring the cacophony from all the others. Finally, she uses her acute sense of smell to double-check before proffering her milk-rich teats. You can get some feel for echolocation by making a noise in a dark room, especially if it's built of stone. Old English churches are perfect.

Thousands of Mexican free-tailed bats emerging at dusk from Bracken Cave, Texas. (Merlin D. Tuttle, Bat Conservation International)

A tiny portion of a bat crèche in Bracken Cave. A mother bat (upper left) must search through millions of baby bats to find and nurse her own pup. (Merlin D. Tuttle, Bat Conservation International)

You'll instinctively sense where and how far away the walls are by cueing in to the direction and timing of echoes.

Taste. To us, seawater tastes salty. To salmon of the Pacific northwest, the water in which they live is rich with subtle tastes and odors, which allow them to locate the specific river in which they were born. When they return to their birthplace to spawn, typically four years later, they unerringly enter the river from which they came, having followed delicate taste cues from the water of their birth.

Green turtles regularly migrate across 1,400 miles of featureless ocean from feeding areas off the coast of Brazil to nesting grounds on tiny Ascension Island. How can they possibly find a 34-square-mile island in the middle of the 10 million square miles of the South Atlantic? They get the general drift, so to speak, from current directions and wave patterns. But the fine-tuning seems to come from their ability to actually taste minute concentrations of chemicals originating on the island's beaches when the turtles are hundreds of miles "downstream" of the island.

Catfish and spiny lobsters are almost unbelievably sensitive to certain tastes. Investigators have shown they are able to detect very low concentrations of a particular amino acid. How low? Imagine stirring one-hundredth of a teaspoon of the acid into an Olympic-size swimming pool filled with seawater. Yes, they'll know!

Eight

For the Week-Hearted

*After I had been there about ten or twelve days, it came into
my thoughts, that I should lose my reckoning of time for
want of books and pen and ink, and should even forget the
Sabbath days from the working days; but to prevent this
I cut it with my knife upon a large post. . . .*

—Daniel Defoe, *Robinson Crusoe*

We live out our lives within a seven-day framework we call the week.
Just as we can trust that the sun will come up tomorrow, we can be sure
that Saturday will always follow Friday and Tuesday will come round,
regular as clockwork, every seventh day. Imagine that you slept right
through a whole day for some odd reason: you might not notice that the
date had skipped from, say, April 15 to April 17, but I bet you'd notice
if Wednesday just disappeared.

I realize how attuned I am to the week when my wife, Louisa, and
I take one of our regular bicycle tours in Europe. Every year or two we
fly with our bikes to Italy or France and spend four to six weeks of
unstructured time cycling, exploring, and drinking cappuccino or café au
lait in little mountain villages. Even then, with no appointments to keep
or schedules to meet, at any moment I could unhesitatingly tell you the
day of the week. For most of us, whether we're working or vacationing,
the day of the week is one of the first things we think of when we wake
in the morning.

Yet those two, the day and the week, are totally different concepts. The day is marked by light and dark, and human bodies respond to it accordingly, slaves to our ancient genetic messages. The 7-day week, on the other hand, is arbitrary and artificial. It follows no natural cycle, as is obvious when you realize that other cultures have gotten along quite happily with 3-day weeks (ancient Colombia), 4-day weeks (much of rural Africa, even today), 8-day weeks (early Rome), 10-day weeks (ancient Peru, revolutionary France), and even 19-day weeks (Baha'i faith)! In rural areas even today, notably in West Africa, the length of the week depends on how many villages make up the local economic unit. Five villages means a 5-day week, so that each village gets to hold a market once a week.

The week, in other words, is a convenient unit of time longer than a day and shorter than a month. It corresponds to no natural period.

Keeping the Faith

Today is Monday. It says so on our bathroom calendar, and the daily newspaper has "Monday" at the top of every page, so it must be true. When we agree to call today Monday (i.e., "moon-day"), we're keeping the faith. This particular faith, which dates back to a hundred or so years before Christ, maintains that every seventh day is ruled by the moon. Without fail, people have acknowledged every seventh day to be the moon's for over 2,000 years. Like an endless chain letter, the cycle of days of the week has been maintained steadfastly by the Greeks, Romans, Angles, Saxons, Vikings, and all the rest who came before us. We just happen to be the latest generation to keep the faith. You might want to think about that when the alarm goes off in the morning and you're trying to remember what day it is!

Some examples of our attachment to the days of the week:

◆ In July 1982, when U.S. Brigadier General James Dozier was rescued from Italian Red Brigades terrorists who had been holding him hostage for nearly two months, his first question to his rescuers was, "What day of the week is it?" It wouldn't seem to make much difference, but knowing it helped reconnect him psychologically with the everyday and familiar world from which he'd been isolated. (It was Thursday.)

◆ In 1582, Pope Gregory XIII instituted the calendar reform still in use today—without changing the sequence of days. In the previous Julian calendar, the average length of the year was about 11 minutes longer than the natural year. The error had built up over the centuries so that by 1582 the date was out of synchronization with the seasons by 10 days. To bring the calendar back into line, the pope ordered that Thursday, October 4, 1582, was to be followed by October 15th. Now, if the 4th of a month is Thursday, the 15th should be Monday, but the pope declared that the 15th was to be *Friday*. Even he was unwilling to mess with the order of days, in particular the Biblical injunction that every 7th day was the Lord's day.

◆ And what did Daniel Defoe's hero Robinson Crusoe call the first man he met after being shipwrecked on a desert island? "Man Friday." Crusoe was definitely into days. He kept track of them by carving notches in a tree trunk, with a double-length notch for Sunday.

Name That Day

Although the structure of our week may have had earlier beginnings in Mesopotamia, the Alexandrian Greeks in the second century B.C. were probably the first to combine the Jewish seven-day week (which goes back at least to the time of their captivity in Babylon, after the destruction of the Temple in Jerusalem, 586 B.C.[10]) with Babylonian astrology.[11] Aeons before the invention of the telescope in 1608, stargazers noted that seven bodies regularly moved through the sky relative to the background stars, which is probably why the number seven has mystical connotations in so many cultures.[12]

---

10. Perhaps earlier, to Moses, who ordered his flock to keep the Sabbath holy. The book of Genesis, with its account of seven days of Creation, dates back to at least 700 B.C. and perhaps to 1000 B.C. in some oral traditions.

11. The earliest *definitive* evidence for the present order of days of the week comes from a wall painting in Pompeii, which must have been done prior to A.D. 79 (when the city was buried in ash during an eruption of Mount Vesuvius). It shows the personifications of the gods controlling each of the seven days in the same weekly order that we use. (See John Percy Balsdon and Vyvian Dacre's *Life and Leisure in Ancient Rome*.) Other evidence indicates that the days of the week in their present order were being used in the Roman Empire, in particular in Alexandria, 100–200 years earlier.

12. Although in Petronius's *Satyricon*, usually dated to around A.D. 61, we read, "On the other [doorpost] was represented the course of the moon and the seven planets, and what days were lucky or unlucky." I'm baffled as to what the eighth body was.

Those old-time astrologers counted five planets visible to the unaided eye,[13] together with the sun and moon. These seven wanderers (the word *planet* comes from the Greek verb *planasthai*, to wander) all appear to move at different speeds through the sky. For instance, relative to the stars, Saturn takes nearly 30 years to make a full revolution, the sun takes a year, and the moon takes about a month. In order, from "slow" to "fast," the seven are: Saturn, Jupiter, Mars, the sun, Venus, Mercury, and the moon.

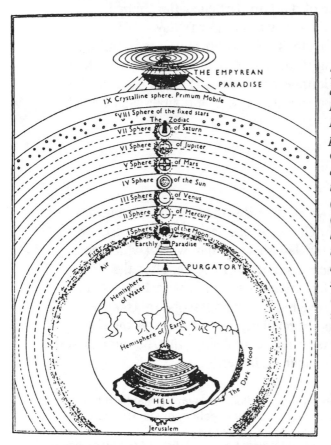

The sun, moon, and planets move at different speeds around the Earth. In The Divine Comedy, *Dante Alighieri (1265–1321) placed them in a sequence of orbits beyond the Earth in accordance with the periods of their rotation, from the moon (about a month) to Saturn (nearly 30 years). Beyond Saturn lies the sphere of fixed stars and the crystalline sphere, on which lies the empyrean paradise surrounded by angelic spheres. Uranus, Neptune, and Pluto were not known in Dante's time.*

To the ancients, "the heavens" were literally a different realm from the Earth, although they were curiously linked: what went on Up There affected what happened Down Here. In particular, each of the seven heavenly wanderers, or their divine personifications, influenced each of

---

13. Uranus is actually visible to the naked eye under clear, dark skies, but it wasn't identified as a planet until William Herschel noted its movement relative to the background stars in 1781. It had been listed in star catalogs many times prior to that, and even Herschel at first took it for a comet.

our days. Thus, Dies Saturna, or Saturday (the Roman first day of the week), came under Saturn's influence. The sun and moon ruled Dies Solis (Sunday) and Dies Lunae (Monday), respectively. The remaining four days of the week, Tuesday, Wednesday, Thursday, and Friday, were assigned to Mars, Mercury, Jupiter, and Venus, respectively. Sometimes, the connection is more obvious in other languages than in English. Here's a small sampling:

"Planet"	English	Meaning	Latin	French	Welsh	Finnish
sun	Sunday	sun's day	Dies Solis	dimanche	Dydd Sul	Sunnuntai
moon	Monday	moon's day	Dies Lunae	lundi	Dydd Llun	Maanantai
Mars	Tuesday	Tiw's day	Dies Martis	mardi	Dydd Mawrth	Tiistai
Mercury	Wednesday	Woden's day	Dies Mercurii	mecredi	Dydd Mercher	(Keskiviikko)
Jupiter	Thursday	Thor's day	Dies Jovis	jeudi	Dydd Iau	Torstai
Venus	Friday	Frigg's day	Dies Veneris	vendredi	Dydd Gwener	(Perjantai)
Saturn	Saturday	Saturn's day	Dies Saturna	samedi	Dydd Sadwrn	(Lauantai)

You can see that four of the names of weekdays in English have succumbed to Norse theology, under the influence of Angles, Saxons, and Jutes who settled England in the so-called Dark Ages. They are:

♦ *Tuesday.* From the Old Norse Tyr (or Tiw), the Teutonic god of war who was identified with Roman Mars. The Old Norse name is cognate with the Latin word *deus*, which in turn comes from Greek Zeus, "the father of gods and men," according to Homer. (To complicate matters, Zeus was identified with Jupiter in the Roman pantheon, but he gets his own day, Thursday.)

♦ *Wednesday.* The day of Woden or Wodan (in Anglo-Saxon mythology), Odin (Scandinavian), or Wotan (German). Odin was identified with Mercury by the Roman historian Tacitus.

♦ *Thursday.* From Thor or Thunor, eldest son of Odin, who was the Scandinavian Vulcan, god of thunder. He's associated with the Roman planet-god Jupiter.

♦ *Friday.* From Frigga, Frig, or Freya (curiously cognate with the English word *free*), the Scandinavian goddess of love and wife of Odin. She's associated with Roman Venus, who in turn is connected with Greek Aphrodite.

Our other days of the week, Saturday, Sunday, and Monday, have obvious derivations (Saturn, sun, and moon) in English, although the first two have been superseded in most other Indo-European languages.

While English still uses the astrological "Saturday," you can see the Jewish "Sabbath" (Hebrew Shabbath) in many other Indo-European languages, for example, sábado, Sábbato, and Szombat, in Spanish, Greek, and Hungarian, respectively. (The connection between the planet Saturn and the Sabbath had been made as early as A.D. 100, when the Jews named the heavenly body Shabtai). Since Saturn traditionally exerts a negative influence, perhaps the Jews thought that by making Saturn's day a holiday they could avoid the problems that would inevitably result from working on that day!

Our pagan "Sunday" has been Christianized in most European languages, for example, as domingo and Domenica in Spanish and Italian respectively, derived from Latin *dies Domenica*, the Lord's Day. In France, your *habit du dimanche* is your "Sunday best" outfit.

Why is Sunday considered to be the Lord's Day by most Christians?[14] The early Christians were Jews, for whom the principal day of worship was, as we've seen, Saturday. One way for them to assert a separate identity for their faith was for Christians to choose a separate day of worship,[15] and they probably chose Sunday because it was the Day

NOVEMBER 1989		NOVEMBER 1989		WEATHER RECORD
S M T W T F S				MON.
·· ·· ·· 1 2 3 4				
5 6 7 8 9 10 11				TUES.
12 13 14 15 16 17 18				
19 20 21 22 23 24 25				WED.
26 27 28 29 30 ·· ··				
·· ·· ·· ·· ·· ·· ··	(310)	MONDAY, NOVEMBER 6 (55)		

9		1
10		2
11		3
12		4
EVENING		

*Does the week start on Sunday or Monday? Both, according to this desk diary! The calendar for the month is shown traditionally, with Sunday as the first day, but the diary entry starts with Monday. Is Sunday really part of the week*end?

---

14. Seventh-Day Adventists and Seventh-Day Baptists consider Saturday to be the most sacred day of the week, based on their interpretation of scriptures.
15. Six hundred years later, the young religion of Islam was faced with the same problem of symbolically separating from the "competition." Friday was chosen.

of the Resurrection. In the Jewish calendar, Sunday is the first day of the week, and the four Gospels agree that was the day Christ rose from the dead: "In the end of the sabbath, as it began to dawn toward the first day of the week, came Mary Magdalene and the other Mary to see the sepulchre." (Matthew 28:1) Today, our legacy from 2,000 years ago is one of ambiguity: does the week start on Sunday, as most calendars insist, or end, as defined in the word *weekend*?

Why a Week, Anyway?

A continuous seven-day cycle that runs throughout history paying no attention whatsoever to the moon and its phases is a distinctively Jewish invention. Moreover, the dissociation of the seven-day week from nature has been one of the most significant contributions of Judaism to civilization. Like the invention of the mechanical clock some 1,500 years later, it facilitated the establishment of what Lewis Mumford identified as "mechanical periodicity," thus essentially increasing the distance between human beings and nature.

—Eviatar Zerubavel,
The Seven Day Circle

The concept of the week is a concept that protects you from the frightening truth that the sequence of days is not circular at all, but linear.

—Corinne D. Bliss,
The Same River Twice

*O*ur discussion of why "our" week lasts seven days begs the question, "Why do we have a week at all?" So we can have regular market days, true. So we can enjoy regular days of rest and worship, yes. But, as novelist Corinne Bliss notes, the week answers to a lot more than practical and spiritual needs. It seems to fulfill a psychological need to forget that time is linear and that each day lived is one day less.

Of all species on Earth, only we humans know that life is, literally, a dead-end, one-way road. This useful (!) information separates us, even more than language and tool using, from every other animal. They, presumably, live in the moment, the eternal now. "There is nothing in the voice of the cicada to indicate how long it will live," runs an ancient haiku.[16] We humans live . . . when? Any time except now, in my experience.

The trouble is, knowledge of our mortality gives us something major to worry about! If cats knew they were going to die, would they be so inscrutably cool? I doubt it. But we do know, and it would be pretty easy to worry ourselves, well, to death, thinking about it. A vast gulf of unfinished business, broken ambitions, and sullied hopes lies between my present state of mind and a sublime, joyful acceptance of the statement, "I'm going to die."

What to do about it? One answer is to forget the whole thing and kid ourselves that we're going to live forever. Which is where the week comes in. It provides us with the illusion that we're just going round and round in seven-day circles of time. From this perspective, no wonder we make it the framework in which we live out our lives. It's our anchor, our cocoon, the place we can go when we get overwhelmed with the enormity of it all. Marcus Aurelius advised us to "Live each day as if it were your last," but the week says, "Take it easy. You've got all the time in the world. Saturday will soon come round again." Isn't that notion of our days eternally rolling around again comforting?

The week does more than cushion us from time's linear flow. Not only does it give us the illusion of immortality (and it's been said that we're nothing without an illusion), but it gives us structure. It tells us that life is predictable and regular. Tomorrow will be Thursday and the weekend is only three days away. I trust and it will be so. A hunter-gatherer society has no more need of a week than does a dog, but for you and me, in our rigidly structured culture, the "mechanical periodicity" of our seven-day cycle saves us from chaos. It gives us order.

Which all sounds pretty Orwellian, doesn't it? Two illusions—that we live our lives in seven-day circles of time and that life is ordered—are civilization's bequest to us. They have come to us by the childishly simple concept of breaking up an (apparently) endless river of days into cycles of seven. Perhaps what we really want is the best of both worlds, a

---

16. Quoted in Raymond Smullyan's *5000 B.C.*

place where we can have structure, but not the structure of the week: rather, a special structure, geared to something higher. Something like Louis MacNeice had in mind:

> *. . . if now alone*
> *I must pursue this life, it will not be only*
> *A drag from numbered stone to numbered stone*
> *But a ladder of angels, river turning tidal.*[17]

17. "Autumn Journal," from *Collected Poems 1925–1948*, by Louis MacNeice. London: Faber and Faber, 1949.

Nine

From Whence We Came

The atoms that compose everything interesting around you—the earth, the sky, your own body—were fabricated in a series of events that took place in hardly more than a few hours.

—James Trefil,
Meditations at 10,000 Feet

Mankind is made of star-stuff.

—Harlow Shapley

*E*ach of us is the end result of billions of years of stellar cooking. Look at your hands, the chair you're sitting in, the walls around you, the ground outside: they're all made of *stuff*. Since the 1930s, we've known that virtually all the stuff that we're made of and that surrounds us was once inside a star. This knowledge is, I believe, one of the richest fruits of modern science: it tells us from whence we came.

Before he lost his head to the guillotine in 1794, the founder of modern chemistry, Frenchman Antoine-Laurent Lavoisier, recognized that stuff came in two varieties: that which could be broken down into simpler stuff (compounds) and that which couldn't (elements, as in *elementary*). This seemingly simple, yet momentous, observation prepared the groundwork for the science of chemistry.

A few years later, in 1803, English scientist John Dalton quantified Lavoisier's work when he revived the ancient Greek concept of the atom (literally, "that which can't be cut"), suggesting that elements were composed of individual and indivisible atoms. His genius was to guess that each element's properties depended upon the unique composition of its atoms, and he formulated a table of atomic weights. Each element, he said, is composed of atoms distinguished from each other by weight. We now know that: (1) atoms consist of light, negatively charged electrons surrounding a comparatively heavy and dense nucleus consisting of positively charged protons and neutral neutrons,[18] and (2) one element is distinguished from another by the number of protons in its nucleus.

You probably remember what the periodic table looks like from your school days, since it's a fixture on the wall of virtually every science lab and has been since John Dalton's day. Dalton's elements, and those discovered since, are arranged in neat rows and columns according to weight and properties. Since the number of protons in an atom's nucleus is unique for each element, that number becomes a useful way to classify elements: it's the element's "atomic number." For instance, the lightest

1 H																	2 He
3 Li	4 Be											5 B	6 C	7 N	8 O	9 F	10 Ne
11 Na	12 Mg											13 Al	14 Si	15 P	16 S	17 Cl	18 Ar
19 K	20 Ca	21 Sc	22 Ti	23 V	24 Cr	25 Mn	26 Fe	27 Co	28 Ni	29 Cu	30 Zn	31 Ga	32 Ge	33 As	34 Se	18 Br	36 Kr
37 Rb	38 Sr	39 Y	40 Zr	41 Nb	42 Mo	43 Tc	44 Ru	45 Rh	46 Pd	47 Ag	48 Cd	49 In	50 Sn	51 Sb	52 Te	53 I	54 Xe
55 Cs	56 Ba	57 La	72 Hf	73 Ta	74 W	75 Re	76 Os	77 Ir	78 Pt	79 Au	80 Hg	81 Tl	82 Pb	83 Bi	84 Po	85 At	86 Rn
87 Fr	88 Ra	89 Ac	104 Unq	105 Unp	105 Unh												

58 Ce	59 Pr	60 Nd	61 Pm	62 Sm	63 Eu	64 Gd	65 Tb	66 Dy	67 Ho	68 Er	69 Tm	70 Yb	71 Lu
90 Th	91 Pa	92 U	93 Np	94 Pu	95 Am	96 Cm	97 Bk	98 Cf	99 Es	100 Fm	101 Md	102 No	103 Lr

Each square represents one element in this periodic table. An element's atomic number, shown in the upper left of each square, equals the number of protons in its central nucleus. Elements in the same vertical column have similar properties. When Dmitry Mendeleyev first formulated the modern periodic table in 1869, he noted two gaps, and on that basis predicted the existence of two undiscovered elements. They were later found: germanium (Ge) and scandium (Sc).

---

18. The proton and neutron each have a mass of about 1,840 electrons. The neutron is slightly heavier than the proton.

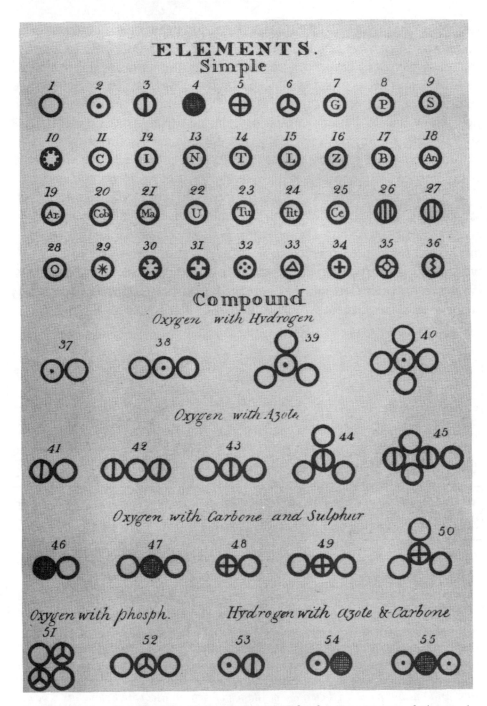

As originally visualized by John Dalton in his 1810 book A New System of Chemical Philosophy, each "simple" element is composed of a unique kind of atom. Above, he shows 36 kinds of atoms, one for each element then known. Below, elements combine to form compounds. Azote (meaning "lifeless") is what we now call nitrogen.

element is hydrogen, atomic number 1. Organic compounds all contain carbon, atomic number 6. Uranium, atomic number 92, is the heaviest naturally occurring element.

Everything you touch, see, smell, and taste consists of mixtures of elements found in the periodic table. Your body, for instance, consists of about 65 percent oxygen, 18 percent carbon, 10 percent hydrogen, and 3 percent nitrogen by mass. The remaining 4 percent consists of traces of almost every other naturally occurring element in that table.

You'll have seen "RDAs" on the back of most food products, from cornflakes to coffee. The recommended daily allowance is what the U.S. government believes is essential for a healthy diet, and it lists many elements we find in the periodic table. Zinc, for instance, maintains our ability to taste and smell and promotes normal growth and sexual development. Iodine is necessary for normal functioning of the thyroid gland, and it keeps skin, hair, and nails healthy. Selenium complements vitamin E in fighting cell damage. We don't need a lot of these elements, but what we do require is essential for our bodies' health and happiness.

After the Big Bang

Since the time of Lavoisier and Dalton, chemists, physicists, and astronomers have made huge strides in understanding where the elements originated. Fifteen or so billion years ago, immediately after the creation event we term the Big Bang,[19] the universe consisted only of the lightest elements: hydrogen, helium, and a trace of lithium. (Hydrogen, helium, and lithium have one, two, and three protons, respectively.) No carbon, no oxygen, no zinc, no uranium: these had to be synthesized from the original elements. The questions are *how* and *where*? The short answers, discovered in the 1930s, are "by nuclear fusion" and "inside stars." So many technical problems had to be solved in order to arrive at a complete understanding that detailed answers have only been available in the last 30 or 40 years. The biggest hurdle investigators had to overcome is right there in your blood: iron.

If the sun is shining and you hold out your hands to it, you immediately feel warm. It's comparable to stretching out your hands in front of a coal fire. Yet the fire is a few feet away, while the sun is nearly

19. Originally a term of derision bestowed on the event by Fred Hoyle, who promoted the rival "steady state" theory. Overwhelming evidence now tells us that the universe did start in the "singularity" we still call the Big Bang.

100 million miles distant. Imagine! Less than a million days have passed since the days of Plato and Socrates, yet we're talking a hundred times that number of miles, and you can still feel the warmth! Based on that observation, you might think that the sun did nothing but pump out energy—but you'd be wrong. Just as your car engine generates heat as a by-product, energy production—what we perceive as light and heat—is just a sideline for the sun and every other star. The *real* work of stars is to synthesize heavy elements from lighter ones. Stars shine as a by-product of this process. Let's see how it works.

In a process diet-pill advertisers might dream about, the sun loses about five million tons of mass every second. Remember $E = mc^2$? The m here represents the five million tons, while the E is the energy it takes to maintain a process known as "nuclear fusion" deep inside the sun that converts several hundred million tons of light hydrogen into heavier helium by the second.[20] Fortunately this process isn't 100 percent efficient, and we're the fortunate recipients of some of the surplus energy that keeps the sun shining.

In a secondary process, as the sun and other medium-sized stars reach old age, they convert the helium "ash" produced in their primes into carbon, which is heavier yet. And that's it as far as the sun is concerned—carbon is the heaviest element that can be synthesized in stars as massive as the sun. In order to produce elements heavier than carbon, stars with a mass greater than about eight times that of the sun are required. Greater mass means higher temperature and pressure in a star's core, which in turn means the ability to synthesize ever-heavier elements—all the way up to iron. Physicist Hans Bethe was largely responsible for figuring out the mechanics of the process in 1938, but after that, little progress was made in understanding where elements heavier than iron came from until 1957.

Beyond Iron

Nuclear fusion, the stellar process we've been talking about, synthesizes the nuclei of heavy elements by fusing those of light elements. The

---

20. The c is the velocity of light, a huge number, implying you can get lots of energy for a little mass. A mere *three pounds* of mass were lost in the first hydrogen bomb test (code-named "Mike"), which vaporized the Pacific atoll of Eniwetok in 1952. The equivalent of three billion "Mikes" are detonated in the sun's core every second.

process runs automatically in massive stars, the "ash" from each phase of the process providing the fuel for each successive phase until iron is synthesized. Iron, whose atomic nuclei are bound tightest of all, is the most stable of elements. At first, it might seem that iron is the end of the line. Until you reach iron, the fusion process *releases* energy, but to fuse iron, you need to *import* energy. But from where? We now know it comes from the material surrounding the star's inner core. Let's see how that works.

At the end of its life, every star becomes unstable. While it lives, any star—our sun, for instance—is in a state of equilibrium: gravity holds it all together and creates intense pressure in the core (hence fusion), while gas pressure (resulting from the fusion) prevents the star from collapsing into itself. Once iron is synthesized in the core of a massive star, however, the game's as good as over. Timothy Ferris writes poetically of the process: "Iron spells death, and death deliverance. The iron core grows like a cancer in the heart of the star, damping nuclear reactions in all that it touches, until the star becomes fatally imbalanced and falls victim to a general collapse."[21]

So if elements heavier than iron can't be synthesized while a massive star lives, when can they be made? In the moments of a star's death. Once the core can no longer resist the intense gravitational pressure of the surrounding material, collapse is inevitable and rapid. Normally, the core of a massive star collapses into an incredibly dense "neutron star." As the outer layers of the star collapse toward the neutron core, that core is in the process of rebounding from *its* initial collapse. The result is cataclysmic, a fury of shock waves and pent-up power released as inward-rushing material meets the rebounding core, "a shock stronger than any other in the known universe," according to Ferris. The energy released is so intense that to us it seems as if a new star—sometimes as bright as the entire parent galaxy to which it belongs—has suddenly appeared in the sky: we call it a supernova. In the process, vast quantities of heavy elements, all the way to uranium, are synthesized in a matter of moments. It took billions of years to synthesize the light elements up to iron, and now it's but a matter of a few minutes' work to create those heavier than iron. I guess that's what they mean by an irony.

To recap:

♦ The lightest elements—hydrogen, helium, and lithium—were present immediately after the Big Bang.

---

21. Timothy Ferris, *Coming of Age in the Milky Way*.

◆ Elements up to and including iron were synthesized by nuclear fusion in the cores of stars.

◆ And elements heavier than iron were synthesized in supernovae, the brief death implosion-explosion shocks of very massive stars.

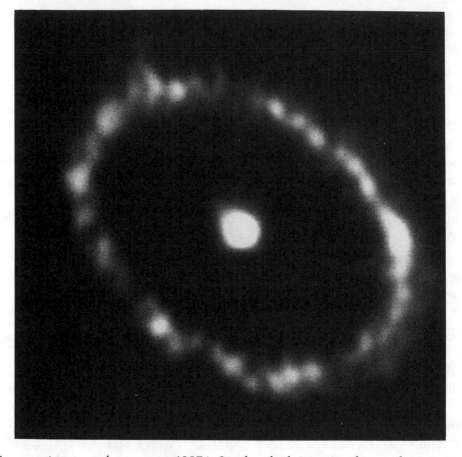

Gaseous ring around supernova 1987A. One hundred sixty-nine thousand years ago, a massive star in the Large Magellanic Cloud, a neighboring galaxy to our own Milky Way, ended its life in a cataclysmic explosion known as a supernova. Light from that event, which reached us in February 1987, has been helping astronomers fine-tune theories of element formation. The ring consists of material ejected from the star in the last few thousand years of its life as a supergiant. It was invisible until radiation from the blast reached it and raised its temperature sufficiently to be observable by Earth-orbiting telescopes. Because the ring is tilted about 43 degrees to our line of sight, we see it as an ellipse. Light took nearly a year longer to travel to us from the far side of the ring than light from the near side. By comparing the "delay time" with the angular size of this Hubble Space Telescope image, astronomers have been able to calculate the distance to SN 1987A with unprecedented accuracy. The resolution of this picture is equivalent to spotting a quarter at 40 miles! (NASA/ESA)

A Next-Door Supernova

In the year 1572, light from an exploding star in our own galaxy reached the Earth. As bright as Venus for several months, it's now known as Tycho's Star after Danish astronomer Tycho Brahe, who described the event. That's the most recent example of a supernova in our own galaxy (we're overdue for another one!). However, astronomers were thrilled in 1987 when supernova "1987A" was discovered in our next-door neighbor galaxy, the Large Magellanic Cloud. It provided, and is still providing, opportunities to test and fine-tune theories about the formation of heavy elements.

Following a supernova, new stars form phoenix-like from the "ashes" of the old star. Nearly five billion years ago, a star we call the sun coalesced out of a cloud of dust and gas, much of which was the remnants of one or more generations of supernovae. Around the protosun swirled material destined to become planets and moons. In addition to the universe's original hydrogen, helium, and trace amount of lithium, the swirling cloud was rich in dozens of other elements. Eventually, on at least one of the planets, life happened.

Billions of years later, one of those life-forms, with iron in its blood, calcium in its bones, and iodine in its thyroid, is holding a book in its hands. Perhaps even now it's looking at those hands and wondering with amazement: "So that's where the stuff in my hands came from!"

A Conversation with
Edward Teller

─────

What is called understanding
is often no more than a state
where one has become familiar
with what one does not understand.

—Edward Teller, from his student
diary, in *The Pursuit of Simplicity*

*D*r. Edward Teller is a physicist and one of the most controversial
scientists of our time. He was born in Hungary in 1908 and educated
there and in Germany before coming to the United States before World
War II with fears of both fascism and communism. He worked on the
atomic bomb and is one of the "fathers," with Stanislaw Ulam, of the
hydrogen bomb. He has been outspoken in his support of a strong U.S.
nuclear weapons program, and he was largely responsible for convincing
President Ronald Reagan to initiate the Strategic Defense Initiative "Star
Wars" program.

Columnist Roger Rosenblatt is one of many observers who have
commented on his complex character, writing, "So closely is he
associated with the Dr. Strangelove character of Stanley Kubrick's movie,

Edward Teller.
(Hoover Institution)

one may forget that Teller was among a minority of compassionate scientists who voted to warn Japan before bombing Hiroshima."[22]

Teller's passion for teaching science to the lay public is best expressed in his book *The Pursuit of Simplicity*, from which I took the quotation in my first question to him.

Barry Evans   You once wrote, "Science is a set of relevant, consistent statements of general validity that also contain an element of surprise." Can you elucidate?

Edward Teller   It is as I said. For instance, what relativity tells us is that simultaneity is not an absolute statement. Quantum mechanics says that the future is not determinable. These are so surprising that most people refuse to even try and think about them!

B. E.   Are scientists as surprised as laypeople?

E. T.   Of course. At least.

B. E.   Is that what motivates scientists?

22. Roger Rosenblatt, "The Men Who Invented the Parentheses," *U.S. News and World Report*, November 28, 1988, page 9.

E. T.   Different scientists are different. . . . Let me make a somewhat negative statement about the topic: For me, personally, to look for surprises not only came in a very natural way, but because what I found all around was full of surprises. But at the same time I don't seem to be attracted to the idea in the way you seem to be looking at it, because all my life, and that means from early childhood [in Hungary], questions of survival came first. What is striking to me in America is that people take everything so much for granted that they begin to worry about dangers that aren't even there.

You see, I grew up in central Europe in a civilization that very thoroughly collapsed with Hitler, and in this country—while I can only feel very grateful for the way people from abroad are received—I had a very special problem. Due to my strong feeling that continued work on [nuclear] weapons is necessary, I got into conflict with my fellow scientists, and that brought up the problem of my survival as a scientist. For me, the world is full of difficulties in many respects. What you describe as "wonder" is something for which I wish I had more time, although I'm surrounded by it.

B. E.   You wrote, "Of all the people who sought simplicity, Einstein was probably the greatest and most successful." Why?

E. T.   When most people think about relativity, they see the complicated mathematics. But in fact, relativity is really a simplified way to look at the inorganic world. Relativity shows that time and space have more similarities than are understood by most people. Geometric concepts can explain gravitation. These are wonderful achievements, and it is the simplicity of it that makes it so convincing.

B. E.   [Physicist] John Wheeler made the point that if our natural speed of movement was close to that of the speed of light, the idea of relativity would be perfectly normal and simple to us.[23]

E. T.   Obviously!

B. E.   You wrote in *The Pursuit of Simplicity* that you considered Henry the Navigator's huge fifteenth-century fortress at Sagres, on

---

23. Because all our movements are very slow compared to the speed of light, it's tempting to think, as Newton did, that space and time are concrete, unchangeable entities. If we routinely traveled close to the speed of light, it would be obvious, as Einstein showed, that space and time are relative and depend on the observer's motion.

the coast of Portugal, the first great research and development project in history. How important was Sagres?

E. T. It was a considerable size, and its consequences have been crucial. It was built at a turning point in history when the West got interested in the world outside and the Chinese lost interest. It is strange. The two events coincided and changed the balance of the whole future.

B. E. The future for us now seems to be very much in the balance, and scientific research is being undertaken at an ever-accelerating rate. What do you consider to be science's greatest unsolved problem?

E. T. My preference would be "life."

B. E. Do you mean the origin of life?

E. T. No, I mean *life*. Life! I don't understand it. I don't understand it at all. If I wonder about something, I wonder more about that than anything else. And I don't need to add "origin of" or "end of" or "purpose of" or anything. Life!

B. E. Will we ever understand what life is?

E. T. There are remarkable steps being made in biochemistry now. The more of life's processes we can reproduce in vitro, the more of a chance we have of understanding it. I am particularly interested in some work by Australian Nobel Prize–winning physiologist Sir John Eccles. This suggests that some important functions of our brains are subject to probability, rather than cause and effect. This may have a profound influence on our understanding of what free will really means.

B. E. Does that trouble you?

E. T. No, it's interesting. And I'm not asserting anything here, I'm only saying it's very interesting.

B. E. I know you're fond of quoting words ascribed to Isaac Newton, "I do not know what I may appear to the world, but to myself I seem to have been only like a boy playing on the seashore and diverting myself in now and then finding a smoother pebble or a prettier shell than ordinary, whilst the great ocean of truth lay all undiscovered before me." Why are these words important to you?

E. T.   It is wonderful admission of limitations. Particularly in view of widespread opinions among physicists that a grand unified theory, or GUT, will give the answer to everything. To my mind the desire for a grand unified theory is a desire to exterminate wonder. If you have all the answers, no more wonder is needed.

B. E.   Didn't Lord Kelvin say a hundred years ago that science has basically got all the answers, and all we need do now is fill in the last few decimal points?

E. T.   Yes, and that is just one of the kinds of predictions you can get from scientists. So you should not be too confident that you can get reasonable answers from scientists!

B. E.   So you would agree with Niels Bohr, whom I believe you knew when you were young, when he said that there is no progress without paradox.

E. T.   He very thoroughly believed in the power of paradoxes, it is true, and I believe he was right to do so.

B. E.   Was there a singular moment in your life when you just stood back and marveled at the fact of being alive?

E. T.   No, for me life is a continuous source of wonder. It is there all the time.

Wednesday's Puzzles

The Power of Visualization

People who are only good with hammers
see every problem as a nail.

—Roger von Oech,
A Kick in the Seat of the Pants

*I*n *Zen and the Art of Motorcycle Maintenance*, Robert Pirsig takes deep, iconoclastic approaches to problem solving. Imagine, he says, that you're working on a motorbike and you manage to ruin the head of a screw holding a side cover assembly to the engine. You're stuck. "Right now this screw is worth exactly the selling price of the whole motorcycle, because the motorcycle is actually valueless until you get the screw out. With this reevaluation of the screw comes a willingness to expand your knowledge of it." In the same vein, I invite you to put a high price on solving these next puzzles. And don't worry about getting stuck! "Stuckness shouldn't be avoided. It's the psychic predecessor of all real understanding," says Pirsig.

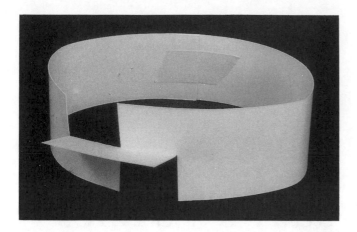

1. This object is well worth the few minutes it takes to make. Leave it on your desk at work and watch how people react to it! You'll need a strip of paper about 12 inches long and 1½ inches wide, scissors, and tape to make one. The only place tape is used is where shown. No other materials are used. Sounds easy? First make it in your mind, to see how it works.

> *Hint 1: Some people seem to have an innate capacity for visualizing three-dimensional objects in their minds. If you're one of them, I envy you!*
>
> *Hint 2: OK, maybe that didn't work. So cut out a strip of paper, about a foot long and an inch wide, and just play with it until you see the trick.*

*Hint 3: Still stuck?
Then it's back to basics.
Create this "hypercard" from a
3½-by-5-inch file card, or even
a business card. Once you see
how that works, the cylindrical
version should be a piece
of cake.*

2. What is the volume remaining in a sphere that has had a cylindrical hole two inches long drilled through its center? (To visualize this, imagine that the bangle shown in the illustration was carved from a sphere with radius *r*.) The assumption you might make here is that you don't have sufficient information. Trust me, you do! Not only that, but an insight can give you the answer in a few seconds. (The volume of a solid sphere, radius *r*, is $\frac{4}{3}\pi r^3$. The volume of a spherical cap is $\pi(rh^2 - \frac{h^3}{3})$, where *r* is the radius of the sphere and *h* the height of the cap.)

Hint 1: If you do trust me, then you can assume the answer is unique. So the answer should be the same, no matter what the diameter of the hole is.

Hint 2: So why not make life easy and assume the hole's diameter is zero?

Hint 3: In which case, the problem reduces to finding the volume of a one-inch-radius sphere.

3. You're given a wooden cube, three inches on each side, and a saw. The assignment is to cut the cube into 27 smaller cubes, each one inch on the side. Obviously you can do it in six cuts (two cuts in each of three directions). Can you reduce the number of cuts required by rearranging the pieces after each cut?

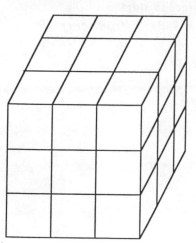

Hint 1: Think about the center cube.

Hint 2: How many cuts do you need to make the center cube, no matter how clever you are at rearranging the rest of the small cubes?

4. What's the diameter of this circle?

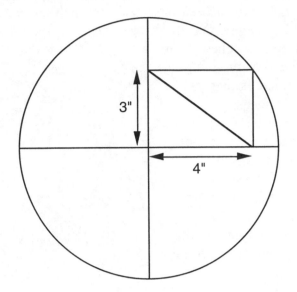

Hint: The two diagonals of a rectangle have the same length.

5. Why is a manhole cover round? Yes, round ones are probably strong and might be cheaper to make, but there's a good practical reason. Again, visualize the situation.

  Hint: Where don't you want the heavy cover to end up?

6. What's the largest number you can make with just three integers? (I suggest you don't try to actually calculate it unless you have a scientific calculator.)

  Hint 1: Three nines might be a good place to start.

  Hint 2: You can do better than 9 × 9 × 9: don't forget powers, for example, 9^9.

  Hint 3: Which is larger, $(9^9)^9$ or $9^{(9^9)}$?

Puzzle answers are at the back of the book.

Wednesday's Quotations

Science and Scientists

The art of conversing with stones is called physics. The question-and-answer periods of the conversations are called experiments. . . . The language spoken is mathematics.

—**J. T. Fraser**

The supreme task of the physicist is to arrive at those universal elementary laws from which the cosmos can be built up by pure deduction. There is no logical path to these laws; only intuition, resting on sympathetic understanding of experience, can reach them . . . this is what Leibniz described as a "pre-established harmony."

—**Albert Einstein**

I realized that if I understood too clearly what I was doing, where I was going, then I probably wasn't working on anything very interesting.

—**Peter Carruthers**

We all agree your theory is crazy; what divides us is whether it is crazy enough to be correct.

—**Niels Bohr (commenting on a proposal regarding the ultimate nature of matter)**

In all the history of mankind, there will be only one generation that will be the first to explore the solar system, one generation for which, in childhood, the planets are distant and indistinct discs moving through the night sky, and for which, in old age, the planets are places, diverse new worlds in the course of exploration.

—**Carl Sagan**

Science involves myths that are of a special type, namely, myths that are predictive, empirically testable *[good theories always make predictions or claims that are testable by experiment] and* cumulative *[a good theory always encompasses all the observational evidence of its predecessor and still manages to add something new].*

—**John Casti,** *Alternate Realities*

If we [discoverers of the DNA double helix] deserve any credit at all, it is for persistence and the willingness to discard ideas when they became untenable. One reviewer thought that we couldn't have been very clever because we went on so many false trails, but that is the way discoveries are usually made. Most attempts fail not because of the lack of brains but because the investigator gets stuck in a cul-de-sac or gives up too soon.

—**Francis Crick**

The more important fundamental laws and facts of physical science have all been discovered, and these are now so firmly established that the possibility of their ever being supplanted in consequence of new discoveries is exceedingly remote. . . . Future discoveries must be looked for in the sixth place of decimals.

—**Albert A. Michelson (From an 1894 lecture, reprinted in his 1903 book** *Light Waves and Their Uses.* **He was probably quoting Lord Kelvin.)**

Among all the great discoveries of the last five hundred years, to me, at any rate, the biggest, most marvelous discovery of all is the discovery of how life came into being—the discovery which we associate with the name of Darwin and DNA. Two hundred years ago you could ask anybody, "Can we someday understand how life came into being?" and he would have told you, "Preposterous! Impossible!" I feel the same way about the question, "Will we ever understand how the Universe came into being?" And I can well believe that the evidence that we need is right in front of us, right now. We just have to look in front of our noses."

—**John Archibald Wheeler**

Luck is an essential part of a career in physics.

—**Leon Lederman**

We cannot yet answer the ultimate questions, but we can discuss the questions intelligently.

—**Alan Guth**

How wonderful that we have met with paradox. Now we have some hope of making progress.

—**Niels Bohr**

Man is not born to solve the problems of the universe, but to find out where the problems begin, and then to take his stand within the limits of the intelligible.

—**Goethe**

Historically, Western science is a johnny-come-lately on the reality generation scene, having arisen in the Middle Ages as a response of the inability of the competition to offer a satisfactory explanation of the Black Death.

—**John Casti**

It is interesting to note the curious mental attitude of scientists working on "hopeless" subjects. Contrary to what one might at first expect, they are all buoyed up by irrepressible optimism. I believe there is a simple explanation of this. Anyone without such optimism simply leaves the field and takes up some other line of work. Only the optimists remain.

—**Francis Crick**

There are some people who see a great deal and some who see very little in the same things.

—**T. H. Huxley**

It is very hard to realize that this all [Earth as seen from an airplane] is just a tiny part of an overwhelmingly hostile universe. It is even harder to realize that this present universe has evolved from an unspeakably unfamiliar earlier condition, and faces a future extinction of endless cold or intolerable heat. The more the universe seems comprehensible, the more it also seems pointless. . . . The effort to understand the universe is one of the very few things that lifts human life a little above the level of farce, and gives it some of the grace of tragedy.

—**Steven Weinberg**

[The brain is] a three pound mass you can hold in your hand that can conceive of a universe a hundred-billion light-years across.

—**Marian Diamond**

But the years of anxious searching in the dark, with their intense longing, their alternations of confidence and exhaustion, and the final emergence into the light—only those who have experienced it can understand that.

—**Albert Einstein**

I like to say that there is no scientific method as such, but that the most vital feature of the scientist's procedure has been merely to do his utmost with his mind, no holds barred.
                        —**P. W. Bridgman (Forgive the sexism here.**
                                      It was written in 1947.)

Science advances but slowly, and with halting steps. But does not therein lie her eternal fascination? And would we not soon tire of her if she were to reveal her ultimate truths too easily?
                                            —**Karl von Frisch**

Thursday

Day of Jupiter

*T*hursday is the last of the midweek "bleached" days. Friday, Saturday, Sunday, and Monday are "colorful" days having "a distinct physiognomy." So says Eviatar Zerubavel in *The Seven Day Circle: The History and Meaning of the Week*. Even though I now work for myself, I've spent enough years in a regular job, working more or less regular hours, to know exactly what he means. Little distinguishes Thursday from the other midweek days (unless you count "The last day to get a date for the weekend," wisdom from an old friend).

By all mythical accounts, Thursday should be filled with mirth. It's named after Thor, long associated with Jupiter, god and planet. And you can surely hear

Jupiter laugh in Gustav Holst's suite *The Planets*, where he's identified as "The Bringer of Jollity."

For historical reasons, we choose one Thursday a year to formally acknowledge our blessings—on Thanksgiving, that oddly placed holiday in November. After a confusing period, the United States finally got around to agreeing that this holiday would be celebrated on the fourth Thursday of November. Abraham Lincoln had proclaimed it to be the last Thursday in November. Franklin Roosevelt decided it should be held on the third Thursday, and finally Congress, in 1941, said, "It's the fourth." And so it is.

Ten

Dividing Time

Dum spectas, fugit hora: carpe diem.[1]

—Sundial in County Durham, England

A newly arrived immigrant had lost his watch, the story goes, so he walked up to a scientist on a London street and asked, "Please, what is time?" "I'm sorry, you'll have to ask a philosopher," was the reply. "I'm just a physicist."

Despite, or perhaps because of, our inability to understand time, we attempt to tame it by dividing it into measurable chunks, some natural and some artificial. It's not always obvious which is which. For instance, the week feels like it *should* be some sort of natural interval, but no such luck. Even the calendar month bears little relationship to natural periods.

The most obvious natural intervals of time are:

♦ The year, the time it takes our planet to orbit the sun relative to the background stars.[2] In accordance with Newton's law of

---

1. "While you're looking, the hour is flying: seize the day." *Carpe diem*, given a new lease on life by Robin Williams in the film *Dead Poets Society*, probably originated with the Roman poet Horace: *"Dum loquimur, fugerit invida aetas: carpe diem, quam minimum credula postero."* ("While we're talking, time will have meanly run on: seize the day, not relying in the slightest on the future.")
2. That is, to relative space in general. This is the sidereal year of 365.2564 days, i.e., 365 days, 6 hours, 9 minutes, and 13 seconds.

universal gravitation (see Appendix 1), this period is determined by our average distance from the sun (or vice versa, that is, our distance from the sun is dictated by the length of our year). The closer a planet is to the sun, the less distance it has to travel and the faster it moves in its orbit, so the shorter its year. Mercury, for instance, orbits the sun in just 88 Earth days. Pluto, on average the farthest planet from the sun, takes 248 Earth years.

◆ The lunar month, the average time from one full moon to the next.[3]

◆ The day, the time the Earth takes to spin once on its axis, relative to the sun. More properly, this is the "solar day." The "sidereal day," measured relative to the "fixed" stars, is about four minutes shorter. The reason is that the Earth's orbit around the sun results in one "extra" spin per year relative to the stars. To see why this is so, imagine that the same face of the Earth always faced the sun, so half our planet was in perpetual daylight while the other half was in perpetual night. If this were the case, we'd all experience zero solar days per year, since (if we lived on the sunlit side) we'd never see day turning into night (or vice versa if we lived on the night side).

However, the stars (which, of course, you could only see if you lived on the dark side!) would appear to rotate once a year, that is, you'd experience one sidereal day per year. Irrespective of how fast or slow the Earth spins, we always get one more sidereal day than solar day per year. That "extra day," divided over a year, is equivalent to about four minutes per day.

The relationship between these three intervals is approximately: 29½ days = 1 lunar month, and 12½ lunar months = 1 year.

The year can also be subdivided into four seasons (delineated by the spring and fall equinoxes and the summer and winter solstices). The month yields to no such natural subdivision, unless you count the hard-to-judge intervals from full moon to half, from new moon to half, and back to full moon. (Such intervals are approximately 7½ days long, another possible origin for 7 days in a week.)

Like those of most other species, our bodies respond to one or more of these natural cycles in accordance with ancient genetic programs:

---

3. This is the synodic month of 29.53059 days, i.e., 29 days, 12 hours, 44 minutes, and 3 seconds.

◆ The *year* defines the breeding season for most large animals, while our "civilized" bodies still try to maintain their prehistoric "fit in July, fat in January" annual cycle. (Is that why our traditional major eating binges take place between Thanksgiving and New Year's Day?)

◆ The *lunar month* is probably responsible for the length of the female menstrual cycle. Our Indo-European language progenitors apparently thought so: the words *moon, month, measure,* and *menstruation* are (probably) all cognate, that is, linguistically related. Spotty evidence seems to show that men also experience monthly mood changes related to hormonal concentration. When we refer to the human gestation period as nine months, we may not realize how accurate we are. On average, we're in the womb to within a few minutes of nine lunar (not calendar) months.[4]

◆ The *day* guides, well, everything. Eating, sleeping, working and playing all take place within the framework of the 24-hour diurnal rhythm. Curiously, when experimenters have undergone extended isolation from the diurnal rhythm in caves, their bodies have usually adopted a cycle of around 25 hours.

Artificial Units of Time

Humankind has adopted several other units of time that have no relation to natural intervals in the way that the year, lunar month, and day do. These include:

◆ The *second*, that is, one-sixtieth of one-sixtieth of one twenty-fourth of a day. It's also approximately the period of our resting heartbeats. The word is derived from the Latin *secunda minuta*, that is, the "second minute," the first minute being the division of the hour into 60.[5]

---

4. My encyclopedia gives the average human gestation period as 265.8 days. Nine lunar months, 9 × 29.53059 days = 265.775 days, is a difference of only 36 minutes. It would be an amazing coincidence if that was a coincidence!

5. Shouldn't that mean that a "trice"—as in "I'll be with you in a trice!"—would be the third division of the hour? It sounds like it, but etymologists prosaically relate it to a short pull on a trise, a pulley in Old Dutch.

♦ The *minute*, 60 seconds. It was considered an impossibly tiny part of time in pre-clock days when these artificial units were first worked out, as can be seen from its cognate *minuscule*, meaning "very small." The divisions of 60 minutes for the hour and 60 seconds for the minute are an ancient legacy from the Babylonians, and before them, the Chaldeans and/or Assyrians. Why did they choose 60? Probably because of its many integral divisors: 2, 3, 4, 5, 6, 10, 12, 15, 20, and 30.

♦ The *hour* is now one twenty-fourth of a day, although it once meant "season" (from ancient Greek *hora*) and may even be cognate with *year*. Why 24? We're not sure. We do know that around 3500 B.C., the Sumerians divided days into 12 hours, starting at sunset. Later, the Babylonians divided the day into 24 hours, starting at midnight, a convention that survives to the present day.

No, the exception doesn't prove the rule! This 24-hour clock on the wall of a church in Florence, Italy, moves counterclockwise. Is it therefore a counterclock?
(Barry Evans)

♦ The *week* is just an arbitrary number of days shorter than a month. I discuss this and the calendar at greater length in Chapter 8, "For the Week-Hearted."

♦ *Months* are, of course, crazy, varying as they do between 28 and 31 days. The problem, known since people first attempted to divide the year into manageable chunks, is that our planet doesn't spin on its axis an integral number of times in its journey around the sun. If it spun exactly 360 times, for instance, life would be easy and calendar makers would be making movies or hunting snarks instead. You could make 12 months of 30 days each (such as the ancient Egyptians did—they just stuck 5 extra days on the end of each year), or 18 months of 20 days each, or any one of many possible combinations. But nature, in its wisdom, isn't that elegant.[6] The Earth spins a little less than 365 and a quarter times a year (more precisely, 365 days, 5 hours, 48 minutes, and 46 seconds[7]), and calendars have been trying to accommodate that odd fraction ever since they've been around.

We use the Gregorian calendar, a 365-day compromise that most of the western world has been using since October 15, 1582, and every four years we stick in an extra day, February 29. That would be fine if the length of the year was exactly 365.25 days. Since it isn't, we resort to the "centuries" trick: only centuries divisible by 400 are leap years. So the years 1700, 1800, and 1900 weren't leap years, while the year 2000 will be.

Messing with the Months

Calendar months probably started life to approximately correspond with the lunar months, but why do they now have such different lengths? Put it down to the stubborn pride of the first Roman emperor, Augustus. His great-uncle, Julius Caesar, had seen to it that the month he named after himself, July, was suitably long for a man of his stature. Since Augustus was left to pick up what we know (of course) as August, which then only had 30 days, he swiped a day from February—which was short anyway—so his month would be at least as important as that of his predecessor![8]

March 25 used to be New Year's Day (also, Lady Day), which explains why September, October, November, and December are confusingly named after the Latin words for seven through ten (rather than nine through twelve). For trivia fans, it's also why, in the United Kingdom, your income tax is due and the financial year starts on April 5 (equivalent to the dreaded April 15 deadline in the United States). Britain and the colonies didn't adopt January 1 as the first day of the

---

6. But stick around for 60 million years and you'll get a 360-day year, based on current estimates for how fast Earth's spin is slowing. Tidal friction due to the moon is the main cause.
7. This is the tropical year, the period of one apparent revolution of the sun around the Earth from equinox point to equinox point.
8. February then had 29 days for three years and 30 days every fourth year.

year until 1752, at which time they also adopted the Gregorian calendar. By then, it was necessary to skip 11 days to bring the calendar in line with nature, leading, so the story goes, to angry mobs demanding that the government give them back their missing days. Be that as it may, the old New Year's Day, March 25, became Tax Due Day, April 5.

―――――――――――――――― Names of Our Months ――――――――――

*H*ere's the origin of all the names of our months, most of which are derived from the early Roman calendar, circa 700 B.C.

English	Latin	Derived From	Cognate Words/Notes
January	Januarius	Janus, two-faced protector of gateways	janitor (from Latin for gatekeeper)
February	Februarius	*februalia*, a period of repentance	from Latin *februare*, to purify
March	Martius	Mars, god of war	martial
April	Aprilis	*aperire*, to open (buds, flowers)	aperitif
May	Maius	Maia, goddess of growth	
June	Junius	*juvenis*, youth	juvenile (or goddess Juno)
July	Julius	(originally *quintilis*, fifth)	Gaius Julius Caesar (102–44 B.C.)
August	Augustus	(originally *sextilis*, sixth)	Augustus Caesar (63 B.C.–A.D. 14)
September	Septembris	*septem* = seven	septet (chorus of seven voices)
October	Octobris	*octo* = eight	octagon (eight-sided figure)
November	Novembris	*novem* = nine	novena (nine-day devotion)
December	Decembris	*decem* = ten	decimal

Eleven

Fighting Entropy

Cold environments are fundamentally more hospitable to complex forms of life than hot environments. Life is, after all, an ordered form of matter, and low temperature favors order.

—Freeman Dyson,
Infinite in All Directions

"*L*ife's tough, then you die," explains the bumper sticker helpfully. "And then look at what happens," I think. "Entropy takes over." Actually, the entire course of our bodies' existence, from birth to death, is spent in a nonstop battle to maintain low entropy. The moment we die, entropy starts increasing. No wonder life is tough! "Fight entropy" (another bumper sticker[9]) might well be the rallying cry of all life on Earth.

Entropy can be loosely thought of as a measure of disorder: chaos and order correspond to high and low entropy, respectively. My favorite example of entropy in action is what happens on the plane when I fly from San Francisco to see my family in England. At takeoff, the wide-bodied jet is a model of orderliness: magazines are in their pockets, cups and glasses are still in the galley, and all of us cattle (as we're fondly referred to by the crew in private) appear reasonably neat and clean. Ten hours later it's a different story. Cups, kids, and trash are all over the

---

9. And yet another, in the same vein, "Stop continental drift: reunite Pangaea!" Pangaea was the single continent from which present-day landmasses originated.)

place, newspapers and magazines litter the floor, and our clothes and minds are all in the later stages of crumpledom. What before was order is now disorder and chaos. Where everything had its place, all is now randomly and messily distributed. That's entropy!

I'm not sure if the founder of the concept of entropy, Rudolf Clausius (1822–1888) would have appreciated my example (assuming he could picture a 400-ton vehicle winging at 500 mph through the skies). He conceived of it as an adjunct to the second law of thermodynamics, for which he was largely responsible.[10] With entropy loosely defined as "a measure of disorder," you can think of the second law as saying that the entropy of a closed system always increases. Technical methods for measuring "disorder" are well established, but let's assume for now that we can go down to our local Radio Shack and buy an "entropy meter." We switch it on at the start of a transatlantic flight and the needle gives a relatively low reading in the cabin. During the flight it slowly creeps up, and by the time we touch down, the needle is high on the scale. We say that the entropy of the system, that is, of the plane's cabin, has increased.

Wait a minute, though. When we're ready to return to the United States, we walk on board, check the entropy, and the reading is once again well down: order has somehow been restored. Where did it come from? From outside the system, in this case, from outside the plane: cleaning staff came on and reinstated the lost order. Somehow they were able to convert their low entropy into low entropy for the plane. Their low entropy came from low-entropy food they'd eaten and from oxygen in the air they'd breathed. (And if they were using vacuum cleaners, the low-entropy electrical energy needed to power them came from the local power station.)

This raises a subtle but important point. We might think we're adding energy to our bodies when we eat, but—unless we're growing or putting on weight—we don't need more energy than we already have: when we eat, we're merely replacing the energy we're giving to the environment, mainly in the form of heat. However, since we are enslaved to the second law of thermodynamics, the energy we take in must have a lower entropy than the heat energy we put out.

10. The second law can be stated in various forms, including these three informal ways: (1) Heat normally flows from hot to cold. (Sometimes stated as, "The only way to make a refrigerator work is to plug it in!" Then it's no longer a closed system.); (2) Engines that work off heat can never be 100% efficient; and (3) An isolated system always moves toward disorder. In case you've forgotten your high school physics, the *first* law of thermodynamics says that energy (or rather, mass-energy, since they are equivalent) can neither be created nor destroyed.

A system, then, can only become more ordered at the expense of things outside the system becoming more disordered. That's why we talk about a "closed" system.[11] Also note that it's easier to end up with disorder than order (look at your desk at 5 P.M.!).

Imagine filling your bathtub and dividing the water into two halves with a dam down the center. Make the water on one side blue (by adding blue dye) and the other side red. Now carefully lift the dam, trying not to stir the water. In minutes your bathtub will be filled with uniformly purple water. Easy, right? Now unmix it, that is, separate the blue water from the red. Tricky.

These examples show us that systems naturally move from order to disorder, or randomness. The unmixed fluids are more ordered (from a physicist's point of view) than when they're mixed: unmixed corresponds to lower entropy than mixed. Let's see how it works with our bodies.

Localized Clumps of Low Entropy

Our bodies and our brains are highly organized compared to the air that surrounds us. This makes us localized clumps of very low entropy in an environment of relatively high entropy. Greater order equals lower entropy, so our hypothetical entropy meter would single out us, our bodies, and every cell within them, as clusters of extraordinarily low entropy in generally high-entropy surroundings. (The human brain represents some of the lowest entropy possible.) Looking at it in a slightly different way, the molecules of our bodies are arranged in a highly selective way so that both our component parts and our entire bodies are individualized. This is not so for air and water, for instance—there's nothing to distinguish one volume of either of them from another, so their entropy is higher than ours.

According to the well-tested second law of thermodynamics,[12] overall entropy is constantly increasing. At first glance, this appears to

---

11. You could argue that the plane could have been cleaned up en route, but the principle's the same: you're using "order" in the food and fuel (if you run a vacuum cleaner off the plane's generators) to create order in the cabin. When the food and fuel run out, nothing can stop the slide toward disorder.

12. It's an empirical law, that is, while it seems to work in practice, it can't be proved theoretically. Statistically, if you waited a very long time, your bathwater might eventually revert back to individual regions of red and blue. In this case, that "long time" is probably greater than the age of the universe, so we can say with confidence that it'll "never" happen.

contradict the fact of our existence! If entropy is on the increase and everything is tending toward a state of randomness, how can such highly ordered bodies as ourselves be here? Where does our low entropy come from?

Directly, it comes from our food. As we've already seen, our bodies import low-entropy energy and export high-entropy energy. In the example of the plane, some of the cleaning crew's low-entropy energy was transferred during the course of their work to the plane and its contents. It's the same for all of us. Those low-entropy cornflakes, fish, loaves, apples, glasses of wine, and all the other stuff we eat and drink are later jettisoned in the high-entropy form of heat, excreta, water vapor, and carbon dioxide. So while the energy we lose equals the energy we gain (unless we're gaining or losing weight), on average the entropy of the *output* energy is higher than the entropy of the *input* energy. The difference is what we've used to keep ourselves alive and ordered. When we die, the process stops, and left to themselves, our corpses naturally revert to a disordered state of high entropy: they rot.

OK, so our source of low entropy comes mainly from the food we eat, but where does that come from? Indirectly it comes from the sun, via photosynthesis. This wonderful process[13] converts low-entropy sunlight (that is, photons of visible light) into plants that we eat (or that animals eat, which we then eat). Photosynthesis reduces local entropy.

Entropy of the Earth

Let's look at this process not from the point of view of our individual bodies, but from the overall energy/entropy balance of our planet. Like each of us, Earth is in an approximate state of energy equilibrium: our planet receives as much energy as it loses. If it didn't, it would heat up or cool down. Instead, everything pretty much evens out. However, the outgoing energy—heat being radiated back into space—has a much

---

13. Wonderful, yes. Efficient, no. When we see a green leaf, our eyes get what the leaf rejects. The leaf absorbs all colors except green, which it reflects. In a sense, we see colors negatively. Since the sun radiates strongly in the green band of the spectrum, it's odd that plants wouldn't use that energy rather than reject—that is, reflect—it. The most efficient color for a leaf would be black, so it absorbs all and reflects no wavelengths. Fortunately for our aesthetic senses, nature (that is, evolution) is far from perfect, as Stephen Jay Gould emphasized in our conversation earlier in this book.

higher entropy than the incoming visible-light energy we receive from the sun: light in, heat out. If you like, the incoming energy is higher "quality" than the outgoing energy. (Technically, the incoming energy has fewer "degrees of freedom.") Heat is, in fact, the most disordered form of energy possible.

Our star, the sun, is the source of Earth's low-entropy energy. In an essentially black, featureless, that is, high-entropy sky, the sun stands out as a gigantic source of low entropy. And that's the trick that keeps us all alive. Visible-light photons are more energetic than heat photons, so fewer photons arrive here than leave (since the overall energy stays the same). Those few higher-energy photons have a lower entropy than the greater number of lower-energy photons leaving Earth. The entropy difference is used primarily by green plants as they separate carbon and oxygen to the benefit of all life on Earth in the process of photosynthesis.

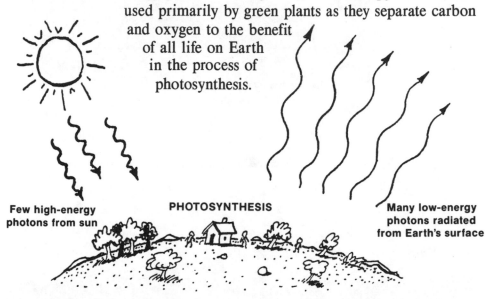

Few high-energy photons from sun

PHOTOSYNTHESIS

Many low-energy photons radiated from Earth's surface

In an otherwise high-entropy sky, the sun is our source of low entropy, sending us comparatively few high-energy, visible-light photons. These photons represent a "high-quality" form of energy, hence they are available for doing work. This includes maintaining photosynthesis in plants. On balance, Earth neither heats up nor cools down: to maintain a constant temperature our planet emits (radiates) the same amount of energy it receives. The outgoing energy is in the form of many low-energy, "low quality," infrared photons—that is, heat.

Fine, but where does the sun's low entropy come from? It originated in the gravitational collapse of the diffuse cloud of gas from which the sun formed 5 billion years ago. And where did the low entropy of that diffuse cloud come from? From the Big Bang itself. Cosmologists have assigned the Big Bang, that unfathomable event that birthed the universe, a vanishingly low entropy, or, if you prefer, an extraordinarily high level of organization. *The organization of our bodies and minds originated in the Big Bang.*

In the 15 billion or so years since the Big Bang, the entropy of the universe as a whole has steadily increased. And no matter what the ultimate fate of the universe, "Big Crunch" or a slow heat death, entropy will continue to increase, despite localized arrangements of low entropy such as insatiably curious human beings, who persist in fighting the overall trend for all its worth![14]

---

14. I'm greatly indebted to Roger Penrose's *The Emperor's New Mind*, which includes an excellent explanation of entropy for nonphysicists.

Twelve

What Can the Matter Be?

World is crazier and more of it than we think,
Incorrigibly plural.

—Louis MacNeice, "Snow"

*L*ook around you, at leaves, stars, roads, automobiles, and people. What do you see? Variety. Multitudes of differences. Yet, beneath all the apparent diversity and complexity, nature is guileless in its simplicity. Everything—*everything*—is made up of an unbelievably few identical building blocks.

Imagine standing in front of a large residential development consisting of many identical brick houses. Each house represents a basic unit of construction. Go closer to one of them. Now it appears that each brick, being essentially identical to every other brick, represents a basic building block. Imagine pulverizing one of those bricks, reducing it to the particles of clay from which it was made. Now it seems as if a clay particle is the underlying basic unit of the housing development. Or is it? What basic units make up clay particles? Molecules of silicon dioxide, for the most part, which are made up of atoms of silicon and oxygen, which consist of protons, neutrons, and electrons—can the subdividing go on forever? Or has twentieth-century science found the absolute, nondividable basic units of the universe?

For thousands of years, people have suspected that simplicity underlies the apparent complexity of our world and that a few basic building blocks make up all of matter. Science has made great strides in the 2,500 years that have passed since a Greek philosopher first proposed that everything in the universe is created from just four basic building blocks. Today, scientists realize how foolish that idea was. Actually, they say, it's only three.

Looking south down the deepest gorge in the world. The packhorse train is crossing the Kali Gandaki, a river that follows the same course it took before the Himalayas were uplifted. In the background is the sixth-highest mountain in the world, Dhaulagiri (26,810 feet), while the Annapurna massif is hidden behind the hill on the left. (Barry Evans)

Kali Gandaki

Come with me now on a roundabout journey, from the remote Nepalese temple of Muktinath, via ancient Greece, to a two-mile-long tunnel near Stanford University in California. Our quest is the holy grail of modern physics: the basic building blocks from which everything is made.

The first leg of our journey to Muktinath is simple once you've arrived in Kathmandu, the capital of Nepal: we take a bus west for eight hours. The road ends at Pokhara, Nepal's second largest city. From here, we're going to have to shoulder our backpacks (or cheat, and hire one of the cheerful local porters for a few dollars a day) and walk three days westward through the hills, until we reach the great river known as Kali Gandaki. One of the world's wildest, it rises high on the Tibetan plateau and cuts right through the Himalayan range until it joins up with the holy Ganges hundreds of miles to the south.[15] We're going to hike north, upriver, following the old salt route through the world's deepest gorge. For hundreds of years, caravans have wended this way over these narrow trails, up and down steps cut into the rock and across great plains of alluvial gravel, to Tibet with their precious cargoes of salt.

Although we rapidly gain elevation as we walk north through the desolate landscape, we're still three miles below the peaks of two of the highest mountains on Earth. To the east lies the great Annapurna massif; to the west is the sixth-highest mountain in the world, Dhaulagiri. Finally we reach Kagbeni, eight days' walk from the closest road. Now we're going to leave the river gorge and head east for another half day to our destination. Barely large enough to be called a village, Muktinath consists of half a dozen stone houses, a couple of primitive hostels, and, a couple of hundred feet higher, a temple—or rather, *the* temple. That's

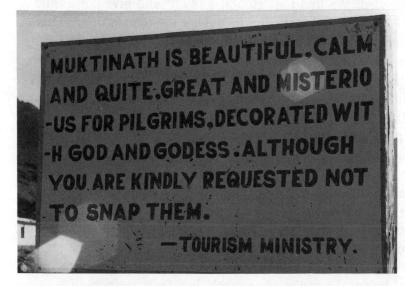

(Barry Evans)

---

15. Neatly confirming the mechanism of continental drift, since rivers don't normally cut through 20,000-foot mountain ranges. The Kali Gandaki was flowing on its present course long before the tectonic plate carrying India collided with the Eurasian plate. When they did collide and the Himalaya range began its slow uplift (which is still happening), the river just kept cutting deeper and deeper while maintaining its course.

The sacred temple of Muktinath. (Barry Evans)

where we're headed. We find the "Hobbit Lady"[16] and give her a little obligatory *baksheesh* to persuade her to unlock the temple door. That's the key hanging from a string around her neck in the photograph.

It's dank and gloomy inside the ancient one-room building. Decaying *tankas*, Buddhist sacred paintings, hang from the stone walls. Between them, statues of Hindu gods sit on narrow shelves, for this place is sacred to Hindu and Buddhist alike. The Hobbit Lady moves silently to an altar and pulls aside the heavy velvet curtain.

We've attained our goal. This is the sight that pilgrims still walk all the way from the plains of India to see. On the trail, we had met one such holy *saddhu*, walking barefoot all the way from India with just a *dhoti* wrap around his loins and a small cloth bag in his hand. He told us that it was no problem for him to eat and sleep, since people felt honored to feed him on his sacred mission and to offer him a bed for the night.

In front of us, from a cleft in the bare rock, a stream of water pours into a channel below. From the same crack, less than an inch away, spurts a jet of blue flame. In this freak of nature, water and methane (marsh gas) spring from the Earth at one and the same place. I know of

16. We nicknamed her this after J. R. R. Tolkien's heroic folk—I hope you can see why from the photograph.

The Hobbit Lady with the key to the temple. (Barry Evans)

nowhere else where such a happenstance occurs. Here in one spot are found the fundamental building blocks of everything, according to ancient Greek belief: fire and water, earth and air. For this reason, the temple of Muktinath is revered throughout the Indian subcontinent.

Earth, Fire, Water, Air

As far as we know, Empedocles (c. 495–435 B.C.) was the first person to categorically propose that all matter is composed of four primordial elements, earth, fire, water, and air. He was heavily influenced by the Pythagoreans,[17] to whom the number four was sacred. All natural phenomena, Empedocles asserted, could be explained by combinations of these four elements and their reactions under the influence of the opposing forces of love and hate (or strife).

---

17. It's curious that Aristotle never referred to Pythagoras, only the Pythagoreans, disciples of Pythagoras the man. On that basis, it's been suggested that Pythagoras was only a legendary figure.

He associated each of his "elements" with one of the four "regular" solids then known:

♦ Fire, representing the igneous state, was represented by the tetrahedron
♦ Earth, the solid state, by the cube
♦ Air, the gaseous state, by the octahedron
♦ Water, the liquid state, by the icosahedron[18]

The Pythagoreans may have discovered the fifth (and last) regular solid by this time, the dodecahedron, and believing this to be dangerous knowledge, they tried to keep it a secret. When one of their number spilled the beans and later died in a shipwreck, legend has it that his fellow Pythagoreans felt justice had been served.[19]

Whether or not the Pythagoreans knew of all five regular solids, it was left to Plato, in *Timaeus*, to outline the full theory, and they have been known as the "Platonic solids" ever since. Later Euclid (around 300 B.C.) rounded out the math in the final book of his encyclopedic work *Elements*. Let's take a closer look at these remarkable bodies that so intrigued the Greeks.

The Five Platonic Solids

A regular polygon is a figure bounded by straight lines of equal length and which has equal interior angles. The first four regular polygons are the equilateral triangle, the square, the regular pentagon, and the hexagon, which have three, four, five, and six sides, respectively. Moving on to three dimensions, a Platonic solid (or regular polyhedron) is a solid body whose sides consist of a number of identical regular polygons. The curious thing is that there are five of them, no more and no less. Go to the farthest galaxy and you'll find five Platonic solids. Theologians have speculated that even an omnipotent God couldn't create a sixth! You can think of them as the only symmetrical solids that would serve as dice:

---

18. If you've ever seen sodium chlorate crystals under a microscope, in the shape of perfect tetrahedrons and cubes, these "elemental shapes" may not seem quite as silly as they otherwise might. Crystals of chrome alum come in the shape of octahedrons.
19. See also Chapter 18, "Pi in the Sky."

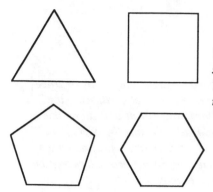

The first four regular polygons: equilateral triangle, square, regular pentagon, and regular hexagon. The faces of each Platonic solid are identical regular polygons.

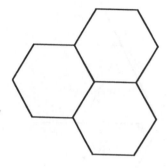

At least three faces must meet at each vertex of a polyhedron (a solid having plane faces). If three hexagons meet, you end up with a flat surface and three regular heptagons (seven-sided polygons) would overlap. Hence a Platonic solid can only use three-, four-, and five-sided regular polygons for its faces.

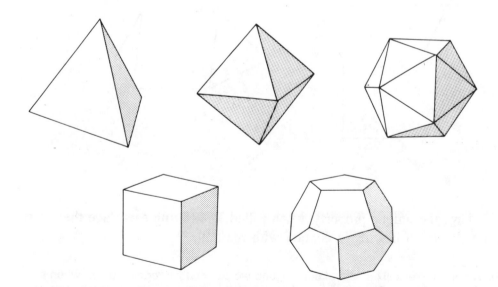

The only five Platonic solids possible, here or anywhere in the universe. Three have faces consisting of equilateral triangles: the tetrahedron (4 faces), octagon (8 faces), and icosahedron (20 faces.) The other two are the cube (6 square faces) and the dodecahedron (12 pentagonal faces).

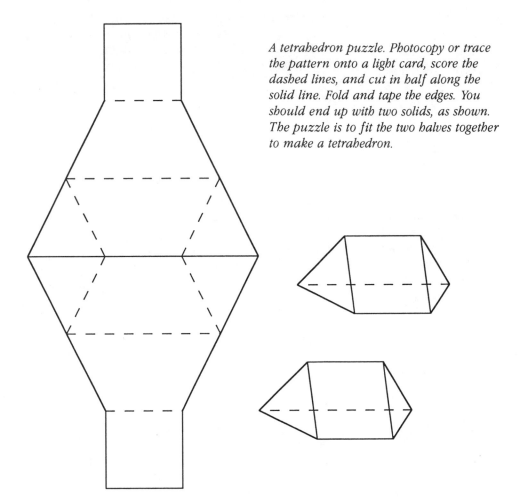

A tetrahedron puzzle. Photocopy or trace the pattern onto a light card, score the dashed lines, and cut in half along the solid line. Fold and tape the edges. You should end up with two solids, as shown. The puzzle is to fit the two halves together to make a tetrahedron.

they have the unique property, when rolled, of offering each face the same chance of landing in contact with the table.[20]

---

20. A normal die is six-sided, of course, and we say that it's "come up six" when six is on the upper face. Because some Platonic solids don't have an upper face, it's easiest to specify the face that ends up in contact with the table. Three-thousand-year-old tetrahedral dice used in the "Royal Board Game" (an ancient forerunner of dominoes) were found in graves in the city of Ur, in modern-day Iraq. They can be seen in the British Museum.

◆ The simplest Platonic solid (or die) is the *tetrahedron*. It's a 4-sided figure (*tetra* meaning four), and it's easy to make one with four equilateral triangles. It's a little trickier making one from two 5-sided solids.

◆ The conventional 6-sided die is our second Platonic solid, the *cube*, bounded by six squares.

◆ The third, with 8 sides, is the *octahedron*. You can think of it as two square pyramids stuck base to base.

◆ The fourth is the *icosahedron*, a 20-sided figure whose faces, like the tetrahedron and octahedron, consist of equilateral triangles.

◆ The fifth, and the one that caused the Pythagoreans so much trouble, is the *dodecahedron*. Perhaps they were unnerved because its 12 sides are pentagons, figures long associated with magic and witchcraft. According to Plato, "God used the dodecahedron in his design for the universe as a whole."

Having already allocated the four elements to the first four Platonic solids, the dodecahedron was assigned a fifth "essence" (hence our word *quintessence*, meaning the most perfect embodiment of something). The fifth essence, or element, was the ether, the supposed constituent matter of heavenly bodies.

Platonic solids made a comeback in the early 1600s thanks to the imaginative efforts of one of the most important Renaissance astronomers, Johannes Kepler. He spent years on the wrong track trying to understand the motions of the planets, and thus, he thought, the mind of God. He believed the Creator had arranged the orbits of the known planets according to ratios dictated by the Platonic solids. To allow him to visualize the divine plan, he constructed model after model in which he tried to fit the remaining five known planets within the orbit of the most distant one, Saturn. Each of the planets occupied the space defined by one of the Platonic solids, as you can see in the accompanying illustration. Or can you? It sure looks confusing. Only when Kepler put his models away and considered the possibility that planets move in ellipses and not, as Aristotle taught, in circles, was he able to move ahead. He soon formulated his three laws of planetary motion, later to be subsumed (and slightly modified) by Newton's law of universal gravitation (see Appendix 1).

Isaac Newton's universal law is a good example of the aspect of science that seeks underlying simplicity in apparent complexity. By demonstrating that the force pulling the apple down from the tree is the

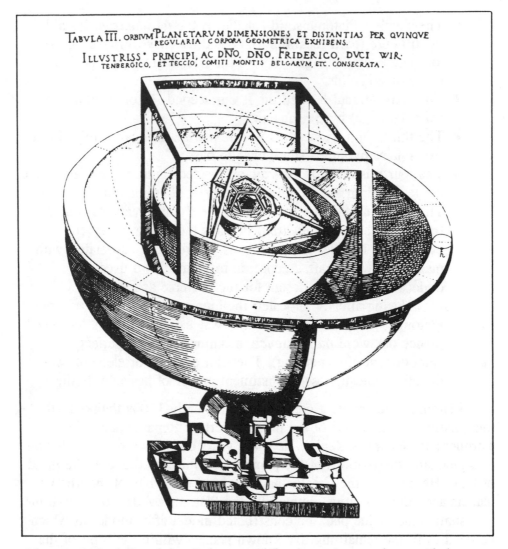

TABVLA III. ORBIVM PLANETARVM DIMENSIONES ET DISTANTIAS PER QVINQVE
REGVLARIA CORPORA GEOMETRICA EXHIBENS.

ILLVSTRISS· PRINCIPI, AC DÑO. DÑO, FRIDERICO, DVCI WIR·
TENBERGICO, ET TECCIO; COMITI MONTIS BELGARVM, ETC. CONSECRATA.

Johannes Kepler believed that God arranged the planets in accordance with the "perfection" represented by the five Platonic solids. He spent years trying various combinations that would model the observed orbits of the known planets. He later realized that his assumption that the orbits are circular was mistaken.

same force keeping the moon in orbit around the Earth, Newton unified two forces—terrestrial gravity and celestial gravity—into one. True, he wasn't able to explain why and how gravity works. That was left to Einstein. But he did simplify the scope of inquiry. Similarly, Michael Faraday's experiments and James Clerk Maxwell's equations, which unified magnetism and electricity into the single phenomenon of an "electromagnetic force," simplified the quest to understand the natural world.

Back to Basics

Since everything we know depends on the nature of the fundamental building blocks of the cosmos, no scientific quest has been more ardently pursued than the one to identify them all. Today, physicists believe that of 12 theoretically possible fundamental particles, 3 exist in nature's ordinary matter. Everything, from this book to your brain to the farthest star, consists of a collection of those three blocks. And nothing else.[21]

How do we know only 12 fundamental particles are theoretically possible? We have strong evidence that they come in families, with four members to a family, so the number of families tells you how many

SLAC, the Stanford Linear Accelerator Center. The two-mile-long linear accelerator is in the background. Starting from the far end, electrons and positrons are accelerated to nearly the speed of light. They are then split into two beams, which make great arcs before colliding in the detector housed in the long building in the right foreground. (Stanford Linear Accelerator Center/Department of Energy)

21. While solar neutrinos by the million pass through your body each second, they can't properly be called "ordinary matter."

The massive Mark II detector detects short-lived decay products from the collisions.
(Stanford Linear Accelerator Center/Department of Energy)

particles are theoretically possible. As a result of elegant experiments carried out in the last few years, most scientists believe that only three families of matter can exist, for a total of 12 fundamental particles.

The experiments have mostly been undertaken at the CERN's (European Center for Nuclear Research) 19-mile-diameter accelerator ring outside Geneva and at SLAC's electron-positron collider 30 miles south of San Francisco. SLAC, the Stanford Linear Accelerator Center, has been responsible for many discoveries in fundamental particle research. There, experimenters slam oppositely charged particles into each other at near-light speed and use a massive detector to observe the decay of the resulting "Z^0."[22]

22. Pronounced "zee-naught," this so-called "gauge boson" mediates one particular force (the electroweak) between fundamental particles.

The trick is to measure the Z^0's rate of decay. Why? Because that rate depends on the number of pathways available for this short-lived particle to decay into. The more pathways, the faster it will decay. The number of pathways, in turn, is governed by the number of theoretically possible kinds of neutrinos. That is, 10 possible kinds of neutrinos would result in 10 pathways, allowing the Z^0 to decay faster than if fewer than 10 neutrino types were possible.

Particle physicists have compiled data from thousands of Z^0 decay events in the last few years. By measuring how long those events take, most are now convinced that no more than three kinds of neutrinos exist. Since one member of each family of matter is a neutrino, the conclusion is that only three families are possible, any time, any place.[23]

We've come a long way from the Greek philosopher's four elemental substances to what is optimistically referred to as our modern perception of fundamental particles and how they interact with each other. The goal of the quest, however, remains the same: to understand all the diverse properties of matter—hardness, color, smell, movement, life even—on the basis of what that matter is ultimately made of. Today, we've come closer to that understanding than Empedocles could ever have dreamed.

— A Thumbnail History of the Quest for Nature's Building Blocks —

Most remarkable will be that a handful of beings on a small planet circling an insignificant star will have traced their origin back to the very beginning—a small speck of the universe comprehending the whole.

> —Murray Gell-Mann, coproponent of the "quark" theory of matter which explains all matter in terms of a few "building blocks," on its implications

c. 500 B.C.   Heraclitus ("the Obscure") of Ephesus proposes that fire is the primary substance out of which all else is made.

---

23. This confirms results from cosmological observations from the most powerful particle accelerator of all, the Big Bang. See David N. Schramm and Gary Steigman, "Particle Accelerators Test Cosmological Theory," *Scientific American*, June 1988, page 66; also see Gary J. Feldman and Jack Steinberger, "The Number of Families of Matter," *Scientific American*, February 1991, page 70.

c. 445 B.C.   Empedocles of Akragas (in Sicily) says that all matter is made up of four elements—earth, fire, water, and air—which change under the opposing forces of love and hate.

c. 440 B.C.   Leucippus and his better-known pupil Democritus propose that the atom (literally, "that which cannot be cut") is the smallest indivisible entity.

c. 385 B.C.   Plato assigns a fifth element (ether) in addition to Empedocles' original four.

1473   Lucretius's *De Rerum Natura* (*On the Nature of Things*) is translated from Arabic into Latin, making Democritus's atomic theory known to the West.

1789   Antoine-Laurent Lavoisier (France) clarifies the difference between compounds and elements, establishing a new chemical nomenclature.[24] He publishes a table of 31 elements.

1805   John Dalton (U.K.) quantifies Lavoisier's idea, and in so doing revives the Greek "atomist" theory in modern form. He proposes that elements are composed of atoms having unique weights, and that different elements always enter into compounds in amounts that are the ratios of small integers. (Today we know of over 100 elements, numbered according to how many protons each of its atomic nuclei contains. About 90 elements occur naturally, from the lightest, hydrogen, with 1 proton, to the heaviest, uranium, with 92 protons.)

1869   Russian scientist Dmitry Ivanovich Mendeleyev realizes that elements come in "families." (Bavarian physicist Johann Døbereiner had suspected something of the kind nearly 100 years earlier.) Mendeleyev formulates his periodic table of elements and predicts that there are some "missing" elements (for example, germanium). Upon discovery, these elements are found to fit the gaps in his table.

---

24. The tip-off came from Henry Cavendish's experiments with water, which Lavoisier correctly interpreted to mean that water was a compound made up of elemental oxygen and hydrogen. As James Trefil points out in *Meditations at 10,000 Feet*, the coining of the word *hydrogen*, i.e., "generator of water" (in German *Wasserstoff*, "the stuff of water") reflected the revolutionary understanding of the composition of water.

1897 — Working at Cambridge, English physicist J. J. Thomson discovers the first "modern" elementary particle, the negatively charged electron, thus showing that atoms can be split into, at least, positive and negative parts.

1911 — New Zealander Ernest Rutherford proposes that the atom isn't a homogenous "plum pudding," as had been previously thought, but consists of a tiny, yet massive, central nucleus of positively charged protons surrounded by "shells" of negatively charged electrons.

1919 — The proton is found, adding credence to Rutherford's theory.

1932 — James Chadwick (U.K.) discovers a third elementary particle, the uncharged neutron.

1937 — The muon, the first member of what we now know to be the second family of fundamental particles, is discovered, confusing the previously simple picture of a triad of particles, the proton, neutron, and electron (prompting physicist I. I. Rabi to ask, "Who ordered that?").

1947+ — The number of "elementary particles" proliferates to over 200 as higher energies are employed, initially by using cosmic ray collisions and later particle accelerators.

1964 — Murray Gell-Mann and George Zweig (both of the U.S.) propose that everything is made up of fractionally charged particles known as quarks and leptons.[25] The proton and neutron, for instance, are each made up of three quarks, while the electron is a lepton.

1974 — Simultaneous discovery of the J/psi particle at the Stanford Linear Accelerator Center (SLAC), California, and the Brookhaven National Laboratory, New York, offers strong confirmation of the quark model and hence of "the standard model."

---

25. Dictionaries and modern folklore notwithstanding, Gell-Mann insists that the word *quark* does *not* come from the line in Joyce's *Finnegans Wake* to which it's usually attributed, "Three quarks for Muster Mark!" That came later, says Gell-Mann, who said he was just looking for "a straightforward, somewhat playful tag." (Ivars Peterson, "Particles of History," *Science News*, September 12, 1992, page 174.) *Lepton* is derived from the Greek for "something small," particularly a small coin.

1989   Particle-accelerator results confirm previous cosmological
               evidence that there are exactly three families of matter, each
               containing two quarks and two leptons (plus their
               oppositely charged antiparticles). Of these 12 theoretically
               possible fundamental particles, only 3 exist in ordinary
               matter: the two quarks (named, for no particular reason at
               all, the "up" and "down" quarks) in the first, or electron,
               family, and the electron.

	ELECTRON FAMILY	MUON FAMILY	TAU FAMILY	Charge
QUARKS	UP	CHARM	TOP* * Not yet observed	2/3
	DOWN	STRANGE	BOTTOM	-1/3
LEPTONS	ELECTRON NEUTRINO	MUON NEUTRINO	TAU NEUTRINO	0
	ELECTRON	MUON	TAU	-1

Increasing mass

Only three families of matter exist, according to both cosmological and particle-accelerator evidence. Each family consists of two quarks and two leptons. To date, all except the top quark have been observed. The constituents of "ordinary matter" are all in the first family: the "up" and "down" quarks and the electron.

A Conversation with
Joseph Schwartz

Works of science are ways of understanding created through human effort which, like works of art, can be interrogated for what they say about ourselves and our development. By finding out about our science we find out about ourselves.

—Joseph Schwartz, *The Creative Moment: How Science Made Itself Alien to Modern Culture*

While I've been enthusing on the value of wonder and awe in introducing or reintroducing science to laypeople, maverick scientist Joseph Schwartz cautions against overselling science. Coming out of the heady climate of particle physics research in the 1960s, Schwartz taught physics at New York's City University and wrote two books. The first, *Einstein for Beginners*, is, in my opinion, the best demystification available of Einstein's theories of relativity. His second book, however, is what really intrigues me.

Like many scientists, science teachers, and science writers, I'm deeply troubled by the sad state of science education in the West and the widening gap between science and the rest of our culture. In his role as a critic of science, Schwartz goes far beyond worrying about these issues: he

167

Joseph Schwartz. (Barry Evans)

looks at how and why science got the way it is. In his book *The Creative Moment: How Science Made Itself Alien to Modern Culture*, he takes several of science's "creative moments" in their historical sequence and shows how "our present fear and awe of science . . . is a symptom of a serious structural problem in the West with ramifications in every area of our cultural life."

I don't agree with everything Dr. Schwartz says, but I wholeheartedly concur with a reviewer who wrote, "This original and thought-provoking book includes a wealth of ideas . . . that force the reader to think critically about the place of science in our lives."

Barry Evans   In *The Creative Moment*, you intimated that your family background was somewhat responsible for your interest in the alienation of science from popular culture. Tell me a little about that background.

Joseph Schwartz   My family were emigrants from Russia. My mother was born in Russia. I grew up in an immigrant family, very traditionally American of that generation; they were part of the last big influx of immigrants before the U.S. Immigration Act of 1924 shut it all down. I was the first in my family to graduate from a university and the first to go to graduate school.

I had plenty of reason to respect the accomplishments of the adults that I grew up with—in terms of the struggles they had made and the success they had won—because it was a time of tremendous progressive advances in America. The entire New Deal was really a result of grass roots pressure, in which my parents and their parents were involved.

In the fifties I went to the University of California at Berkeley, and I loved it; Berkeley was a terrific school and a terrific environment. I was interested in physics and I went to graduate school there. I got my Ph.D. working in Luis Alvarez's particle physics group—a Nobel Prize–winning team. I think all of us who had that experience were changed one way or another forever.

B. E.   What experiences led to your becoming first a science demystifier and later a science critic?

J. S.   Coming out of that quite elitist, and extremely successful, environment, I was not able to explain what I was doing to my Yiddish-speaking grandparents. It bothered me a great deal that physics, which I loved so much, was essentially opaque to them. They were smart and successful in their own way, yet here was this highly valued activity, which was so exciting to me, completely divorced from their experience. The result was a kind of an alienation from them and from friends of my parents' generation, people whom I greatly respected. I also experienced an odd kind of adulation toward me, being very successful academically: being looked up to without any real understanding of what was involved.

Then, quite suddenly, I realized I was getting from other well-educated people of my own generation this same reaction, "Oh you're a physicist! How interesting!" And then they would change the topic. This contrasted with the usual interest shown in what people were doing. In science this sort of interest was out of bounds. Instead I experienced fear and ignorance.

So I think that the confluence between those two groups, my contemporaries and my grandparents, influenced my decision to move into the realm of trying to understand what it was all about.

B. E.   Are we talking here about C. P. Snow's "two cultures"?

J. S.   Phenomenologically he was accurate, particularly in the British scene, in describing an elite science culture and an elite arts culture, where "art people" were running the country while "science people" were taking a backseat. But he didn't really explain why that should happen.

B. E.   Is that the sort of feeling that inspired you to write your cartoon-style book explaining relativity, *Einstein for Beginners*?

J. S.   Yes, and I had a lot of fun doing that, with a wonderful artist, Mike McGuinness. I thought, "I'll toss this chip into the fire and see what happens."

B. E.   Did it have the desired effect?

J. S.   I think it had a positive effect, but it was such a small thing compared to the overwhelming weight of ignorance and fear. It still left me wanting to understand what *really* was going on in conversations with my contemporaries and with my grandparents.

B. E.   And that led to your latest book?

J. S.   Eventually, yes. In order to understand what goes on now, I think it's important to look at some of the choices that the science community as a whole made at certain critical points. I try to tell the stories of some of those choices.

B. E.   You picked Galileo and his struggle with the church as your first "creative moment." Perhaps you could summarize the story for us.

J. S.   Galileo's story was told in the nineteenth century as "the church suppressing the truth." That was at a time when the church was acting as a brake on the development of the scientific culture. Back then, it was important to tell the story in such a way as to say, "Look, we can't really have this suppression of the truth." But I think the historical record, when looked at from the point of view of our present problems, shows something much more important, that is, how Galileo himself furthered the inaccessibility of science.

What I've tried to say in the Galileo story is that, in many ways, he symbolizes the choice that many scientists have made at critical points in history. In Galileo's case, instead of communicating his discoveries with the most progressive and forward-looking members of his community—that is, the businessmen, tradesmen, and artisans of the Republic of Venice— being born a patrician and feeling invulnerable to the pressures that the church could place upon him, Galileo moved from Padua (where he'd been a popular teacher for many years) to Florence (where he no longer had to teach). For a while he still wrote in very accessible language, then he was threatened with the Inquisition for saying that the Earth orbited the sun.

To try to evade persecution, he then argued that the book of nature is written in mathematics and that you can't decipher it without knowing mathematics. In effect he was saying to the church hierarchy, "You just leave it to us and we'll get on with it." That line of argument was quite effective in dealing with the higher levels of the church, but ultimately it wasn't effective enough in the lower levels to keep him from the Inquisition.

The critical point in history, from our point of view, wasn't so much the Inquisition and the trial, but this whole business, in 1623, of arguing, "Leave me alone. What other scientists and I are doing is in mathematical language. You don't have to worry about it, and just let us be."

B. E.   You go on to say that Galileo's tactic became commonplace.

J. S.   It was certainly picked up over the next 50 years and was consolidated by Newton in his *Principia*, which is expressed in a highly mathematical language (particularly the new calculus) and was not written to be understood. It was written as a mathematical model.

Today we still have this legacy of highly mathematicized physical science. It's very off-putting to nonscientists, and it still serves very obscurantist functions. The point is that these were *choices* made by scientists of the period, in order to avoid the problems that their work was encountering. Galileo, rather than continuing to create a science of very broad, popular appeal, decided to try to win the elite over. I think he lacked the political consciousness to stay with language where he would have support from large social groups who would support him. He chose not to do that.

B. E.   He must have moved a long way from his extremely popular book *Siderius Nuncius* [*The Starry Messenger*], published in 1610.

J. S.   Yes, when Galileo was younger, he was a very successful science writer. In *Siderius Nuncius*, his descriptions of what he had seen with one of the earliest telescopes, of moons orbiting Jupiter and so on, were very accessible. He included no mathematics and it was full of sketches. The book became a sensation among educated Europe because it was decisive evidence in favor of Copernicus.

B. E.   Coming back to the present, what dangers do you see in the popularization of science today?

J. S.   Some excellent scientists are writing well for the lay audience, but even the best of them, in my opinion, don't have enough of a critical attitude towards science. They communicate too much of a sense of awe.

B. E.   But don't we science writers need to get readers excited with awe and wonder for them to take interest in science in the first place?

J. S.   I think we've gone as far as we can with awe and wonder, and that's not very far at all. You have *A Brief History of Time*, a really terrible book, topping the bestseller lists precisely because it *is* so incomprehensible. We have relativity, a masterpiece of human understanding, still being a synonym for the awesome and mysterious. We have men in white coats selling us everything from carcinogenic face creams to destructive advice on how to raise our children.

No, I think one of the very *worst* things we can be doing is exciting readers and students with awe and wonder! I think we should be aiming to create a critically aware populace that is capable of blowing loud raspberries when confronted with arrant nonsense, a population that is confident enough in its own powers of perception and understanding to demand the best, and only the best, from our scientists. I am describing a population that is grown up in relation to science, not a population of four-year-olds still encased in the magic world of childhood. Anything that takes us away from increasing our maturity, from realizing our powers as individuals and as a species, is to my mind irresponsible. Especially today when you see the magnitude of the crisis we are facing.

B. E.   What questions should your utopian, critically aware populace be asking?

J. S.   "What problems are being worked on?" and "Why are they being worked on?" We need a much fuller, more embedded sense of the scientific enterprise, in the same way we have an embedded critique of art. We don't simply *look* at paintings. There's really a vast intellectual edifice of art history and art criticism—why paintings get painted at certain times, what it expresses about the culture, a much more interpretive criticism. We don't have that in science, that critical eye.

B. E.   What would you like to see more of in science education?

J. S.   Firstly, the inclusion of more of how we know what we know, including the story of the wrong turns on the way. In particular, to bring the human element into science education, showing students that knowledge is created by human effort. It doesn't appear by magic.

Secondly, I'd like to see much more lab work. The trouble with much lab work today is that students are penalized if they get the wrong answer. So they fake the results. When I was teaching at City University, we tried an experiment. We cooked the instrument so it couldn't give the result it was meant to give, yet the kids would still make it come out right. We weren't trying to penalize them by catching them out, but we wanted to show what sort of pressures the kids felt they were faced with in terms of coming up with the right answer.

The point is that knowledge is open-ended, yet what generally motivates kids these days isn't so much wanting to know more as wanting to confirm what they've already been taught.

B. E.   So should we be teaching children that it's OK to spend as much time as they want on the process, and not to worry too much about the answer?

J. S.   Certainly in the lower grades. We should teach kids how to observe and to write down what they observe, what they feel about it and what they think might be going on, without having them worry all the time about what the "right answers" are.

B. E.   What about facts they really do need to know?

J. S.   Against that process I've outlined, teachers should be introducing the idea that there really is something to be learned and that there is a body of knowledge that the kid needs to know.

B. E.   With what result when they grow up?

J. S.   So they can be doing with science what is regularly done in art: interpreting, questioning, and criticizing. In a word, *democratizing* science.

Thursday's Puzzles

Instant Solutions

The most basic principle of lateral thinking is that
any particular way of looking at things is only
one from among many other possible ways.

—Edward de Bono, *Lateral Thinking:*
Creativity Step by Step

*T*hese puzzles can be solved instantly, or at least in a few seconds, if the right insight is gained.

1. I have two glasses. One contains 10 ounces of water, the other an equal amount of wine. I pour 1 ounce of water into the wine, mix thoroughly, then I pour 1 ounce of the wine-water mixture into the water. Is there now more water in the wine or wine in the water?

    Hint 1: The numbers are red herrings, as is the word thoroughly. *It works with any transferred amount, mixed or not.*

    Hint 2: Imagine you have two equal piles of marbles, one containing 10 red marbles and the other containing 10 black. Mix them up and divide again so you've now got two mixed piles of 10 marbles each. If 3 black marbles have "contaminated" the red pile, how many red marbles are now in the black pile?

2. The local tennis club had 125 entrants for its annual singles elimination tournament. In the first round, 62 games were played to eliminate about half the contestants (the odd man had a bye, that is, he moved to the second round without playing). In the second round a further quarter were eliminated, and so on until the winner emerged. How many matches were played?

> *Hint 1: The same insight that gives the answer to the previous question applies. The answer takes less than a second to compute.*
>
> *Hint 2: To get one winner, how many people have to* lose *a match?*

3. You roll a normal die 9 times and it comes up six each time. What's the chance it will come up six the 10th time?

> *Hint: Does a die have a memory?*

4. This is a cube. At what angle do the two diagonal lines meet?

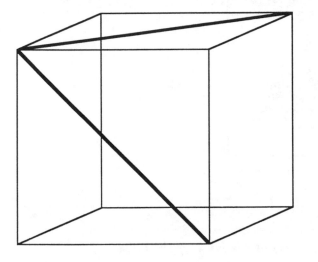

Hint: Connect the two lines along the right face of the cube.

5. Sam Loyd (1841–1911) was arguably America's, if not the world's, greatest puzzlist. He's said to have sold a hundred thousand copies of this puzzle in a few weeks. First, see if you can solve it simply by looking at it. Then photocopy it and cut out the three parts. The puzzle is to place the three pieces so the riders are riding the donkeys.

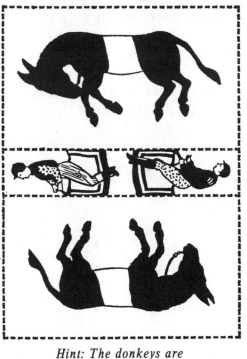

Hint: The donkeys are practically flying!

Puzzle answers are at the back of the book.

Thursday's Quotations

Now

If you are not happy here and now, you never will be.

—**Taisen Deshimaru**

Live this life as if you live eternally, and live this life as if you die tomorrow.

—**The Prophet Muhammad**

Life is not a problem to be solved but a reality to be experienced.

—**Søren Kierkegaard**

There is an objective reality, but we're nowhere near to grasping it in its totality . . . and if we did get to the truth, would we ever know it?

—**Michael Redhead**

When I turned away in this manner, the silence gathered and struck me. It bashed me broadside from the heavens above me like yard goods; ten acres of fallen, invisible sky choked the fields. The pastures on either side of the road turned green in a surrealistic fashion, monstrous, impeccable, as if they were holding their breaths. The roosters stopped. All the things of the world—the fields

*and the fencing, the road, a parked orange truck—were stricken
and self-conscious. A world pressed down on their surfaces, a world
battered just within their surfaces, and that real world, so near to
emerging, had got stuck.*

*There was only silence. It was the silence of matter caught in
the act and embarrassed. There were no cells moving, and yet there
were cells. I could see the shape of the land, how it lay holding
silence. Its poise and its stillness were unendurable, like the ring of
the silence you hear in your skull when you're little and notice
you're living, the ring which resumes later in life when you're sick.*

—**Annie Dillard, "A Field of Silence"**
in *Teaching a Stone to Talk*

*A Zen-master was delivering a sermon to some monks outside his
hut. Suddenly he went inside, locked the door, set the hut on fire,
and called out, "Unless someone says the right thing, I'm not
coming out." Everybody then desperately tried to say the right thing
and, of course, failed. Along came a latecomer who wanted to know
what all the fuss was about. One of the monks excitedly explained,
"The master has locked himself inside and set fire to the hut and
unless somebody says the right thing, he won't come out!" Upon
which the latecomer said, "Oh my God!" At this the master
came out.*

—**Raymond Smullyan**

Eat the present and break the dish.

—**Egyptian saying**

*In order to be utterly happy the only thing necessary is to refrain
comparing this moment with other moments in the past.*

—**André Gide**

Like everyone else, I lived in a house bricked up with seconds and minutes, weekends and New Year's Days, and I never went outside until I died, because there was no other door. Now I know that I could have walked through the walls.

—**Peter Beagle**, *The Last Unicorn*

The present is the object of vision.

—**Annie Dillard**

Friday

Day of Venus

*I*f Tuesday is male (by virtue of its association with Mars and the shared symbol of the male gender), Friday is female. Since Roman times the day has been associated with Venus, goddess of love. The astrological-astronomical symbol for Venus the planet, a cross surmounted by a circle, is also our symbol for female.

Venus was originally an obscure Italian deity whose name meant beauty, but after being associated with the Greek goddess Aphrodite, her stock rose. Later, Nero even claimed descent from her!

T h i r t e e n

The Amazing Accelerator

*We who stand securely see things the wrong way around because
the ground beneath our feet is all the time pushing us away
from a natural state of motion. That natural state of motion
is free fall, or, better said, free float.*

—John Archibald Wheeler, *A Journey
into Gravity and Spacetime*

*Y*ou're on the freeway in a new car. This is some set of wheels. Not only
does it look terrific and feel fantastic, but it's got amazing acceleration:
zero to 20 mph in one second, zero to 40 in two seconds, zero to 60 in
three seconds . . . wow! zero to 100 in five seconds! Can this baby move!
In one minute you're doing 1,200 mph, and you're still accelerating.
Every second your speed picks up by another 20 mph.

Imagine what it might feel like, this sensation of constantly
accelerating, every second moving another 20 mph faster. Imagine . . .
no, don't even imagine. *Just notice.* Your fantasy car is free. Assuming
you're not reading this while skydiving or orbiting in a spaceship, you
are, this moment, experiencing an acceleration of about 20 miles per
hour every second, or (using feet and seconds) 32 feet per second per
second.[1]

---

1. The difference between velocity and acceleration is this: velocity (roughly
synonymous with speed) is how fast you're traveling, e.g., 60 miles per hour, which
is equivalent to 88 feet per second; acceleration is how fast your velocity is
changing, e.g., gravity at the surface of the Earth causes a falling stone to

Stop reading for a moment, close your eyes, and fully experience the force of gravity on your body. Do you feel it? (You can open your eyes now.) This force of gravity you're aware of, right now, is completely indistinguishable from what you would feel if you were in outer space and being accelerated "upward" (that is, in the direction of overhead) at a rate of 32 feet per second every second.

The phenomenon is called the principle of equivalence, first formulated by Albert Einstein in about 1910. To make it clearer, let's perform something Albert particularly enjoyed: a thought experiment. This one's called "Escape the aliens."

Suppose you wake up one morning and realize to your horror that, yet again, you've been kidnapped sometime during the night. (You must be getting tired of this by now if you're reading the book sequentially!) This time, instead of being in your bedroom, you find yourself in some sort of sealed chamber. It's plenty big enough to move around in and has all the comforts of home, but there's no way you can communicate with the outside. Pinned to the wall is a note saying, "Good morning! You've been kidnapped by us, a mean bunch of aliens who want to test your intelligence. This chamber is either (1) sitting on the Earth's surface, or (2) accelerating through space at 32 feet per second per second. Your task is to determine which is true, (1) or (2). If you pass the test, we'll set you free. If you fail, we'll kidnap Tammy You-know-who and put her in here with you. Have a nice day."

You're understandably frantic. What should you do? It sure feels as if you're on the Earth, but you know that a constant acceleration of 32 feet per second per second in the direction of "up" would feel exactly the same as if you were on solid ground. Surely, you think, there must be some experiment to determine which is true for you, gravity or acceleration. The chamber is equipped with every imaginable piece of apparatus, and they've even kidnapped a few world-class scientists to advise you. You ask them how to learn the truth. "There's no way to communicate with the outside world?" they ask. Nope, everything is totally, utterly sealed. They confer, then the leading scientist pulls

---

accelerate by 32 feet per second every second (neglecting air resistance), so its velocity would be 32 feet per second after it's been falling for one second, 64 feet per second after two seconds, 96 after three, and so on. The difference between being accelerated and moving at a constant velocity is obvious in an elevator. You experience the change in velocity, i.e., acceleration, as a force on your body when the elevator is starting and stopping. When you're traveling at a constant velocity between floors, there's no force due to the movement: it feels as if the elevator is stationary.

A stone dropped at the surface of the Earth falls with an acceleration of about 32 feet per second every second.

Gravity

Acceleration

If you drop a stone while being accelerated through space at 32 feet per second per second, the stone's motion will be the same as on Earth—you wouldn't know if you were in space or on Earth.

something out from his pocket and hands it to you. "It's the best we can do," he says. It's a quarter. You understand. "Heads we're on the Earth, tails we're in space," you say, as you toss.

The Principle of Equivalence

The principle of equivalence says, essentially, that there's no way to distinguish between gravity and acceleration because they're the same thing. Notice I said earlier that skydivers and Earth-orbiting astronauts were exempt from the acceleration-gravity feeling. Ignoring air resistance, they felt the same thing: weightlessness, that is, nothing. They're in free-fall. To glimpse what this acceleration-gravity equivalence is all about, imagine that you're the skydiver. As you jump and start to fall, you see your buddy standing in the door of the plane. From your point of view, she's shooting skyward at an ever-increasing velocity, accelerating at 32 feet per second per second (neglecting air resistance)! "How does it feel?" you yell. "Just like I'm standing on the ground!" she shouts back.

This is such an important point, let's make it a little clearer. I want you to drop a video camera over a cliff, as before, assuming there's no air resistance.

From the point of view of a falling video camera in "free-fall," you appear to be accelerating upward at 32 feet per second per second. Gravity imparts that acceleration to your body via the surface on which you're standing.

The camera, pointing up, transmits what it sees, that is, you, standing on the top of the cliff looking at a monitor. The camera doesn't "know" it's falling, in fact it feels no gravity at all (just like a skydiver falling in a vacuum). From the camera's point of view (which you experience vicariously on the monitor), you look like you're on a rocket ship, or in that car we were talking about, accelerating heavenward at 32 feet per second per second. What we call gravity the free-falling camera sees as acceleration!

The principal of equivalence, which is one of the foundations of Einstein's 1915 general theory of relativity, solves an old problem that was first explicitly recognized by Galileo Galilei (1564–1642) and later

Isaac Newton (1642–1727). (Pat Linse)

explained to some extent by Isaac Newton (1642–1727). Ask most people about Galileo and they'll bring to mind a picture of him dropping different-sized rocks from the top of the Leaning Tower of Pisa and noting that they reach the ground at the same time. That story is assumed to be apocryphal these days, although Dutchman Simon Stevin (in virtually the first original exploration of mechanics since Aristotle) noted in 1586 that two lead spheres, one 10 times heavier than the other, hit the ground at the same time after being dropped simultaneously from a height of 30 feet. (Had he dropped them from a greater height—for example, from the top of the 180-foot Leaning Tower, he would have seen the heavier one hit first. Can you see why air resistance affects a smaller rock more than the larger one?[2])

However, Galileo assumed that in a vacuum, rocks of different masses would all land simultaneously,[3] and he undertook many

---

2. Mass (which governs gravitational force) increases in proportion to the cube of any dimension, but surface area (which governs air resistance) increases in proportion to its square. So the more massive a body, the less affect air resistance has on it compared to the force of gravity.

3. Galileo wrote, in *Dialogues Concerning Two New Sciences*, ". . . in a fall of one hundred cubits, a ball of gold would surely not outstrip one of copper by as much as four fingers. Having observed this, I came to the conclusion that in a medium totally devoid of all resistance, all bodies would fall with the same speed."

experiments rolling spheres down inclined planes that tended to support his conjecture. Later, Newton stated the problem explicitly: a body wants to fall because of gravity and resists falling because of inertia. That is, any body has a natural resistance to change in motion, so a body at rest remains at rest, while a body moving with uniform velocity remains at that velocity. Now, he said, the only property of a body that affects its motion under the influence of gravity is its "gravitational mass," while the only property affecting its resistance to motion is its "inertial mass." If light rocks and heavy rocks hit the ground at the same time, the inescapable conclusion is that a body's gravitational mass is exactly the same as its inertial mass. What a coincidence! Experiments in this century have confirmed this assumption to better than 1 part in 10,000.

In Newtonian physics, there's no obvious reason why the two masses should be the same. "It's just a happy coincidence," prerelativity scientists may have thought, and pondered. But with Einstein's principle of equivalence, the mystery was solved: they are the same because gravity and inertia are the same.

Back to Your Chamber

To understand what a profound result this is, let's go back to you in your sealed chamber. You've been thinking about it and suddenly you hit on what seems like a brilliant answer to the problem of deciding whether you're sitting on the surface of the Earth or accelerating through space. Your solution is the old "light beam on the wall" trick! If you're being accelerated, a beam of light shining across the room would be bent down a tad by the time it's reached the other side. (We'll neglect the problem of actually measuring such a tiny deflection).

To see why this is so, imagine that the beam comes from outside and shines through a slit in the right-hand wall and out of a slit in the left-hand wall. An external observer would see the beam exit the left wall a little lower than where it entered the right wall, since in the interval the chamber moved "up" from his point of view.

So, you reason, all you have to do is see if a beam of light is deflected as it passes across the chamber: if it is, then you're accelerating through space. If it isn't, you're sitting quietly on the surface of the Earth.

The brilliant scientists keeping you company (who are, by now, beginning to annoy you with their negative attitude) shake their heads. "What's the problem?" you ask. "Curved space," they say. They explain

Acceleration

If you were being accelerated through space at 32 feet per second per second, and someone shone a flashlight through a slit in the right-hand wall, the beam would appear to "fall" toward the left.

Acceleration

You don't need someone outside to shine the flashlight, though. You can do the same thing yourself while inside.

If you did this on the surface of Earth, you'd see the same thing because Earth's gravity deflects the beam, so this experiment wouldn't tell you whether you were in space or on Earth.

that your assumption, that a beam of light wouldn't be deflected if your chamber was on the Earth, is wrong. Why? Because light is bent by the Earth's gravitational field. Why? Because light travels through space, and space is bent by mass, in this case, the mass of the Earth. Mass tells

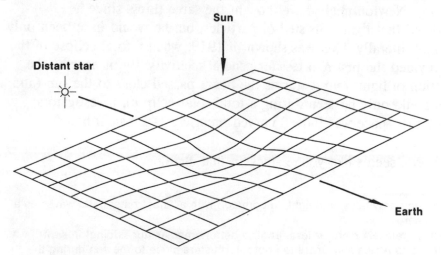

Light from a distant star is deflected as it passes close to the sun. It's convenient to imagine the sun "warping" space in its vicinity. The starlight doesn't "know" it's being deflected, it "thinks" it's just traveling in a straight line.

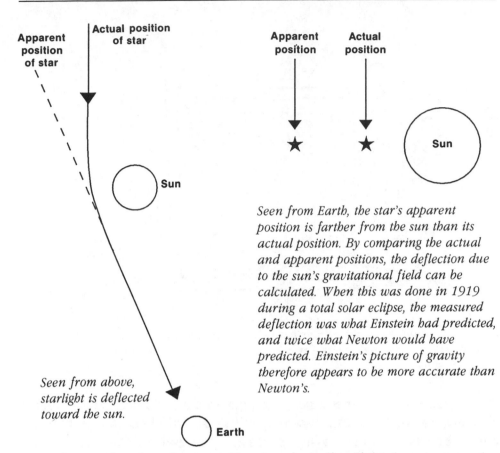

Actual position of star

Apparent position of star

Sun

Seen from above, starlight is deflected toward the sun.

Earth

Apparent position

Actual position

Sun

Seen from Earth, the star's apparent position is farther from the sun than its actual position. By comparing the actual and apparent positions, the deflection due to the sun's gravitational field can be calculated. When this was done in 1919 during a total solar eclipse, the measured deflection was what Einstein had predicted, and twice what Newton would have predicted. Einstein's picture of gravity therefore appears to be more accurate than Newton's.

space how to bend, and space tells mass, including light, how to move.[4]

Now Newton might have thought the same thing, since he considered that light consisted of particles, but he would have been only half right, literally. This was shown in 1919, when a total eclipse of the sun provided the first real test for general relativity. By measuring the deflection of light from a star as the beam passed close to the sun (and which could only be seen during a total solar eclipse), investigators showed that space was indeed curved precisely as Einstein had predicted.[5]

Sorry, seems like you're stuck in that chamber.[6]

---

4. All energy gravitates, and light, in common with all electromagnetic waves, is a form of energy.

5. That is, precisely more or less. English astronomer Arthur Eddington sent expeditions to Africa and Brazil to photograph stars close to the sun during the eclipse. Subsequently, star positions were compared with photographs taken six months later, when the sun wouldn't affect their light paths. The trouble is that when the researchers measured the positions of the stars on the two sets of glass plates, the possible error due to unsharp images on the glass plates was about the

Albert Einstein (1879–1955).
(Pat Linse)

Stopping the Earth (aka Spinning the Cosmos)

Here's another way to think of gravity and inertia. We noted earlier (See Chapter 5, "Crisis on the Scales") that our planet bulges at the equator. Why? Because of inertia, just as the inertia tries to throw you off a spinning disk. "But didn't Einstein say that it doesn't matter which 'frame of reference' you choose?" you say. "That is, isn't it as correct to think of the Earth as standing still and the sun, moon, and rest of the universe spinning around it as it is to imagine the Earth spinning relative to them?

---

same as the distances they were trying to measure (since the predicted deflection is vanishingly small). So when Eddington announced that Einstein's prediction had been confirmed, he was taking a small leap of faith. Later, and better, eclipse measurements gave more reliable confirmation. Today, general relativity is known to be accurate to at least 1 part in 10,000.

Following Eddington's announcement, Einstein was asked what he would have done if the results had shown him to be wrong. In an unusually candid moment, he replied, "I would have felt sorry for the good Lord! The theory is, of course, alright." He already knew his theory was on solid ground, having confirmed it with reference to the precession of Mercury's orbit around the sun.

6. If you really want out, I think I can help. Assuming you could really measure the deflection of a light beam with such uncanny accuracy, perhaps you could also detect the difference in the force of gravity between the floor and ceiling of your chamber. (A very sensitive pendulum might do it.) If you're being accelerated, there won't be any difference, but on Earth, because the ceiling is farther away from Earth's center than the floor, gravity will be stronger at floor level. You're as good as free! (You can easily extend this picture to understand how the moon causes tides by replacing your chamber with Earth and Earth with the moon.) Alternatively, plumb bobs hanging on either side of your chamber would be parallel in space but would make a minute angle toward Earth's center on the surface.

Isn't that why it's called the theory of relativity? Everything's relative, right?" Sounds good so far, what's the problem?

The problem is this: if you think of the Earth as fixed, with everything else spinning around it, what's making it bulge at the equator? Obviously, there are no inertial effects because it isn't spinning. If you don't see the answer, stop for a moment and consider the problem. All the clues to solve it are in this section.

Got it? The answer is *gravity*. Gravity is what's making the Earth bulge at the equator: the gravitational attraction of the sun, moon, and stars as they spin around the Earth. Get it? Einstein said gravity and inertia are one and the same thing. The inertial force that causes a spinning Earth to bulge is exactly the same as the gravitational force from a spinning universe.[7] The point is that inertial forces don't occur in isolation, they need something—in this case, the rest of the universe—to work. Gravity? Inertia? Same thing. Both are manifestations of a single phenomenon: curved space.

--------------------- **Foucault's Pendulum** ---------------------

This dialogue occurs early in Umberto Eco's novel, *Foucault's Pendulum*:

> *"What does [Foucault's pendulum] do? Just hang there?"*
>
> *"It proves the rotation of the earth. Since the point of suspension doesn't move . . ."*
>
> *"Why doesn't it move?"*
>
> *"Well, because a point . . . the central point, I mean, the one right in the middle of all the points you can see . . . it's a geometric point; you can't see it because it has no dimension, it can't move, not right or left, not up or*

---

7. Which leads us to another phenomenon. If the Earth was perfectly spherical and homogenous, its axis wouldn't "precess," so that if your astrological sun sign was Leo, the sun would have been in Leo when you were born. In Babylonian times, that would have been true, but precession of Earth's axis has caused the astrological zodiac to be off by one sign from its astronomical counterpart. Also, the sun would still be in Cancer and Capricorn (as in "tropics of") on the solstices. Nowadays, it's in Gemini at the summer solstice and Sagittarius at the winter solstice.

down. So it doesn't rotate with the earth. You understand? It can't even rotate around itself. There is no 'itself.' "

"But the earth turns."

"The earth turns, but the point doesn't. That's how it is. Just take my word for it."

"I guess it's the Pendulum's business."

Idiot. Above her head was the only stable place in the cosmos, the only refuge from the damnation of the panta rei, and she guessed it was the Pendulum's business, not hers . . ."

In truth, Eco's bestseller doesn't have a lot to say about the physics of Foucault's pendulum, but what he does say—essentially the quote above—is significant. Other than its metaphorical influence on the crazy and intricate plot (and neglecting a ghastly murder), the pendulum doesn't put in much of an appearance. But it does give us the opportunity to revisit what's really going on in so-called empty space.

Suspend a pendulum over the North Pole in winter, when it's continuously dark, and let it swing for a while. Overhead, the stars slowly rotate clockwise around the sky, taking nearly 24 hours to make a

A pendulum swinging over the North Pole is affected symmetrically by Earth's rotation so has no preferred frame of reference relative to the Earth. Instead, it responds to the distant stars, and moves around with them.

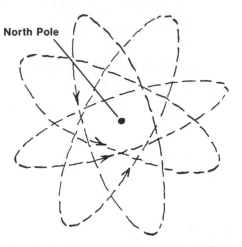

North Pole

From an earthbound observer's point of view, the pendulum swings around with the stars, taking 23 hours and 56 minutes to make a full circle.

full circle.[8] As you watch the stars, you can see the pendulum out of the corner of your eye: it's moving around with the stars. The Earth is rotating counterclockwise beneath it. Suspended from a point in space, where the effect of the spinning Earth is symmetrical (since a point immediately above the North Pole lies on the Earth's axis), the pendulum is guided in its motion by an imaginary grid of gravity that fills space. The framework for the grid is the universe as a whole, a fraction of which is perceived by us as stars overhead. It's from that grid that the pendulum takes its orders.

If you were to install the pendulum over the equator, the Earth's spin, now asymmetric, would force it to swing in tune with the Earth. Instead of rotating around with the stars it would stay swinging, from our frame of reference on the ground, in one plane. The period a pendulum takes to swing around in a full circle varies, therefore, from nearly 24 hours at the pole to infinity at the equator. For instance, a Foucault pendulum in Paris (in the Conservatoire des Arts et Métiers, for instance, the location of *the* pendulum in Eco's book) takes nearly 32 hours to complete its cosmic circle.[9]

"I can easily believe, Holy Father, that when people read that I ascribe certain motions to the earth, they will shout out that me and my theory should be rejected," wrote Nicolaus Copernicus from his deathbed

---

8. Actually, 23 hours and 56 minutes, the length of the sidereal day, which differs by four minutes from the solar day due to Earth's orbit around the sun.

9. To figure its period anywhere on Earth, just divide its 24-hour pole period by the sine (opposite over hypotenuse, remember?) of the latitude. Paris is approximately at latitude 49 degrees, whose sine is about 0.755; 24 divided by 0.755 is nearly 32.

As the Earth spins counter-clockwise (as viewed from above the North Pole), this Foucault pendulum in San Francisco takes its orders from the universe as a whole. From our point of view, the plane of its swing rotates clockwise, causing the heavy bob to knock down pegs positioned around the compass rose. (Lloyd Ullberg, copyright © San Francisco Academy of Sciences)

to Pope Paul III in 1543. The "motions" he refers to are, of course, the Earth's spin on its axis and its orbit around the sun. Centuries were to pass before people could actually see the spin, via the pendulum Léon Foucault installed in the church of Sainte Geneviève in Paris in 1850. He used a 62-pound cannonball suspended from 200 feet of piano wire. Observers could see for themselves that after one hour the plane of the pendulum's swing had veered about 11 degrees clockwise. Here, 300 years after the death of Copernicus, was a visible demonstration of his proposition: our planet really *does* spin![10]

---

10. It's not easy to make a Foucault pendulum, by the way. (I tried and failed.) If you're interested, I recommend C. L. Stong's book *The Amateur Scientist* (New York: Simon & Schuster, 1960). Stong wrote "The Amateur Scientist" column in *Scientific American* for many years.

Fourteen

Dragons in the Fire

*Lowell always said that the regularity of the [Martian] canals
was an unmistakable sign that they were of intelligent origin.
The only unresolved question was which side of the telescope
the intelligence was on.*

—Carl Sagan, *Cosmos*

*H*umans delight in finding order in chaos. As a child, before clean air
laws put an end to coal-burning open hearths in England, I'd spend
endless hours creating fantasy worlds of people and places in our living-
room fireplace. There, black lumps of impure carbon that we call coal
slowly burned, oxidizing into carbons monoxide and dioxide and glowing
every shade of red and orange imaginable, while yellow flames licked
their way up to the chimney. My mind transformed the chaos of
combustion into the order of a fairy-tale land: kings and queens, dragons
and unicorns, castles and cathedrals all came to life as I stared into the
fire.

Clouds are another fertile source for imagining order where little
actually exists. It's easy to lie back and find old ladies' faces, galloping
camels, and who-knows-what-all romping around in cirrus and cumulus
agglomerations of water vapor floating overhead. Psychiatrists
administering the Rorschach test exploit our minds' endless capacity for

seeing something meaningful where none exists. Where one person sees her father's face in a symmetrical but random blob of ink, another sees rabbits mating, mirroring, the theory goes, the inner workings of the mind. And how's this? Just yesterday, our local newspaper ran a photograph of a tree that is receiving homage after the face of the Virgin Mary appeared on its trunk. (No, I don't understand how pilgrims know what her face looks like.)

THURSDAY, JULY 23, 1992

San Francisco Chronicle

BAY AREA
AND CALIFORNIA

Pilgrims Flock to Watsonville Oak Tree
Faithful claim to see Virgin of Guadalupe's outline on bark

Seeking order in the relative chaos of the bark of a tree. "An estimated 4,000 people have flocked every day this week to what many claim is the outline of the Virgin of Guadalupe on the limb of an oak tree. . . ." (San Francisco Chronicle, July 23, 1992)

If we can find order in fire, clouds, ink blobs, and tree trunks, imagine what we can do with the surface of Mars seen through a telescope. At its closest, Mars is about 35 million miles from Earth. Seen through the best telescope on Earth, under optimum viewing conditions, it's a tiny rusty disc. Moments of "good seeing" reveal a few large,

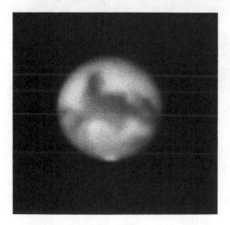

Even under the best seeing conditions, like in September 1988 when the planet was less than 40 million miles from Earth, Mars has few distinguishing features and no canals. This photograph was taken from France through an eight-inch telescope. It shows the bright southern polar cap at the bottom. The dark "spur" heading north from the dark equatorial band is the high plateau of Syrtis Major. The lighter area to the upper right is centered on Schiaparelli's Planitia Elysium, the Elysian fields of Mars. (Gérard Therin)

indistinct features.[11] From 1894, when he founded the Flagstaff Observatory, to his death in 1916, Boston banker Percival Lowell's obsession was mapping orderly patterns on Mars. Perhaps because he lived in the great canal age, from Suez (completed in 1869) to Panama (1914), he thought he saw canals on Mars.

The stage had been set in 1877, when Italian astronomer Giovanni Schiaparelli (uncle of famous Parisian couturiere Elsa Schiaparelli) claimed he saw *canali*, that is, channels, on Mars at one of its close approaches. Sacrificing, perhaps, an accurate translation for the sake of a good story, newspaper editors in the United States told their readers that canals had been found on Mars. While a *channel* might mean a natural

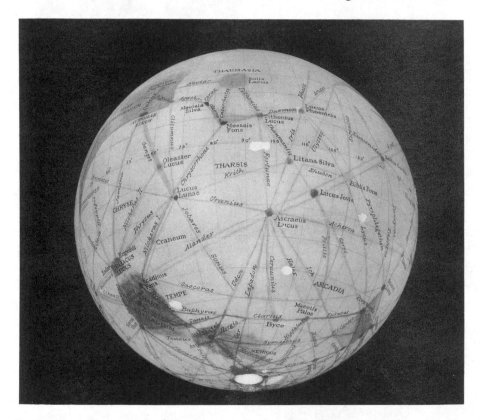

Percival Lowell's network of Martian canals, from his observations of the planet in 1903. (Lowell Observatory)

11. In the last few years, charge-coupled devices (CCDs) in lieu of conventional cameras have enabled astronomers at high-altitude observatories to obtain images of Mars of unprecedented resolution. See, for instance, William Sheehan and Stephen James O'Meara, "Exotic Worlds," *Sky and Telescope,* January 1993, page 22.

gorge (indeed, Mars's Valles Marineris is a 3,000-mile-long series of valleys), a *canal* can only imply the presence of intelligence. So when Lowell put his eye to the telescope, he already knew what he wanted to see. Before long he'd published maps showing a vast network of canals, an irrigation system bringing life-giving water from the Martian polar caps to parched equatorial deserts.[12]

Or so he thought. H. G. Wells's *The War of the Worlds* notwithstanding, I for one was saddened 30 years ago when a series of Mariner spacecraft sent back close-up views of Mars and confirmed what every astronomer (other than Lowell) had known all along: there are no canals on Mars. Just as we create monsters in the fire and dragons in the

Latest indication of intelligent life on Mars? The "Great Stone Face," (half-way up the photo and slightly to the right of center) imaged by the Viking 1 orbiter in 1976. It's possible to find "faces" in almost any eroded terrain, on Mars or here on Earth. North is at the top. (NASA, frame M1174-016)

---

12. Lowell knew, of course, that the comparatively thin line of an actual canal would be impossible to see from such a distance, so he postulated that he was seeing broad strips of vegetation running alongside the canals, just as you can see in satellite photographs of the Egyptian Nile.

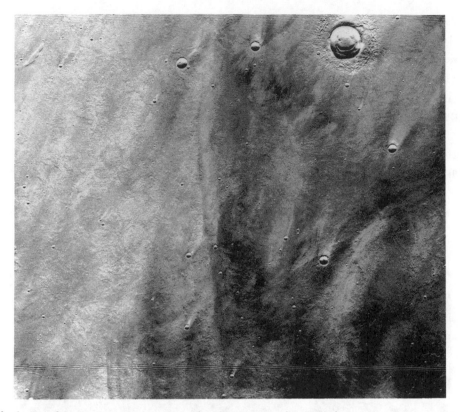

The largest known "Happy Face" in the solar system (top right). Another sensational find by the Viking 1 orbiter, it's actually a five-mile-wide impact crater on Mars. The eyes and mouth are fractures in the surface, probably created by the same meteor that formed the crater. South is at the top. (NASA, frame M3637-003)

clouds, Lowell had created his Martian canals in the mind.[13]

More recently, wishful thinkers have found abundant evidence of intelligent life on the surface of Mars. Not content with finding cities ("Did NASA Photograph Ruins of an Ancient City on Mars?" asked the *National Enquirer* in its October 25, 1977, issue), they found faces as well. The "Great Stone Face," with its attendant pyramid-shaped formations, is a feature approximately one mile across on which shadows give the illusion of a single eye, nose, and mouth. The "Happy Face" is a five-mile-diameter crater with fractures for eyes and a smiling mouth. Despite NASA's patient explanations that such formations can be

---

13. While it's easy to poke fun at Lowell, he did a great deal to advance the young science of astronomy in the United States, making important contributions to our understanding of how planets evolve. Also, Lowell's Flagstaff Observatory was where Clyde Tombaugh discovered Pluto in 1930. (The symbol for Pluto, an overlapping *P* and *L*, is—not coincidentally—Lowell's initials.)

attributed to natural processes—in fact, they can be *expected* to occur, given sufficient features to examine—they are still occasionally touted as evidence of extraterrestrial intelligence.

Wanna Bet?

Such wishful thinking is by no means confined to children, imaginative astronomers of a bygone age, and amateur ET-seekers. The same propensity for seeking—and finding—order in chaos can be seen in "technicians" of the stock exchange, real-money Monopoly players who plot elaborate charts and graphs in vain attempts to predict the future value of shares on the basis of past performance.[14] So too with horse race bettors who use "systems" that will, they hope, allow them to pick the day's winners. I recently saw a computer-age example of such blind optimism, a program that was said to increase one's chances of winning the lottery.

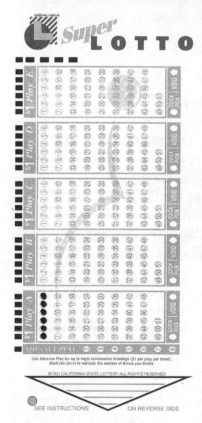

Let's look more closely at that last one, since it's so easy to analyze. California, like many states, has a weekly lottery. You can win the jackpot prize by picking the 6 winning numbers out of 51. The fact that it's run by the state should be a tip-off to its real purpose. It's not there to enrich the life of Joe Q. Public or to entertain the masses, of course (despite what the advertisements tell us), but rather to help counter the state's worsening budget deficit. The lottery is a very efficient revenue-making machine, paying out only 50 cents for every dollar "invested." (Thirty-four cents of every

My system for playing "Super Lotto" is guaranteed to be at least as good as any other! The numbers 1 through 6 have exactly the same chance as any other six.

---

14. A point of view obviously not universally shared! In *Searching for Certainty*, John Casti makes a persuasive case that "The Value Line" system of rating a stock's future value consistently outperforms random investments.

dollar goes toward education, with the balance paying for administration and commissions. Compare that to Las Vegas casinos, which only "charge" you about 5 cents on the dollar to play their slot machines.)

If you're a lottery player and you play a system of "lucky" numbers, you won't believe this (you've heard it too many times before, right?), but this is the truth, trust me: *no system of picking numbers is better than a random choice.* The odds of numbers 1, 2, 3, 4, 5, and 6 coming up are exactly the same as for any other set of 6 numbers. What are those odds? One in about 18 million.[15] Are these good or bad for the chance of winning a jackpot of a few million dollars? Look at it this way: they're about the same as the odds of having two people randomly pick exactly the same word on the same page in the same volume of the first 13 volumes of the *Encyclopaedia Britannica.*[16] Good luck!

Of course, there's someone out there saying, "Baloney! My cousin Fred won the jackpot only last year." It's hard to believe that the odds are so pitifully low when you, or someone you know, or someone they know, wins.

Amazing Coincidence in Central America!

The following incident happened to my wife, Louisa, when we were vacationing in Belize a few years ago. We'd taken a local boat from one island to another. As we were walking down the gangplank, Louisa looked with astonishment at a woman standing on the jetty. "Susan!" "Louisa!" School friends, they hadn't seen each other in over 10 years.

We sat around later trying to imagine what were the chances of such a reunion happening. Astronomical odds, we concluded, for that

---

15. The odds of one of your chosen numbers coming up in the first of six drawings are 6 in 51. The odds of getting it right on the second drawing are 5 in 50 (you have 5 drawings left and 50 numbers from which to choose). The odds of picking a third winning number are 4 in 49, and so on. So your chance of picking all 6 winning numbers is given by the fraction $(6 \times 5 \times 4 \times 3 \times 2 \times 1)/(51 \times 50 \times 49 \times 48 \times 47 \times 46)$, that is, 1 in 18,009,460.

16. Imagine a friend goes to the 32-volume *Encyclopaedia Britannica*, opens any one of the first 13 volumes at random, and notes a single word on that page. Your friend replaces the volume and then you do the same. The odds against you both picking the identical word on the identical page are the same as the number of words in 13 volumes of the *Encyclopaedia*, that is, about 18 million to 1. (The entire set contains about 44 million words.)

particular event. But what are the odds of, sometime in our lives, bumping into someone we recognize from the past? Turns out, pretty good. What with all the people we know (typically, a few hundred) and all the strangers we encounter every day (typically, dozens), the chance of some incident like Louisa's jetty reunion occurring to any one of us during the course of a lifetime is a lot greater than it *not* occurring.

Here's Edgar Allan Poe's perceptive take on coincidences: "There are few persons, even among the calmest thinkers, who have not occasionally been startled into a vague yet thrilling half-credence in the supernatural, but coincidences of so seemingly marvelous character that, as mere coincidences, the intellect has been unable to receive them."[17] In other words, it's only human to feel lucky when you bump into an old school friend or if you finally win the lottery.

The Chaos Game

If you enjoy finding order in chaos, you may enjoy a real curiosity, a "game" where order appears to tumble quite unexpectedly out of the midst of chaos. Here's how it works. On a sheet of paper, pick three "vertex" points at random, A, B, and C. Then pick a fourth random point O (for Origin). Now roll a six-sided die. A one or two indicates vertex point A, a three or four indicates vertex point B, and a five or six indicates vertex point C. The rule is this: Each time you roll the die, mark a spot on the paper halfway between your last spot and whichever vertex—A, B, or C—the die commands.

To begin, if you roll a three, measure halfway from O to B and mark a spot on the paper. Shake again and roll a two: mark a spot halfway between the last spot and A. Shake again and get a one: mark halfway between the last spot and A. Roll a six: mark halfway between the last spot and C. And so on. What will you end up with? A mess of dots all over the paper, right? After all, every new dot is determined randomly, by the roll of the die.

Wrong. What you actually get is a beautifully ordered geometric pattern. If you have a computer with BASIC or some other programming language, I urge you to write a program for this routine so that you can

---

17. From "The Mystery of Marie Roget."

If chaos lurks in apparent order, order hides in apparent chaos. The "chaos game" yields a beautiful pattern on my computer screen, no matter where the starting points are placed or in what order the die determines the dots are to be placed. (Barry Evans)

An orrery, a mechanical model of the solar system. The sun is at the center, Mercury at 2 o'clock, and Venus at 4 o'clock. The Earth and moon are at noon. Mars, Jupiter, Saturn, and Uranus are at 5, 3, 8, and 9 o'clock, respectively. (This orrery was made before the discovery of Neptune in 1846.) It used to be thought that the solar system epitomized the phrase "as regular as clockwork." We know now that the regularity is an illusion and that, in the long run, chaos lurks in even this system. (Copyright © National Maritime Museum, Greenwich, U.K.)

plot a few thousand points effortlessly. It's a spooky feeling watching your pattern appear as if by magic on a computer screen.[18]

Is the Solar System Chaotic?

Is the particular distribution of planets just one of many possible stable arrangements, or is it that one arrangement that survives because it happens to result in a stable solar system? Such questions remain largely unanswered.

—Ivars Peterson[19]

*H*istorically, our solar system represents the very finest that order has to offer. Until recently, the planets in their majestic orbits around the sun, moving to the tune of Newton's law of universal gravitation, seemed to be the very model of orderliness and predictability. If you've ever played with an orrery, one of those neat working models of the solar system, you'll have some idea of how the solar system used to be imagined. You can turn the handle of an orrery either way and imagine that at any time, past or future, the configuration of the planets—where they were and where they will be—is completely predictable. The phrase "as regular as clockwork" comes to mind. We'll take a look at our modern understanding of the solar system's inherent unpredictability in a moment, but first I want to tell you about Bode's law, which is neither Bode's nor a law.

Bode's Law

Historically, six planets have always been known: Mercury, Venus, Earth, Mars, Jupiter, and Saturn. Being easily visible in the night sky, their

---

18. It seems magic only because it's easy to confuse *randomness* with *chaos*. Although the points are plotted in a random order, they are not plotted chaotically. In fact, the program gives strict orders, in that it allows the points to assume some locations while forbidding others.
19. Ivars Peterson, "Chaos in the Clockwork," *Science News*, February 22, 1992, page 120.

motions have been noted for thousands of years. In 1766, 15 years before the discovery of the seventh planet (Uranus), Johann Titius of Wittenberg formulated a law of planetary orbits. Published a few years later by Johann Bode, it's come to be known as Bode's law. It says that the ratio of the mean distances at which the planets orbit the sun are proportional to 4 plus numbers from the sequence 0, 3, 6, 12, 24, 48. You can see how well it works from the following table, using modern values for mean distances from the sun. Distances are shown relative to that of Earth, whose distance is set at 10 arbitrary units for convenience.

Planet	Distance (Earth = 10)	Bode Number
Mercury*	3.9	4
Venus*	7.2	7
Earth*	10.0	10
Mars*	15.2	16
Asteroids	28.0 (average)	28
Jupiter*	52.0	52
Saturn*	95.2	100
Uranus	191.8	196
Neptune	300.3	388
Pluto	396.2	772

*Planets known when Bode's law was formulated.

As you can see, the law fits quite well for the six historically known planets. In 1781, William Herschel discovered Uranus, which also fits it rather nicely. Now, if the law were really a law, astronomers reasoned that there must be an undiscovered planet between Mars and Jupiter. A hunt soon began for the "missing" object, and sure enough the first minor planet (or asteroid), Ceres, was discovered on New Year's Day, 1801.[20]

What a way to start the nineteenth century! No wonder we can detect a certain lack of humility in some scientists and philosophers who thought they must have been on the verge of discovering all the underlying mechanisms governing the universe. We can, for instance, smile at mathematician Pierre-Simon Laplace for saying that the future was completely determined and could be predicted if we knew the

20. If you'd like to know more about this, see Clifford J. Cunningham, "Giuseppi Piazzi and the 'Missing Planet,' " *Sky and Telescope*, September 1992, page 274.

position and velocity of every particle in the universe (quantum mechanics finally scotched that dream). At the time, such hubris seemed justified.

Bode's law ultimately flunked the test. It strikes out somewhat with Neptune and utterly with Pluto. Astronomers are still trying to decide whether it's all just a fluke or whether there might be some automatic stability underlying the "law."

The Real World

In any case, the fact that there are only a few planets, together with a few thousand little asteroids that (mostly) orbit between Mars and Jupiter, might have been a tip-off to astronomers of old how the solar system really is: unpredictable and chaotic. The "cleanliness" of the solar system (particularly with one planet, Jupiter, providing nearly all the angular momentum of the system) suggests, in retrospect, chaos. That is, chance collisions would have eliminated other planets that may have formed, or were in the process of forming, early in the history of the solar system. Despite its superficial orderliness, chaos is inherent in the system.

What seems to have happened to early planets and protoplanets that are no longer around can still happen in the future. The new science of "chaos theory" tells us that in the long run almost anything can happen to an apparently orderly system such as the solar system.

The essential point about chaos theory is that some systems are extremely sensitive to initial conditions, and because we can never measure such conditions with perfect precision, it's theoretically impossible to predict the outcome of the system. This isn't due to a lack of computing power: it's absolutely impossible to predict what's going to happen.

The "butterfly effect" was a term coined by meteorologist Ed Lorenz in the early sixties, when he realized the weather was such a system. Whether or not a butterfly flaps its wings in Tokyo on a certain day defines two possibilities for a set of initial conditions. Whichever one is true (flap, or no flap) could theoretically determine whether or not a hurricane devastates the Caribbean months later.

Similarly, our inability to precisely measure the orbital elements (that is, the position and velocity in three dimensions) of a planet means that we can never be sure if some resonance between the outer planets will, for instance, one day eject Pluto out of the solar system altogether.[21]

A psychologist could probably explain our attraction to finding order in chaos (rooted, perhaps, in the ancient Greek myth that held that *cosmos*, that is, order, was originally made out of the primeval chaos). Einstein's famous comment in the face of quantum mechanics—that he couldn't believe God played dice with the universe—is now considered rather quaint. At all levels of existence, in long-enough periods of time, the bottom line is unnervingly simple: *the future is unpredictable; everything is chaos.*

---

21. Resonance is the phenomenon whereby a relatively small force can have disproportionately large results. A violin bow stroked lightly across a taut string causes it to resonate and give off a sound (via the instrument's sound box) at the string's natural frequency. Perhaps the most dramatic example concerns the demise of the Tacoma Narrows, WA, bridge in 1940: although the bridge could readily handle the momentary sideways force of a gale, its designers hadn't reckoned on steady winds setting up resonance at the deck's natural frequency. A famous movie of the event shows the deck abruptly start to thrash about wildly as that frequency was established. Seconds later, the bridge collapsed.

Similarly, computer simulations show that the outer planets could conceivably cause Pluto to resonate into a highly elliptical orbit as a prelude to leaving the solar system altogether. Pluto is already a wayward sphere, an oddball (literally) that defies most of the norms of a well-behaved planet. It's in a highly elliptical orbit, spending about a tenth of its 248-year orbit closer to the sun than Neptune. Its orbit is also sharply inclined to the ecliptic. While the other planets orbit in approximately the same plane as Earth (the ecliptic), Pluto's orbit is inclined at about 17 degrees. In addition, it has the largest moon in the solar system compared to its parent planet. Some astronomers believe Pluto may be the remnant core of a large comet, perhaps a twin of Neptune's moon Triton.

Fifteen

The Right (and Left) Stuff

A wise man's heart is at his right hand:
but a fool's heart at his left.

—The Book of Ecclesiastes

*F*or some of us, a mirror opens up a secret world of nose hairs, mascara, and intimate grooming. For others, a mirror is vanity made visible. For children, it's the key to (secret) backward writing.[22] Etymologically, it's cognate with miracle and mirage, from Latin *mirari*, wonder. Remember this from Lewis Carroll's *Through the Looking Glass*?

> There was a book lying near Alice on the table, and while she sat watching the White King . . . she turned over the leaves, to find some part that she could read, "for it's all in some language I don't know," she said to herself.
>
> It was like this.

JABBERWOCKY
'Twas brillig, and the slithy toves
Did gyre and gimble in the wabe;
All mimsy were the borogoves,
And the mome raths outgrabe.

---

22. Also for Leonardo da Vinci.

*She puzzled over this for some time, but at last a bright thought struck
her. "Why, it's a Looking-glass book, of course! And if I hold it up to a
glass, the words will all go the right way again."*
This was the poem that Alice read.

JABBERWOCKY
*'Twas brillig, and the slithy toves
Did gyre and gimble in the wabe;
All mimsy were the borogoves,
And the mome raths outgrabe.*

Why did Alice's mirror reverse the writing from left to right, but
not from bottom to top? You might ask yourself a similar question next
time you look at yourself in a mirror. What do you see? Not what
someone else sees. If you face a friend, your friend sees your left side on
their right, while in the mirror, you see your right side on your right.
Again, why does a mirror reverse left and right but not from top to
bottom?

Don't skip over this question! In his delightful book *The
Ambidextrous Universe*, Martin Gardner writes
of this and similar questions, "They are
indeed puzzling. . . . Try them on your
friends. Chances are they will be
just as puzzled. You will get plenty
of embarrassed laughs and
stammering attempts at explanation,
but it will be surprising if anyone
gives a clear, straightforward
answer."

*Two mirrors placed at right angles
will show your hand unreversed,
that is, as others see you.*

While you're mulling, you may want to see yourself as others see
you. If a mirror reverses left to right, a second mirror should reverse right
back to left. Try it. Get a second mirror and hold it as shown in the
accompanying figure. Now you can see yourself with your left eye on
your right (try winking at yourself), the same as everyone else sees you.

Do you notice any difference from your (single) mirror image? Which "you" do you prefer?

Here's another curious left-right phenomenon to explore. Have someone take a close-up photograph of you. Do the same for him or her. After you get the film processed, get the processor to print the photos both normally and with the negatives reversed. You'll now have one "normal" photo of yourself and one with left and right reversed (so it looks like the person you see in the mirror). Cut the two photographs carefully down the middle of your face, match the two left halves, and tape them together. Do the same with your right halves.

What do you see? You may not recognize yourself, since we're only approximately bilaterally symmetrical.[23] Chances are, you've created two very distinct faces, neither of whom is quite the real you. In a nonscientific survey, eight friends and I decided our (combined) left sides generally showed a darker, more mysterious personage than our (combined) right sides.

Faces sinister and dexter. On the left, normal photographs. In the center, two right halves butted together (the "left" side of the faces are the right halves printed backward). On the right, two left halves butted together (the "right" sides are left sides printed backward). Note the difference in character between the two left halves and two right halves. (Barry Evans)

---

23. Females more so than males. In humans, the only obvious outward exception to bilateral symmetry is that a man's left testicle hangs lower than his right.

Our conclusions reflect the real world, in which many cultures discriminate against the left side. People from most societies shake with their right hands, sometimes for sanitary reasons: the Hindu, Buddhist, and Muslim religions specify that the right hand is clean and the left unclean. Soldiers from every country salute with their right hands. Tools are generally made for right-handers, and most writing is left to right (which is easier for right-handers). When I was at school in England (in the fifties), lefties were discriminated against: writing with the left hand was actively discouraged and even forbidden. Today most products, from subway turnstiles to coin phone boxes to cameras to corkscrews, are designed for the right-handed majority.

The Judeo-Christian tradition is decidedly proright from the word go. God reaches out his right hand to touch Adam's left, giving him life, in Michelangelo's fresco on the ceiling of the Sistine Chapel. Later (as recorded in Genesis), when Joseph's father blesses Joseph's

Heaven up, Hell down. The Last Judgment *by Jan van Eyck, painted about 1422, leaves nothing to the imagination. In keeping with our cultural bias favoring the right side, this and many other "Last Judgment" paintings show God using his right and left hands for Heaven and Hell, respectively.* (The Metropolitan Museum of Art, Fletcher Fund, 1933).

younger son with his right hand, "it displeased him [Joseph]," since the right hand was reserved for the firstborn. Christ "sitteth on the right hand of God," as do the saved sheep: the goats, that is, the damned, are relegated to God's left en route to everlasting fire. We shake with our right hands, and in a court of law you'll be asked to raise your right hand before giving evidence.

Language is particularly adept at showing what the majority of people think of the left side. Our word *sinister*, for instance, comes from the Latin for "left," while *dexterous* is derived from Latin for "right." The English word *right* is from the Latin word *rectus*, meaning "straight" or "just." A "left-handed" compliment is insincere. An "alright" guy is, well, alright. The French word *gauche*, which has found its way unchanged into English, means "left." The word *droit*, meaning "a legal right," is just that, as in the motto of the royal arms of Great Britain, *Dieu et mon droit*, "God and my right." "Left" in Italian, Portuguese, and Spanish is *mancino* ("maimed"), *canhoto* ("weak"), and *zurdo* (from *azurdos*, "to go the wrong way"), respectively. Finally, the Arabic word *simal* means both "left hand" and "bad omen."

How did humans originally acquire their right-handed bias? It's not seen in other primates, who are either ambidextrous or tend to left-handedness. One (rather flimsy, you may think) speculation is that if early man tried to defend his heart on his left side, perhaps with some sort of shield, he would have naturally held a weapon in his right hand. (Amazons cut off their right breasts, which might otherwise have impeded their sword arms, according to legend.) Another hypothesis is that humankind's predominant right-handedness results from our capacity for language, a specialization found in the left hemisphere of our brains.[24]

Still worried why a mirror reverses left and right but not up and down? Congratulations! It takes a special kind of mentality to treat the question as nontrivial. Truly, research papers have been written on the subject. The difficulty is basically one of semantics. "Left" and "right" mean different things in different contexts, while "up" and "down" are unambiguous, just like "north" and "south" have specific meanings. To appreciate this, put a red spot on your left, or port, cheek and a green one on your right, starboard, cheek. In a regular mirror, red is always opposite red, green opposite green, hair opposite hair and chin opposite chin. In a double mirror, red and green are reversed. Rotate it 90 degrees, and now hair and chin are reversed! What could be simpler?

Now, remind me again: why is up overhead?

---

24. For more, see Michael C. Corballis's *The Lopsided Ape: The Evolution of the Generative Mind*.

A Conversation with
Francis Crick
————

*Rather than believe that Watson and Crick made the
DNA structure, I would rather stress that the structure
made Watson and Crick . . . [because of] the intrinsic beauty
of the DNA double helix. It is the molecule that has style,
quite as much as the scientists.*

—Francis Crick,
What Mad Pursuit

Dr. Francis Crick is an Englishman whose home is now La Jolla,
California. He is best known for discovering, with James Watson, the
double-helical structure of the DNA molecule in the summer of 1953.
Crick, Watson, and x-ray crystallographer Maurice Wilkins shared the
1962 Nobel Prize in chemistry for what has been termed "the greatest
biological advance of the twentieth century." Since 1976, Crick has
worked at the Salk Institute for Biological Studies, concentrating on the
study of the visual systems in mammals.

Barry Evans I'm interested in the relationship between a person's
education and lifelong sense of curiosity. Reading your book *What
Mad Pursuit*, I sensed that you managed to retain a strong curiosity
all the way through school.

Francis Crick, 1992. (The Salk Institute)

Francis Crick   I was fortunate in my education. Up to the age of 14, I went to a local grammar school. The teaching there wasn't that special, but I was sufficiently interested to read things myself, keeping my curiosity going. I don't recall ever having been put off by school, although I know many people who were.

I went to a boarding school between the ages of 14 and 18. The school taught science well, which was unusual at that time. Although we had to absorb a lot of facts, especially chemistry (which I never really mastered!), the teaching was at a sufficient level to keep one's curiosity aroused. I don't think that's so difficult to do if a student still has his curiosity. It is quite easy to kill it. But I think a person who has some curiosity will survive unless it's really sat upon.

B. E.   Do we all have curiosity innately?

F. C.   I think some people have much more than others. Some people are prepared to take the world as they find it and accept ideas that are given to them, and other people are more curious. It's one of the characteristics of primates, in fact mammals as a whole, that they actively explore the environment, especially the younger ones. For instance, we see it in a kitten. A kitten will romp around and explore its environment while an old cat just sits around and purrs in front of the fire. Curiosity does decline somewhat with age unless it's kept going.

B. E.   I was fascinated to read in your book *What Mad Pursuit* that you were a generalist through most of your twenties, and that this enabled you to pick a field which perhaps you wouldn't have chosen if you had specialized earlier. In your case, being a generalist for so long seems to have been an advantage.

F. C.   Most scientists start off with a general interest in science, and many of them keep it up. A person working in biology will often have an interest in astronomy and cosmology, for example, which he won't necessarily contribute to, but he'll read articles in *Scientific American* and so on. I think it's harder to keep abreast of all fields nowadays. Scientific life is so competitive and young people have to work so hard that it's not as easy to do as in the past.

B. E.   A hundred years or so ago, there were few professional scientists, just gentlemen philosophers.

F. C.   Yes, there was a period—when it was called natural philosophy—when you could take all knowledge for your province. But obviously nowadays that's impossible. Even in a general area like biology you can't follow in detail what is going on because so much is happening. For example, I've had a fair grounding in molecular biology, but I don't follow a lot of the work in molecular biology because I'm mainly interested in one facet of the field, that is, the brain. It's not even possible for me to cover all the things I'm interested in about the brain. I concentrate largely on the visual system, and don't know much about the motor system, for instance.

B. E.   Some kids tend to naturally gravitate towards science and spend their whole lives at some level wondering about what's going on around them, while others don't. If there is really a genetic advantage to curiosity, then I assume we start out more or less at the same level. I'm wondering if curiosity is something we acquire as kids or something we start off with that's later taken away from us when we're young?

F. C.   It's likely to be a bit of both. I'm just thinking of my own children. My son showed a lot of curiosity from an early age. Our two daughters, very much less so. Curious children try to teach themselves. I think the difference is not whether they get exposed to some sort of teaching, but whether they find it easy or difficult. If they find it easy, it's great fun and they go on and do more, but if they find it difficult, they struggle so hard to grasp what they're told that they don't even want to know anymore. They've worked hard enough already. I think it's partly a matter of innate intelligence. You'd have to ask a psychologist who works with young people. I hardly see young people except for my grandchildren.

The coeducational boarding school in England that my son

James Watson and Francis Crick with the demonstration model (referred to in the interview) of their DNA double-helix model, summer 1953. (Photo by A. C. Barrington-Brown. From *The Double Helix* by J. D. Watson. New York: Atheneum, 1968. Courtesy of Cold Spring Harbor Laboratory, Research Library Archives.)

went to wasn't very good on science and was better in art and drawing and theater. When he started doing physics, I guess around the age of 10, they spent the whole of the first term learning various methods of measuring density! That's enough to kill any child's interest. Yet he survived, and now he's got a good degree in theoretical physics. I think some children are so motivated they'll survive anything, while others are easily put off.

B. E. Do you believe your scientific discoveries resulted from an innate creativity?

F. C. In my case, my parents realized from an early age that I was very curious about the world. Although they had no scientific background of any sort, either of them, they went out of their way to help me by putting books in my way and allowing me to experiment, within reason. On the other hand, girls used to be discouraged. I don't detect my two granddaughters being discouraged in that way, but I don't know about my daughters. They could have been.

B. E. Let's talk about DNA and the way you hit on the double-helix arrangement. Was there a day when you and Dr. Watson knew you had solved the structure, even though you didn't have the details yet?

F. C. Yes, when he discovered the base pairs, although we still weren't sure it would work out.

B. E.   You hadn't built the model at that time, right?

F. C.   What people don't realize is that the model in the picture you sometimes see, with me looking a bit silly and holding a slide rule, wasn't built until well after the paper was published. We built the model for an open day. Before that, we actually worked on a model that consisted of only a half a base pair, because that's all you need to do the crystallography. So we did build a model, but it wasn't the model most people have in mind.

B. E.   So there was one moment when you knew you'd discovered the structure?

F. C.   Watson found the base pairs before I came in one morning. He was playing with cardboard cutouts of the bases when he happened to form those two pairs. Then when I came in, he showed them to me and I pointed out that they had the right symmetry, that is, if you flipped them over, the way they joined onto the chains was the same. I had previously deduced that they should have that symmetry because of the fact that the atoms in the two chains run in opposite directions. So we had that bit of knowledge already.

What we didn't know was this: if we put the base pairs into the structure, was it possible to build that structure to fit the small amount of x-ray data we had, or at least make it look plausible? In fact, we didn't know it would fit that data until we built the model, which took us a day or so. So sometime in that period, there was a definite moment when we thought "My gosh, it's going to come out." Even after that Jim wasn't sure that it was right. He was worried that we didn't have the structure and we'd make fools of ourselves.

B. E.   You mentioned in your book that he was rather cautious.

F. C.   Strictly speaking, we didn't know for about 20 years if it was completely right! It just became more and more plausible. The experimental work then was done on fibers, which are always subject to uncertainties of interpretation.

B. E.   The history of science is replete with counterintuitive discoveries. For instance, the replication of mitochondria using independent DNA, the fact that many of the atoms of our bodies originate in supernovae, and so on.

F. C.   I'm not sure I would call those counterintuitive. I would call them surprising. If you want to ask me what is counterintuitive, I would go to relativity and quantum theory. "Counterintuitive" often refers to discoveries that depend on observing events which our ancestors and ourselves didn't normally look at. In other words, the way our brain works is that it has been shaped to deal with concepts that are useful in everyday life and that are reinforced in the education we get. When we get into regions where the ordinary person doesn't have the experience—the paradoxes of quantum mechanics, for example—then our everyday ideas don't fit. The whole idea of something being both a wave and a particle is very counterintuitive, whereas the things you've mentioned I'd call surprises.

As far as your examples go, I remember being surprised when I heard that heavy elements were synthesized in supernovae. I'm not sure when I learned about DNA in mitochondria. I think my knowledge came in several stages, because when I started to look at mitochondria in cells in tissue culture, there were already people who suggested that they divided, though that was very controversial. Once you bought the idea that they divided, then it wasn't too far off from asking if they had their own DNA. And then there were people who had shown that there were genes in the cytoplasm. I don't think it came as the same sudden shock as it did in the case of the synthesis in the supernovae.

B. E.   How about the idea that a meteorite probably hit the Earth 65 million years ago and was responsible for the death of the dinosaurs?

F. C.   That was surprising. But when I heard of it, I immediately liked it. And the evidence has gotten better and better. There are still some paleontologists who don't like it, but it can be a very stubborn profession in my view.

B. E.   Perhaps that's the nature of studying old things!

F. C.   Different subjects attract people with different temperaments.

B. E.   Can you offer me any examples from your own field which, if not exactly counterintuitive, were surprising to you?

F. C.   Yes. The base pairs of DNA, which we discussed earlier, is one example. "Who would have thought that?" was our attitude, so that when it happened we were taken by surprise and it made a bigger impression.

Another example—and I can still remember where I was in the room because it was so striking—was when the idea emerged in conversation that the messenger RNA was something separate, and that the RNA of the ribosome was not the message. When I woke up that morning I had one set of ideas, and when I went to bed everything looked different. My view of the world had changed in a single day.

Friday's Puzzles

Oddballs

*There is no problem so big that it can't be
solved with high explosives.*

—Unknown sage

*T*hese five oddballs are "story" puzzles, my favorite kind. With a little
imagination, you can put yourself in the middle of these situations and
enjoy being there.

1. You're about to take off from the Beijing airport on a long-
   distance flight when a hitchhiker asks you for a ride. "Sure," you
   say, "hop in!" "Don't you want to know where I'm going before
   you agree to take me?" asks your passenger. "No," you answer.
   "Wherever it is, it won't take me out of my way." What's your
   destination?
2. Here's another Sam Loyd puzzle. You may have heard the story
   of how Christopher Columbus demonstrated his capacity for
   thinking beyond normal boundaries by challenging his cronies to
   balance an egg on its "pointed" end. After they'd all failed, he
   tapped the end, flattening it slightly, to easily balance it. "That's
   not according to the rules!" they said. "The rules have changed,"
   he replied.

   Loyd said that what really happened is that once they'd all

got into balancing eggs on their ends, Columbus challenged his
arch-rival to a game: "I'll put the first egg down on the table,
then you put one down, and we take turns until there's no room
left for another egg. Whoever puts the last egg down wins." How
did Columbus ensure that he won? Assume all eggs are the same
size and that the table was either round or square.

> Hint 1: *Without knowing the rationale behind the solution, you may
> deduce that if there really is a solution, there must be a spot
> on the table that's unique for CC's method to work.*
>
> Hint 2: *Think "symmetry."*

3. You may have read Marilyn von Savant's column in *Parade* when
she asked, "Should a contestant on Monty Hall's "Let's Make a
Deal" TV show, given the opportunity to switch their door
choice after Monty has revealed a goat behind a non-picked
door, do so?" The column generated more mail and argument
than anything the magazine had ever printed. Here's a much
earlier version of this puzzle, posed by Lewis Carroll in *Pillow
Problems*.[25] I've rephrased it slightly.

   A friend has a bag containing one ball, known to be either
white or black. She then puts a white ball into the bag, so now it
contains *either* one black and one white ball *or* two white balls.
She shakes the bag and takes one ball out: it's white. She now
offers you a wager to guess what color the ball remaining in the
bag is. What odds should you accept, that is, what is the chance
of the remaining ball in the bag being white?

> Hint 1: *At first glance it appears that, since the state of the bag
> after the operation is identical to its original state, the
> chance that the ball in the bag is white is one in two. But
> this is wrong—consider all the possibilities.*
>
> Hint 2: *There are three possibilities, not two.*

4. The scene is a pebbly beach, where a young woman has been
kidnapped by an evil prince. "I will give you a chance for
freedom," he tells her. "In this bag, I will put one white pebble
and one black pebble. You will put your hand in and draw out
one pebble. If you pick the white pebble, you will go free, but if
you pick the black pebble, you will marry me." She noticed,

---

25. Originally printed in 1893, reprinted by Dover Publications, 1958.

however, that he cheated and put two black pebbles into the bag. What did she do?

5. Years ago, when I first saw this puzzle, I liked it so much that I thought, "If I ever put together a book of puzzles I'll call it something like *The Monk's Journey.*" About a year later, pottering at the local library, I saw that someone had beaten me to it.[26] It's a beautiful puzzle, requiring just a little logic and, as ever, the ability to visualize the situation:

At 6 o'clock one Sunday morning, a monk leaves his monastery at the bottom of the mountain and walks up the only path to the top, arriving at 6 P.M. Sometimes he walks fast, sometimes he dawdles, and often he stops for a rest. After a night of meditation, he leaves the top at 6 A.M. on Monday and, again varying his speed, reaches the monastery at 6 P.M. that night. Is there a place on the path that he occupied at exactly the same time on both Sunday and Monday? If so, prove it.

Hint 1: *Suppose on Monday a brother monk also started up the mountain, following exactly the same schedule the first monk had on Sunday . . .*

Hint 2: *. . . would they meet?*

Hint 3: *Graph theorists might plot the monk's (or monks') journeys as two lines on a graph, where time is plotted along one axis and distance from the bottom of the mountain along the other. Do the two lines cross?*

Puzzle answers are at the back of the book.

---

26. Ivan Morris, *The Lonely Monk and Other Puzzles*. Boston: Little, Brown, 1970.

Friday's Quotations

Life and Death

I have no money, no resources, no hopes. I am the happiest man alive.

—Henry Miller

Each pleasure we feel is a pleasure less, each day a stroke on the calendar.

—John Fowles

Earth's sweetest joy is but disguised pain.

—William Drummond

Pain will come, just like pleasure. Hate will come, just like love. And when both are accepted, unaffected by the mind, then there will be peace.

—Baba Hari Das

A balance that does not tremble cannot weigh. A man who does not tremble cannot live.

—Erwin Chargaff

All animals except man know that the ultimate purpose of life is to enjoy it.

—**Samuel Butler**

Changes happen because that's the way the universe is. . . . The screeching sound you hear is only your own heels, digging into the pavement, futilely trying to resist the irresistible.

—**Stan Hampson**

Change is the law of life. And those who look only to the past or present are certain to miss the future.

—**John Kennedy**

At times of change we are between shells, like caterpillars and butterflies. It is then that we are most vulnerable—but also open to new feelings, new impulses, new inputs.

—**Gail Sheehy**

Get a job you love and you'll never have to work again.

—**Unknown**

Sunt lacrimae rerum. ("There are tears at the heart of life itself.")

—**Virgil**

No one's as miserable as the truly sated.

—**Sally Belfrage**

O God, I love so many things, it will take years to take them away one by one.

—**Leonard Cohen**

We're all going extinct all the time.

—**Jerre Lipps**

Life . . . preferable after all to total nonexistence, the state of being eternally unborn, of never having had the opportunity to contemplate the exquisite joys and sorrows of life, brief as it is.

—**C. L. Sulzberger**

Mere existence is so much better than nothing, that one would rather exist even in pain than not exist.

—**Samuel Johnson**

You wish that I leave this magnificent spectacle: I leave it. And I thank You a thousand times over that You have deigned to admit me there where I can see Your works manifested and to see before my eyes the order with which you govern the universe.

—**Epictetus**

Saturday

Day of Saturn

*"T*o a dog, every day is Saturday," according to *San Francisco Chronicle* columnist Herb Caen. At the week's end, any beliefs we may have about the week being a natural, preordained period of time come to the fore: it's almost unthinkable that we wouldn't take two days off out of seven. And, like dogs, most of us tend to frisk around on Saturdays, free of the cares of the workaday world. It's a day on which to wag our tails.

Sixteen

It Goes Without Saying

*This chapter is dedicated to all those who do not have
a chapter dedicated to themselves.*

A commentator on National Public Radio said yesterday, "The
conventional wisdom in Washington is that conventional wisdom is
wrong!" Hearing that, I thought, "Epimenides lives!"

Whatever his other attributes, I think it's fair to say that the apostle
Paul wasn't known for his sense of humor. Yet this wry line appears in
his pastoral letter to Titus: "One of themselves, even a prophet of their
own, said, 'The Cretans are always liars . . .'" He was probably referring
to Epimenides, the Cretan (or Cretian) poet who is reported to have said,
"All Cretans are liars." Did he lie? Is conventional wisdom wrong?

Epimenides may have been the originator of the self-referential
paradox, a statement that falsifies or mocks itself. Consider the following
curiosities, most of which are variants on your basic "I never tell the
truth" theme of twisted self-reference:

- This sentence is false.
- Socrates said, "What Plato is about to say is a lie." Plato
  responded, "Socrates has spoken truly."
- "If I've told you once, I've told you a thousand times: don't
  exaggerate!" ("And try to not ever split infinitives.")

♦ Answer this question with "yes" or "no": Will your next word be "no"?
♦ According to Ionesco, "Only the ephemeral is of lasting value."

Then there's the related "Am I dreaming?" category of puzzlers:

♦ In Lewis Carroll's *Through the Looking-Glass*, Alice dreams that the Red King is asleep. Tweedledee tells her that the king is dreaming about her and, "If that there King was to wake, you'd go out—bang!—just like a candle!" Who is really dreaming?
♦ A much earlier version of this story is attributed to the fourth-century B.C. Taoist philosopher Chuang-Tzu: "I dreamed that I was a butterfly, but I awoke and found I was a man. Or is it that I am a butterfly who dreams he is a man?"

Sometimes, sentences seem to have a life of their own. The ones that follow are mostly gleaned (and sometimes adapted) from two columns written by Douglas Hofstadter for *Scientific American* over a decade ago:[1]

"You are under my control because you will read until you have reached the end of me."

"Hey, out there—is that you reading me, or is it someone else?"

"I had to translate this sentence into English because I could not read the original Sanskrit."

"If I had finished this sentence . . ."

"This sentence apologizes for the fact that its writer stole the idea for such a sentence from a column in *Scientific American*."

"It goes without saying."

Do you get packages with instructions like this? Similarly, a sign on a vacant lot in Toronto said only, "Penalty for removal $25."

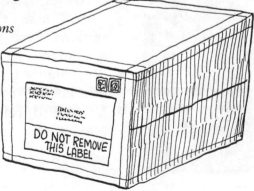

---

1. Hofstadter wrote *the* book on self-reference: *Gödel, Escher, Bach: An Eternal Golden Braid*. The relevant columns appeared in *Scientific American* in January 1980 and January 1981.

I'm not sure how to categorize the following, so I won't:

♦ Years ago I was terrified before going on radio for the first time. "Don't worry," said my host. "No one listens to this station."

♦ A physicist is an atom's way of knowing about atoms.[2]

♦ "I think I'm brain-dead!"

♦ Speaking of Douglas Hofstadter (we were, weren't we?), he coedited a book entitled *The Mind's I*, for which artificial intelligence guru Marvin Minsky wrote a cover blurb: "This great collection of reflections provides you with your own quite special ways to understand things such as why, if you don't read this book, you'll never be the same again."

♦ It's written (right here) that Epimenides, whom we've already met, asked the Buddha, "What is the best possible question, and what's the best answer to it?" The Buddha replied, "You've just asked the best possible question, and I'm giving you the best possible answer."

♦ Philosopher-magician Raymond Smullyan tells the story of how, when he was a graduate student, he applied to be a vacuum cleaner salesman. "Do you object to telling a little lie every now and again?" he was asked. He did, but wanting the job, answered, "No." He worried later that the answer he gave was a lie . . . therefore it was the truth![3]

♦ Writing is sometimes trickier than saying. What punctuation mark should go after the word *please*? I just asked Louisa, "Do you want to put the water on for tea, please" "Was that a question?" she asked.

♦ Descartes walked into a bar. "Would you like a beer?" asked the barman. "I think not," answered René, and disappeared.

♦ A chicken is an egg's way of reproducing itself.

♦ What are the three misteaks in thi sentence? (See Puzzle Answers at the back of the book.)

♦ My (stuffed) baby gorilla's name is "Nameless."

"Nameless." (Barry Evans)

2. George Wald, quoted in Roger von Oech's *A Whack on the Side of the Head*.
3. This and many other paradoxical stories appear in Smullyan's *What Is the Name of this Book?* If you enjoy this sort of mindgame, check out his *5000 B.C. and Other Philosophical Fantasies*.

The Million-Dollar Challenge

If you're still reading this,[4] I hope you're ready for my number-one candidate for the oddest paradox of all: Newcomb's paradox. It first appeared about 20 years ago and was popularized in Martin Gardner's "Mathematical Games" department in *Scientific American*.[5] Here it is, in modified form:

ET, an extraterrestrial visitor, arrives on Earth with the uncanny ability to predict how we will choose between two alternatives. ET's test apparatus is simply two boxes on a table. Box A is transparent and holds $1,000. Box B is opaque and either holds nothing or $1,000,000.

Your choice is to take both boxes or box B only. You can see $1,000 in box A, but box B is closed. It either contains nothing or $1,000,000. If you take both boxes, you can reasonably anticipate that box B will be empty. If you take box B only, it will probably contain $1,000,000.

Everyone who wants to play is given exactly the same information by ET: "You are free to choose one of two alternatives. You may either (1) take the contents of both boxes, in which case I'll leave box B empty, or (2) take the contents of box B only, in which case I'll put a million dollars in it."

You're invited to observe for a while. You see each player introduce himself or herself to ET outside the door, then ET goes inside and always puts $1,000 in box A and sometimes puts $1,000,000 in box B.

4. Ignore this footnote.
5. Gardner's original column on the paradox appeared in July 1973, with a follow-up in March 1974.

The player comes in and either chooses both boxes or box B only. You watch carefully for many plays, thousands, if you like. Every time a player picks both boxes, they find ET has left box B empty; every time a player picks box B only, they find ET has put a million dollars in it. It never fails.

Your turn has arrived. You introduce yourself to ET outside the room, then ET goes in ahead of you. When ET is done putting money in the boxes, you go in and look at the table. You can see $1,000 in box A. Box B may or may not hold $1,000,000. What do you do? Think about it for a minute and decide, one way or the other, before reading on.

(Commercial break.)

Do you see the beautiful paradox? You might think either of two things:

1. Every time someone picks box B only, they get a million dollars, so I'll pick box B.
2. Either there's a million bucks in box B or there isn't. If the money's in there, it's not going to disappear. Therefore I'll take everything that's there by choosing both boxes.

Try honing that second choice (taking both boxes) by imagining you have a friend on the other side of the table who can see into the back of box B. What would your friend tell you to do? "Take both boxes," of course. You'll be $1,000 better off either way! (In fact, why bother to have your friend look? You already know what he or she is going to say.)

Have you changed your mind yet?

The ensuing spate of readers' letters after Gardner's original column (which I've merely summarized) was extensive, cerebral, and passionate. Few readers found it trivial. By a two-to-one margin, most readers voted to take box B only. Many saw it as a perfect metaphor for the venerable "free will versus determinism" argument, with people who labeled themselves free-willers usually opting for both boxes and determinists choosing to take box B only. Not always, though. Isaac Asimov[6] wrote:

---

6. Asimov, who wrote nearly 500 books in his lifetime, is supposed to have been asked by a friend a few weeks before his death, "What are you going to do in the short time you have left?" Asimov replied, "Write faster!"

I would, without hesitation, take both boxes. . . . I am myself a determinist, but it is perfectly clear to me that any human being worthy of being considered a human being (including most certainly myself) would prefer free will, if such a thing exists . . . suppose you take both boxes and it turns out (as it almost certainly will) that God [Gardner's version posited an omniscient God instead of ET as the challenger] has foreseen this and placed nothing in the second box. You will then, at least, have expressed your willingness to gamble on his nonomniscience and on your own free will and will have willingly given up a million dollars for the sake of that willingness—itself a snap of the finger in the face of the Almighty and a vote, however futile, for free will. . . .

That was the last sentence of this essay.

Seventeen

Politics of a Supermolecule

Water bears the Earth and supports the universe.
It is the element which generates all others.

—Thales of Miletus, c. 600 B.C.

*T*hey don't serve iced coffee, so, unlike its East Coast namesake, you can't get anything you want at Alice's Restaurant. But it's a fine place, anyway, in the hills above Woodside, California, and most Sunday mornings Louisa and I will cycle up the 12 miles and 1,300 vertical feet from Palo Alto to breakfast there. In summer we usually start early before it gets hot, but still the first thing we do on arrival is to ask for a glass of water for each of us, to replace what we've sweated out en route. One glass isn't much, 10 ounces perhaps. If it weren't for hydrogen bonds, we'd be drinking several times that.

Most liquids other than water are composed of virtually discrete, that is, separate, molecules. Molecules of, say, benzine, don't have much attraction for their neighbors, and each is pretty much independent. While molecules of flowing benzine can be thought of as sliding around each other, water molecules can be pictured as rolling, because each water molecule has a relatively strong attraction for its neighbor. If it didn't, water would be a gas, much the same as methane, ammonia, oxygen, and carbon monoxide—all of which have about the same molecular weight. The attraction between one molecule of water and its

234

Alice's Restaurant, Sky Londa, California. (Barry Evans)

neighbors is due to hydrogen bonds, so-called because of the curious configuration of hydrogen atoms found in water. On the other hand, the bonds aren't *that* strong. If they were, an ocean liner would be locked into a solid, unyielding mass of water, and you could literally "walk on water." For that, you need to freeze the water into ice, which is where hydrogen bonding really comes into its own.

If we imagine that the molecules of most liquids behave like regular marbles, then water molecules might be imagined as magnetized marbles. Have you played with these little toys? A small bar magnet is embedded in each plastic marble, and a gang of them behaves rather like a single organism. Move one and the others follow, constantly taking up new configurations. The analogy is far from perfect, since the poles of a bar

A hill of magnetic marbles, showing how each one clings to its neighbor. The marbles are a poor analogy for water molecules, since the marbles' internal bar magnets are linear—that is, the poles are 180 degrees apart. In a water molecule, the poles (i.e., hydrogen atoms) are 105 degrees apart. While magnetic marbles form loops, water molecules form interlocking tetrahedra.
(Barry Evans)

magnet are 180 degrees apart, so magnetized marbles adopt patterns such as strings and closed loops. In a water molecule, the angle its two negatively charged hydrogen atoms makes with the positively charged central oxygen atom is about 105 degrees. (See the sidebar to this chapter.) This allows a molecule's hydrogen atoms to be "shared" with the oxygen atom of the adjacent molecule, hence the "hydrogen bond." The net result of hydrogen bonding is that each molecule tends to the center of a tetrahedron formed by its four neighbors. In liquid water, this framework is ephemeral; in ice, it's fixed.

Water's Skin

The affinity between neighboring molecules is greater in water than in almost any other substance. You can compare it with, say, that of rubbing alcohol by trying to float a paper clip on the surface of a saucer of each liquid. Hydrogen bonds create a surface-tension "skin" on the water, allowing the clip to float, while the clip sinks in the weakly bonded alcohol. Hydrogen bonding is also what allows water to remain liquid at

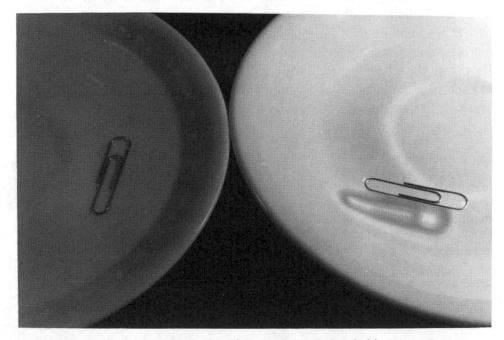

Paper clips readily float on water (right) but sink in alcohol (left). Relatively strong hydrogen bonds link water molecules, experienced here as a "skin" of surface tension. In alcohol, adjacent molecules are weakly linked. (Barry Evans)

room temperature, and it enables us to cycle to Alice's on just a few ounces of water. Visualize the process by considering how water and cooking oil evaporate. (I suggest you do this in your imagination rather than in the kitchen!) Imagine you are heating a small pot of water and a small pot of oil side by side on a stove. Once the oil reaches its boiling point, it immediately smokes heavily, and in moments it's turned into a blue, acrid vapor. When the water reaches its boiling point, it just sits there bubbling on the stove. Eventually it will boil away into steam, but it takes much longer, and hence more energy, to convert it from liquid into vapor.

Technically speaking, we can infer that water's *latent heat of vaporization* is higher than that of oil. In fact, weight for weight, its heat of vaporization is higher than that of any known substance. The extra energy provided by your stove is needed to break the hydrogen bonds between individual molecules of water. Similarly, when I sweat, my body has to provide a lot of energy, in the form of heat, to vaporize liquid water from my skin. That's why sweating cools me so efficiently. In the absence of hydrogen bonds, I'd have to drink a lot more liquid, perhaps seven times as much, to cool my body.

Without that bonding, water would be a gas anyway. So you can think of a glass of water not as trillions upon trillions of independent molecules,[7] but as a single weakly bonded "supermolecule." Consider the water sitting in the pipe leading to your kitchen-sink faucet. When you turn the faucet on, you're releasing one "tentacle" of a gigantic molecule of water! That tentacle is connected to all the water in the network of distribution pipes linking your entire community. When someone else—a stranger on the far side of town, say—opens her faucet, she releases another tentacle of the huge monster. If both of you simultaneously put your hands under the flow, you're curiously connected to each other via the same supermolecule.

If your community is like ours, your water comes from a reservoir in the hills. (Water for much of the Bay Area, including the city of San Francisco, comes from the Hetch Hetchy Reservoir, where runoff from the Sierra Nevada is dammed in the Tuolumne River gorge.) Normally, a dam cuts off the reservoir from water in a downstream river, but the two bodies of water—reservoir and river—are inevitably linked. Sometimes it's obvious, such as when water flows in a continuous stream over a spillway; sometimes it's more subtle, since a trickle is always making its way under and around the dam through pores in the subsurface. Either

---

7. A four-ounce glass of water contains about 10^{23} molecules.

Water can be thought of as a huge "supermolecule" because each individual water molecule has relatively strong hydrogen bonds with its neighbors. When you put your hand under a running faucet, you are "linked" to someone doing the same thing across town. If your water flows from a reservoir connected to a river, then you're united to, for example, someone washing in the Amazon.

way, it means that your tentacle is linked not only to water flowing from every other open faucet in town, but to the reservoir and the river and thence to the ocean.

The oceans of Earth, of course, are really just one big ocean: there's no boundary where you can say "the Pacific stops there and the Atlantic starts here." So now we're talking about a *really* big molecule! When you put your hand in the flow from your faucet, you're physically linked through this single supermolecule with, you might imagine, a Tanzanian swimming in the sea off Africa or a Yanomamo tribesman washing in a tributary of the Amazon 2,000 miles upstream of the Brazilian coast.

Perhaps hydrogen bonds make the notion of individual nations and political boundaries rather moot. The jingle "Reach out and touch someone" takes on a whole new meaning. Perhaps we really are one humanity.

The Water Planet

Nothing personal, but do you slosh when you walk? No? That's amazing, considering how much water you carry around. About two-thirds of a man's weight is water (for women, it's less), so a 150-pound male carries about 100 pounds of water, or 12 gallons.

You'll find me from time to time in our local drugstore, staring at the shelf on which they keep the plastic gallon bottles of "crystal pure" (whatever that is) water. I'll be trying to imagine the contents of 11 of those bottles inside me! It's almost impossible. Try it yourself. If you're a man, you carry around the contents of a gallon bottle for every 12½ pounds of your weight. For a woman, it's more like a gallon for every 15 pounds you weigh. (Once our water content was even more extreme: a three-day-old fetus is 97 percent water, and no, I don't know how they calculated that.)

Just about everywhere you look, water is abundant. Our planet is home to over 300 million cubic miles of water, a volume that could cover the United States to a depth of nearly 100 miles. Ninety-seven percent of it is in the oceans, while most of the remaining 3 percent is in the polar ice caps. Inland seas, lakes, and stream channels together account for a mere fiftieth of 1 percent, while just one thousandth of 1 percent is in the atmosphere. That doesn't sound like much, but it's a— perhaps, *the*—major influence on our weather. It translates to about 3,000 cubic miles of water. If you leveled California and poured it all in, you'd need a 100-foot-high dam to stop that much water from flowing away.

Just as sweating is our bodies' way of keeping us water-cooled, evaporation from the oceans is our planet's primary means of keeping itself cool. Much of the Earth would be intolerably hot if it weren't for water being "sweated" from the tropical oceans, thus cooling the entire equatorial region and moderating temperature differences over the whole planet. In addition, water's great capacity to retain heat,[8] also a consequence of hydrogen bonding, helps temper our climate. (It's also why a hot water bottle stays warm for so long in bed.)

Have you noticed how sea breezes blow in from the water to the

---

8. That is, its *specific* heat.

land at night? Oceans act as great reservoirs of heat, so at night they readily share the solar energy that they received by day with the cooler land, which loses heat much faster.[9] By day, the reverse happens: heat flows from the warmer land to the cooler water, where it's easily absorbed. The whole process serves to moderate coastal land temperatures.[10]

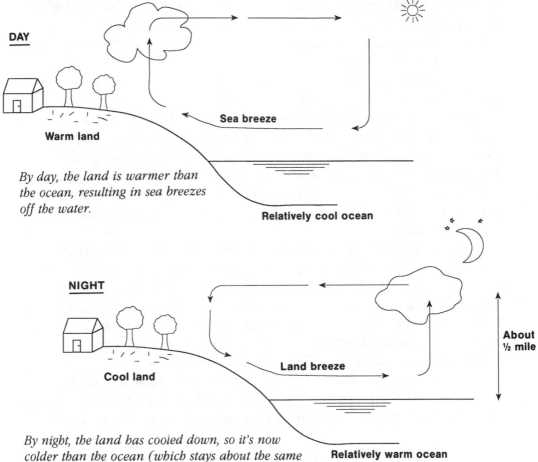

DAY

Sea breeze

Warm land

By day, the land is warmer than the ocean, resulting in sea breezes off the water.

Relatively cool ocean

NIGHT

About ½ mile

Land breeze

Cool land

By night, the land has cooled down, so it's now colder than the ocean (which stays about the same temperature, due to its high capacity to retain heat).
Now winds blow off the land toward the sea. Clouds form when rising moist air cools.

Relatively warm ocean

---

9. Temperature differences over land between day and night are frequently over 20, and sometimes over 30, degrees Celsius. Over water, a day-to-night temperature difference of more than 1 degree is exceptional.

10. Earth's Southern Hemisphere, with about twice the ocean area of the Northern Hemisphere, has generally warmer winters and cooler summers than in the north because the oceans act as a vast heat reservoir. This effect is somewhat offset by our elliptical orbit around the sun: we're about 3 percent closer to the sun in January than July.

Water vapor in the atmosphere helps moderate our climate in several ways. At night, it acts as an insulating blanket, trapping heat radiating from the Earth below. Seasonally, it helps transport heat from the tropics to the polar regions, cooling the former and warming the latter. (This long-range convection of heat doesn't just happen in the air: the Gulf Stream, for instance, transports heat across the Atlantic from the Caribbean to Europe. Without it, Great Britain would be much colder.)

It's hard to overemphasize how special water is:

- As we've seen, water has a remarkably high capacity to retain heat.
- Water is densest at 4 degrees Celsius. "Big deal," you might think. But that's 4 degrees above freezing, so ice, having 90 percent of the density of liquid water, floats. That's what keeps fish alive in winter (they're safe below the insulating layer of ice). Also, if ice sank to the bottom, it might not melt in summer. Over time, the polar oceans would freeze solid from the bottom up.
- It has a particularly high boiling point. For instance, it boils at about 260 degrees Celsius hotter than methane (a gas at room temperature), with which it shares a similar molecular weight (water 18, methane 16). Again, without hydrogen bonding, water would be a gas.
- It's a near-perfect solvent, for everything from sugar to rocks. ("In time and with water, everything changes," said Leonardo da Vinci.) That's why water is so suitable as a medium for life, in this world and, perhaps, others. In water, life can evolve, propagate, and make merry.

I hope I've convinced you by now that water's unique. It sure is nice to have this particular supermolecule around. Most scientists interested in the search for extraterrestrial intelligence (SETI) simply write off any chance that life will be found on a planet on which there's no liquid water. Mars (probably) and Venus (possibly) once had oceans three or four billion years ago. Earth did then and does now, and terrestrial life, from the smallest cell to the largest whale, thrives in it.

Supercool in Yosemite

Finally, a stranger-than-fiction story. It was cold at dawn one mid-October morning in 1967 in the Yosemite backcountry. Very cold. When my friend Richard emerged from his tent near the shore of Boothe Lake, hoarfrost covered the rocks and leaves. He walked down to the edge of the lake with his fishing pole and cast a long line, perhaps fifty feet out. As the fly and float hit the water, he heard an odd sound, "like the crackling ice cubes make when you dump them into liquid," he remembers. As he started to wind his line in, he noticed something odd happening to the surface of the water immediately behind his fly: it was freezing solid. By the time he'd wound the whole line in, perhaps 30 seconds had passed since his fly had touched the water. In that time, the entire lake, all 10 acres of it, had frozen over.

Having majored in physics, Richard knew what had happened but couldn't quite believe it. Feeling a little foolish, he cast again. This time, his fly and bubble hit ice with a hard "clunk" and bounced all the way back to shore as he wound in his line.

Supercooled water is water that's still liquid below the freezing point. It's not difficult to superfreeze water in the controlled conditions of a laboratory, where you can minimize vibration and air movement while you lower the temperature of a flask of distilled water to well below 0 degrees Celsius. When ready, you can blow on the surface, or rock the flask slightly, or drop in a "nucleating agent" such as a tiny grain of sand, and the water will instantly freeze into ice. Very pure water can be supercooled in the lab to minus 40 degrees Celsius without freezing.

But for the same phenomenon to occur spontaneously in natural conditions in a 10-acre lake in the wilderness is, well, phenomenal. It requires extremely pure water and not a breath of wind. Apparently the conditions were perfect on that chilly October morning when the lake froze—in seconds.

The Magic of Hydrogen Bonds

*A*s we've seen, most of water's special properties can be explained by two words: *hydrogen bonds*. Of the four possible ways by which molecules can be bonded, hydrogen bonding is the most powerful.[11]

---

11. The other three are collectively known as the "van der Waals forces." They are the dipole-dipole, dipole-induced, and London dispersion forces. Dipole-dipole forces also act between water molecules, but hydrogen bonds are more important. Dutch physicist Johannes van der Waals (1837–1923) received the 1910 Nobel Prize in physics.

In water, it works like this: a molecule of water consists of a central oxygen atom and two hydrogen atoms, the latter making an angle with the oxygen atom of about 105 degrees. While each hydrogen atom is basically "loyal" to its oxygen atom, it also participates in a quasi-chemical bond with the oxygen atom of an adjacent water molecule. One author put it this way, "In a sense the hydrogen atom acts as if it doesn't know which oxygen atom it belongs to and, consequently, becomes indentured to both."[12] The result is that it's harder to pry a molecule of water away from its neighbor, and a high boiling point is the result. Normally, the boiling point goes down as molecular weight decreases, but water is one of the few exceptions to the rule,[13] thanks to hydrogen bonding.[14]

A molecule of water consists of two small hydrogen atoms and a large central oxygen atom.

The hydrogen atoms make an angle of 105 degrees with the oxygen atom, as shown. Electrons are shared between the oxygen and hydrogen atoms ("covalent bonding"), and they're indicated by a cloud. Because the electrons spend most of their time near the oxygen atom, the lobes opposite the hydrogen atoms are negatively charged, while the hydrogen-atom arms are positively charged (since the nucleus of a hydrogen atom is a positively charged proton).

12. Frank L. Pilar, *Chemistry, the Universal Science*, page 187.

13. Together with hydrogen fluoride and ammonia, which also rely on hydrogen bonding.

14. The property of hydrogen bonding is also essential to life as we know it (and perhaps extraterrestrial life, if it exists). The bonds are perfect for long chain protein or carbohydrate molecules, since they are just strong enough to hold the biological systems together but just weak enough to allow those systems to adjust to the dynamic processes of life. Hydrogen bonds between adenine and thymine, and between guanine and cytosine, hold the "rungs" of the double-helical DNA molecule together: no hydrogen bonds = no DNA = no life as we know it.

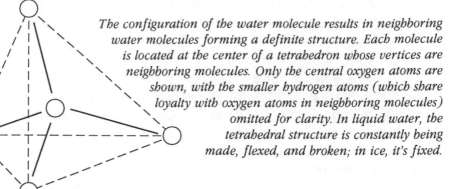

The configuration of the water molecule results in neighboring water molecules forming a definite structure. Each molecule is located at the center of a tetrahedron whose vertices are neighboring molecules. Only the central oxygen atoms are shown, with the smaller hydrogen atoms (which share loyalty with oxygen atoms in neighboring molecules) omitted for clarity. In liquid water, the tetrahedral structure is constantly being made, flexed, and broken; in ice, it's fixed.

Water's peculiar behavior near zero degrees Celsius is explained by another quirk in its character. The 105-degree angle between its hydrogen "arms" is responsible for water's unique tetrahedral array when it freezes.[15] Viewed from one angle, a series of tetrahedrons looks like a honeycomb structure consisting of six-sided hexagons, the reason why most snowflakes are six-sided.[16] When ice melts, this tightly knit structure becomes even tighter, up to four degrees Celsius, after which it relaxes. But at four degrees, the molecules are packed in the most

Water's tetrahedral structure is locked in ice. Two layers of a sheet of ice are shown, the black and gray spheres representing oxygen atoms (the smaller hydrogen atoms have been omitted for clarity). Atoms on the top and bottom layers are black and gray, respectively.

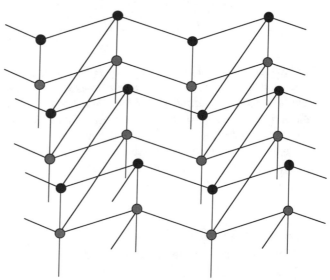

15. Water-ice comes in a total of nine forms. The other eight, in which the hydrogen bonds are distorted, are only stable at very high pressures.
16. A fact known for centuries. For example, Johannes Kepler (of planetary-laws fame) published a pamphlet speculating on the "six-corneredness" of snow. While six sides are normal, three and five-sided snowflakes are not uncommon.

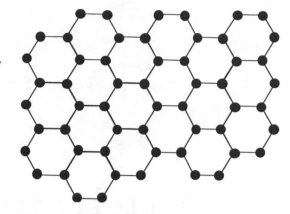

*Seen from above, the structure
is hexagon-shaped. That's why
snowflakes are six-sided.*

compact form available to them, so that's the temperature at which water
is at its densest. Ice that is less dense, therefore, floats on water.

In liquid form, water molecules generally link up, via hydrogen
bonding, with four neighbors in a far more ephemeral tetrahedral
structure than in ice. Scientists were puzzled why this didn't result in
water being much "stiffer" than it actually is, more like a gel. Only in
1991 was this mystery solved. It seems that every so often a fifth
molecule intrudes, leading to two weak hydrogen bonds instead of a
single strong one. This keeps the configuration in constant flux, resulting
in water being as fluid as it is. It also explains why water flows faster
under pressure: the mechanism allows the molecules to bunch closer.[17]

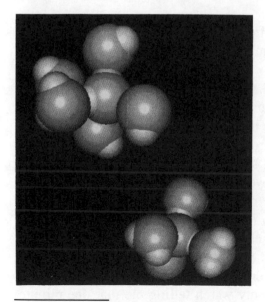

*In ice and usually (but momentarily)
in water, water forms a tetrahedral
structure, that is, any one molecule sits
at the center of a tetrahedron while its
four neighbors are at the vertices. This
"normal" configuration is shown at the
bottom right. Occasionally, a fifth
molecule intrudes, as shown at the top
left. In this computer simulation, the
hydrogen atoms show as "ears" on the
much larger oxygen atoms. (H. Eugene
Stanley and Stefan Schwarzer)*

17. Francesco Sciortino, Alfons Geiger, and H. Eugene Stanley, "Effect of Defects
on Molecular Mobility in Liquid Water," *Nature*, November 21, 1991, page 218.

Eighteen

Pi in the Sky

Hiding between all the ordinary numbers was an infinity of transcendental numbers whose presence you would never have guessed until you looked deeply into mathematics.

—Carl Sagan, *Contact*

Look around you without moving from your chair and see how many circles you can find in exactly one minute. Go!

How did you do? I counted 44. I could have found many more by simply counting the "*o*'s" on the computer screen in front of me (you may have counted *o*'s on this page), but even without those, my world (and, I venture, yours) is fat with circles: each of five lamp fixtures, the end of a bolster pillow, the discount sticker on a catalog, the yogurt container with some brownies left over from the weekend, the tops of about ten pens stuck in a jar on my desk, the rim of the cup of tea by my side, knobs on the stereo system in the corner, the outlines of twin loudspeakers showing through their cloth covering, holes for round pegs in the frame of the futon, an ancient bell push in the wall (we live in an old house), two cylindrical candles on the table, an empty soda can, doorknobs, and the double zeros on my watch telling me that one minute had elapsed.

Circles are ubiquitous because they're simple and symmetrical. Each is the same shape as every other, in any orientation (an upside-down circle is still a circle). Two other reasons why circles feature so ubiquitously in our lives are economy and strength. They're related: not only does a 12-ounce cylindrical soda can use less material than one with a square cross section, but it's stronger, lacking the stress-attracting corners of the square.

Let's see just how efficient the circle is. One day you get a call from your eccentric Uncle Ebenezer, who owns about half of Montana. "Come on out, I've got something for you!" he says. You meet him at a lonely spot in the prairie where he's driven a stake into the ground. "Everything within one mile from this stake is yours!" he says, beaming. "Er, thanks Uncle Eb," you say.

You get a mile-long length of rope from the local mile-long-rope store, tie one end to the stake, then pull the rope taut and walk in a circle around the stake. Now, how much land do you own, and how much fencing material do you have to buy to enclose it? (Between the rope and the fence, maybe this isn't such a great deal!)

Claiming your land in Montana.

The area of a circle, you may remember from high school, is πr^2, while the circumference is $2\pi r$, right? The radius, r, is 1 mile (the length of the rope), so the area of your land is pi (π) square miles and the circumference is 2π, or about 6.3 miles. You think, "Why couldn't the old geezer have given me a square plot of land?" Then you realize what a

Area = π square miles

Area = π square miles

*Comparing the amount of fence needed
to enclose the same area of pi square miles. A
circular plot needs about 6.3 miles of fence, while a square one needs about 7.1 miles.*

favor he's done you. To enclose a square plot having an area of π square miles, you'd have needed $4\sqrt{\pi}$, or about 7.1 miles of fence.

So that's one property of a circle: no other shape encloses area more efficiently. A circle is about 13 percent more efficient than a square. That's why pipes are round: a round water pipe is more economical than a square one. It's also more efficient at carrying water: the less the perimeter, the less the friction.

How about the circle's three-dimensional analog, the sphere? The same principle applies, that is, nothing is more efficient at enclosing a volume. (A sphere is about 28 percent more efficient than a cube, for instance.) A beach ball knows this without being told. The material resists stretching, so the ball assumes the shape that minimizes the surface area for any volume of air, that is, a sphere.

It's the same with raindrops, where the surface tension of the water acts like the rubber of a balloon—at least in a free-fall environment, like in a space shuttle.[18]

Mathematical Pi

So what exactly is this number pi, or π in Greek orthography? It's usually given as the ratio of a circle's circumference to its diameter

---

18. Raindrops falling under the influence of gravity through the atmosphere are distorted by air resistance, but not in the way most people think. They are usually depicted in cartoons as teardrop-shaped, round at the bottom, and tapering gracefully to a point at the top. In fact raindrops, as pictured by high-speed photography, are nearly round when small and hamburger-bun shaped when large. See James E. McDonald, "The Shape of Raindrops," *Scientific American*, February 1954, page 64.

(which is, of course, twice its radius).[19] Given that the circumference of a circle is pi times the diameter ($2\pi r$), it's easy to show that the area is πr^2, as shown in Appendix 4. A sphere's surface area and volume are $4\pi r^2$ and $\frac{4}{3}\pi r^3$ respectively. Any time you deal with a circle or sphere, you deal with pi.[20]

You can easily check the value of pi for yourself. Wind a length of thin thread or dental floss around a cookie can, mark it off where it overlaps its own end, and see how many diameters go into your marked-off length. You—or anyone, anywhere in the universe for that matter—will find that it's about 3. (For greater accuracy, wrap your thread 10 times around and divide your answer by 10.) More precisely, $\pi = 3.14159265358979\ldots$ where the three periods (ellipses) indicate that the digits go on for a long time. No, not just a long time. Forever.

Wrapping twine around a cookie can to estimate the value of pi. Dental floss would give a more accurate result because it's thinner. (Barry Evans)

---

19. The Greek symbol π, corresponding to the English letter *p*, denotes the initial letter of the word *periphery*.

20. Pi also crops up unexpectedly in all sorts of places other than circles and spheres. One example, out of many: the probability that any two randomly chosen integers don't have a common divisor is 6 divided by π^2. For instance, 8 and 27 have no common divisor, but 21 and 497 do (7). The more pairs of random integers you test, the closer the odds of them not having a common divisor approaches $\frac{6}{\pi^2}$, or about 61%.

A Transcendental Number

The next digit of pi will always be unknown until every prior digit is known. You can't predict, say, the millionth digit of pi without calculating each of the prior 999,999 digits.[21] Pi is, in fact, a "transcendental number." (See the sidebar to this chapter.)

So the *exact* value of pi will never be known. Calculate it to a million decimal places (a trivial task for a supercomputer[22]) and you've got pi accurate to one in a million. Calculate it to a trillion places and your accuracy is now no better than one in a trillion. It's a never-ending quest.

It's also an ancient one. Four thousand years ago, the Babylonians thought pi equaled $3\frac{1}{8}$ (3.125), while some clever Egyptian discovered the approximation $4(\frac{8}{9})(\frac{8}{9})$ (3.160 . . .). In a famous Biblical verse (2 Chronicles 4:2) pi apparently equals 3: "He made a molten sea of ten cubits from brim to brim . . . and a line of thirty cubits did compass it round about." In the third century B.C., Archimedes employed the now-common approximation of $3\frac{1}{7}$ (3.143 . . .), while Ptolemy, around A.D. 150, used the fraction $3\frac{17}{120}$ (3.14166 . . .). Indian scholars once thought pi neatly equalled the square root of 10 (3.16 . . .).

A much better approximation for pi was found 400 years ago (and probably much earlier by Chinese mathematicians) by Dutch engineer Adriaan Anthoniszoon, 1527–1607. It's easily remembered by writing the first three odd numbers in pairs (113355), then placing the last three over the first three. Thus, $\frac{355}{113} = 3.1415929$ . . . , giving pi correct to six decimal places.

Only when transcendental numbers were fully understood, less

---

21. For ordinary mortals, that is. Martin Gardner's numerologist buddy (and *alter ego*), Dr. Irving Joshua Matrix, predicted in 1966 (in Gardner's *New Mathematical Diversions from Scientific American*, New York: Simon & Schuster, 1966) that the millionth digit of pi was 5. Eight years later, his prediction (who am I to call it a fluke?) was found to be correct. The prediction was "based" on the 3rd book, 14th chapter, 16th verse (pi is approximately 3.1416) of the King James Bible. The verse mentions the number "seven." The seventh word, "right," has five letters. Gardner, who has practically made a career of demolishing unscientific claims, must have been delighted with Dr. Matrix's none-too-scientific prediction!

22. The evolution of electronic computers, which have been with us for less than 50 years, can be roughly measured by pi's expansion. In 1949, the first computer calculation of pi gave it to 2,037 digits: at the size of this text, the expansion could have been written out on a strip of paper 10 feet long. In 1991, pi was calculated to over 2 billion digits, requiring a strip 2,000 miles long!

than 300 years ago, did mathematicians realize that the digits of pi went on forever without any rhyme, reason, or repetition.[23] In order to calculate pi to whatever accuracy we choose (short of "perfect"!), we, or rather, our computers, use the notion of converging infinite series. What's a converging infinite series? To understand, let's first look at its opposite, a diverging infinite series. The numbers 1, 2, 4, 8 . . . go on forever. If you added them as you went, you'd get 1, 3, 7, 15 . . . , getting a larger and larger number as you progressed. So we say that the series $1 + 2 + 4 + 8$ . . . diverges.

How about the series, $\frac{1}{1} + \frac{1}{2} + \frac{1}{4} + \frac{1}{8}$ . . . ? It also goes on forever (indicated by the ". . ." , meaning "and so on"), getting closer and closer to 2 but never quite reaching it. We say the series *converges* on 2, that is, it's a converging infinite series. Similarly, many infinite series converge on, but never quite reach, pi. Alternatively, we could say they equal pi after an infinite number of terms.

My favorite series for pi (perhaps because its Scottish discoverer James Gregory, 1638–1675, also invented the reflecting telescope, thus giving impetus to the young science of astronomy)[24] is this:

$$\pi = 4 \left(1 - \frac{1}{3} + \frac{1}{5} - \frac{1}{7} + \frac{1}{9} - \frac{1}{11} \ldots\right)[25]$$

---

23. In his novel *Contact*, astronomer Carl Sagan has his hero's computer discover a wonderful pattern—a perfect circle—secreted deep in the digits of pi, waiting for beings, on this world or another, to discover: "Hiding in the alternating patterns of digits, deep inside the transcendental number, was a perfect circle, its form traced out by unities in a field of noughts. The universe was made on purpose, the circle said."

Needless to say, no one has yet found such a pattern in pi's endless digits. (The serendipitous occurrence of six consecutive nines, that is, 999999, in the first 800 digits of pi doesn't count!)

24. In truth, Gregory didn't actually write down this series. That was left to Gottfried Leibniz 10 years later. Gregory discovered the general formula that gives rise to the series, but there's little doubt he was aware of this "special case."

25. If you have a computer with BASIC, you can easily program it in accordance with Gregory's simple series to compute pi, at least to the accuracy of your computer or, more likely, the limit of your patience. (It converges very slowly, taking nearly 10 million iterations to compute pi to a mere seven decimal places! Can you see why?) You'll have to leave your computer running overnight to get any appreciable degree of accuracy. (If you have a screen-saving utility, turn it off.)

```
10 N=1: P=0: S=1          40 N=N+1: S=−S
20 PRINT N; TAB(20); 4*P  50 GOTO 20
30 P=P+(1/(2*N−1))*S      60 END
```

To make the program run faster, print out only every 1,000th (or 10,000th) iteration by adding a FOR-NEXT loop:

```
25 FOR M=1 TO 1000
45 NEXT M
```

The number hidden in every circle and sphere, from nickels to softballs, is found in this trifling, but infinite, summation!

Finally a quick anti-pi puzzle. What's the area of the vase shape? Hint: you don't need to use pi. (If you give up, see Puzzle Answers at the back of the book.)

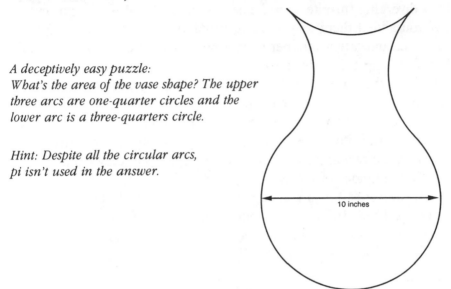

A deceptively easy puzzle:
What's the area of the vase shape? The upper three arcs are one-quarter circles and the lower arc is a three-quarters circle.

Hint: Despite all the circular arcs, pi isn't used in the answer.

10 inches

Don't Disturb My Figure!

Archimedes of Syracuse, the greatest mathematician of his age, calculated many difficult volumes and areas, including the volume and surface area of a sphere, which we've already mentioned. He was able to compute a sphere's volume after accomplishing an astonishing feat for that time (about 240 B.C.): he showed that the volumes of a cone, hemisphere, and cylinder having the same height and radius are in the ratio 1 to 2 to 3. And this was nearly two millennia before the invention of calculus!

Archimedes' passion for mathematics led, at least according to

Archimedes' theorem. The volumes of a cone, hemisphere, and cylinder having the same base and height are in the ratio 1 to 2 to 3.

legend, to his murder. In 212 B.C., when the Roman army finally ended the two-year siege of Syracuse, a Roman infantryman found the 73-year-old mathematician drawing in sand outside his house as he worked on his latest problem. "Don't disturb my figure!" growled Archimedes, prompting the impatient soldier to slay him.

The Roman commander Marcellus, who had ordered that the renowned mathematician was not to be harmed, had a tomb erected for the old man on which were carved a hemisphere, cone, and cylinder, symbolizing Archimedes' "favorite theorem." When Cicero visited Sicily 150 years later, he found the monument, overgrown with thorns. No trace of it remains today.

True or false? The death of Archimedes in 212 B.C. at the hands of a Roman soldier—at least according to later writers, who may have wanted to glorify Greece at the expense of Rome.

"It Must Be the Truth"

Finally, here's something strange and beautiful. I don't understand it, and I'm not sure anyone else does either. To really grasp the strangeness and beauty, you have to understand that there are, in all of mathematics, five numbers that are unique (quinque?). They have been called "the most important constants in the whole of analysis" by Philip J. Davis and

Reuben Hersh in their book *The Mathematical Experience*. The five numbers are:

◆ zero (0).
◆ one (1), the smallest integer.
◆ pi (π), the ratio hidden in every circle and sphere, as we've seen
◆ "*e*" (approximately 2.7), the root of natural logarithms. Essentially, *e* establishes an exponential or "snowball" rate of growth that is proportional to the value of a growing quantity (so called because the larger a snowball is, the faster it grows). As such, *e* turns up in such everyday matters as the interest on mortgage payments, gambling odds, suspension bridges, and spiders' webs.[26]
◆ "*i*," the square root of minus 1. This *i* is a curious number, since, as you know, negative numbers like minus 1 don't have square roots. (A negative number multiplied by itself yields a positive product.) However, *i* does allow for a whole branch of "complex" numbers, whose applications include a theoretical understanding of alternating-current electricity.

At first (and second and third!) glance, these five numbers have little

---

26. Perhaps the easiest way to grasp the fundamental nature of *e* is to consider how compound interest increases the value of money. Suppose you put a dollar into a bank that pays compound interest of 10% per year, compounded every *year*. At the end of a year, 10% of $1.00 is added to your original dollar, so it's now worth $1.10. At the end of the second year, 10% of $1.10 is added, so now it's worth $1.21, and so on. By the end of 10 years, your original dollar is worth $(1 + \frac{1}{10})^{10}$, or $2.5937.

A rival bank announces that it also pays compound interest at the rate of 10% per year, but that it will compound your money every *six months*. At the end of the first six months, your dollar is worth $1.00 plus 5% (if they pay 10% per year, they'll pay 5% every six months), i.e., $1.05. At the end of the first year, 5% of that amount is added, for a total of $1.1025, and at the end of ten years, your original dollar is worth $(1 + \frac{1}{20})^{20}$ or $2.6533, about $0.06 more than you got from the annually compounding bank. It seems that the more frequently your dollar is compounded, the more you'll end up with.

Suppose a third bank goes for broke and advertises that it pays compound interest of 10% per year compounded *daily*. Since there are about 3652 days in 10 years, at the end of 10 years your dollar is worth $(1 + \frac{1}{3652})^{3652}$, that is, $2.7179. Notice what's going on here? Although it's true that the more frequently your money is compounded the more you get, there seems to be a limit to it. In fact, if you compound the money *continuously*, instant by instant, at the end of 10 years you'd end up with $(1 + \frac{1}{n})^n$ where *n* is infinitely large, or $2.7182818284 \ldots$, that is, *e* dollars. Note the serendipitous repetition of 1828 (which doesn't continue, alas!).

in common. Yet this one equation links them, crisply and elegantly:

$$e^{i\pi} + 1 = 0$$

What does it mean? You've got me. In their book, *Mathematics and the Imagination*, Edward Kassner and James R. Newman have this to say about it: "Elegant, concise and full of meaning. We can only reproduce it and not stop to inquire into its implications. It appeals equally to the mystic, the scientist, the philosopher, the mathematician." They then tell of how Harvard mathematician Benjamin Peirce explained it to his students one day after working through the proof on the chalkboard: "Gentlemen, this is surely true, it is absolutely paradoxical; we cannot understand it, and we don't know what it means, but we have proved it, and therefore, we know it must be the truth."

Surely someone must have innocently asked, "Sir, what is truth?"

----------------------------- **Transcendental Numbers** -----------------------------

Number is the measure of all things.

—Pythagoras

A number is either rational or irrational, and some irrational numbers are transcendental. Starting from basics:

An *integer* is a whole number, for example, 777, −19, 0, 5.

A *rational number* can be expressed as the ratio (hence, *ratio*-nal) of two integers, for example, $\frac{2}{7}$. A rational number's decimal expansion is predictable, so for instance $\frac{2}{7}$ equals 0.285714285714285714 . . . . Notice the pattern: six figures keep repeating, so it's easy to show that the 100th digit of the expansion is 7 (without calculating the previous 99), since the 96th, like the 6th, 12th, 18th, and so on, is 4.

An *irrational number* can't be expressed as the ratio of two integers. An irrational number's expansion is infinite and nonrepeating. For example, the square root of two ($\sqrt{2}$, that is, the number that multiplied by itself equals 2) is 1.41421356 . . . . There's no pattern to be found here, no matter how many digits you inspect. The only way to know the

100th digit of the expansion is to figure out all previous 99.[27] Yet it's
theoretically possible to construct a line of length precisely the square
root of two with the classical tools of a compass and straightedge, since
the square root of two is the diagonal length of a square with sides of
unit length. (Practically, by making the square large enough, you can
measure the square root of two as accurately as you want.)

Around 450 B.C. a member of the "Pythagorean Brotherhood" was
probably the first to realize that the square root of two was irrational,
prompting a crisis among these philosophers who believed that all
things—or at least all other numbers—could be derived from whole
numbers. The Pythagorean proof of the irrationality of the square root of
two, a brilliant example of *reductio ad absurdum* ("reduction to
absurdity"), is given in Appendix 3. Even if you are not mathematically
inclined, do spend a few minutes going over it. It's easier than it looks,
and it has a beautiful "aha!" ending.

To the Pythagoreans, for whom the essence of everything lay in
natural numbers, the discovery of "unnatural" numbers was disastrous,
and they tried to keep the knowledge secret. According to one legend,
when Hippasus revealed it he was banished by the brotherhood and later
drowned by the gods in a shipwreck, to no one's surprise or regret.[28]

A *transcendental number* (for example, pi) is a class of irrational
numbers that not only can't be expressed as the ratio of two integers (like
all irrationals), but neither is it the root of an algebraic equation with
rational coefficients. For instance, the square root of two is the root of
the equation $x^2 = 2$; no such equation exists for pi.

In the absence of any "finite" equation (pi, remember, can only be
expressed as the sum of an infinite series of terms), no geometrical
construction is possible to precisely establish pi. In other words, it's
impossible to construct a line whose length exactly equals pi (relative to
a line of unit length), as opposed to a line of length that equals the
square root of two, for example, which can be constructed as the
diagonal of a square having sides of unit length, as we've already seen.
Mathematicians from the time of Anaxagoras (500–428 B.C.) to quite
recently have spent prodigious efforts attempting to solve the equivalent

27. Curiously, it is possible to find numbers that are both irrational and predictable.
For instance, it's obviously easy to predict the next digit in the irrational number
0.12345678910111213141516171819202122 . . . , since it's simply a string of
consecutive integers pasted together.
28. See also Chapter 12, "What Can the Matter Be?"

problem of "squaring the circle," that is, constructing a square having the same area as that of a circle.[29]

Only after the existence of transcendental numbers was proved (by Joseph Liouville in 1840), and pi shown to be one such number, did mathematicians know for sure that squaring the circle was an impossible task. Although professional mathematicians frequently receive letters asking them to review "solutions" to the problem, most such solicitations are ignored, since the proofs of its impossibility are rigorous.

---

29. This is one of the three "classic" problems the ancient Greeks set themselves, using only a compass and straightedge. The other two are (1) doubling the cube (otherwise known as the "Delian problem," which involves constructing a line whose length, compared with a line of unit length, is the cube root of two, so that a cube with sides that length would have double the volume of a unit cube); and (2) trisecting the angle (dividing any angle into three equal angles). It's been known since the early 1800s that these problems are impossible to solve because you can't extract cube roots with a compass and straightedge. Obviously doubling the cube is therefore impossible, and since the trisection of a 60-degree angle requires extracting a cube root, at least some angles can't be trisected.

A Conversation with
Philip Morrison

——

Doing science is like growing a garden. You sow seeds, you have to water them, you've got to tend them, and when you bring in the harvest, you have to think of next year. And not everybody gets magnificent flowers and fruits.

—Philip Morrison,
Nova: Adventures in Science

*F*or nearly three decades, Dr. Philip Morrison has been known to millions of readers of *Scientific American* as a gifted book reviewer with an extraordinarily broad range of interests. He is also a professor of astrophysics at MIT and an expert on quasars and other active galactic nuclei: bodies as small as the solar system emitting the energy of hundreds of galaxies.

During World War II, as a group leader in the Manhattan Project, he helped design and build the first atomic bombs and rode in the sedan carrying the plutonium core of the first bomb, code-named "Trinity," from Los Alamos to the test site in Alamogordo, New Mexico. Soon after the war ended, he was sent to Hiroshima to report on damage. Since that time, he has written and spoken on the dangers of nuclear war and the irrationality of the vastly oversized atomic arsenal maintained by the United States.

Philip Morrison. (Donna Coveney/MIT)

Of his many achievements, two are particularly noteworthy in the context of the themes of this book, wonder and curiosity. The first is his 10-minute movie *Powers of Ten*, a fixture at many science museums across the country, in which viewers are "flown" in a continuous sequence of film from deep space to the nucleus of an atom. The second is his recent PBS television series "The Ring of Truth," in which he investigates how we know what we know.[30]

Barry Evans Dr. Morrison, how did you originally make the decision to become a scientist?

Philip Morrison As far as I can recall, I got my first radio set when I was five years old, very early in the history of broadcast radio in this country. I happened to live near the first radio station in Pittsburgh. Before they started broadcasting, they made a couple thousand receivers and put them on the market in the stores, and my father bought me one. I thought that was the most fascinating thing in the world. By moving a little wire whisker over the crystal, you could or could not receive signals. The signals came from all over the country depending on the time of day or night. Most interesting! I became entirely absorbed in radio.

B. E. Was the intriguing part of it the fact that the waves were invisible?

P. M. Yes, the fact that there were so many invisible properties that were so important, and you could learn to control them and to understand a little bit how they worked. So indeed I became a radio amateur and quite a serious one. When I went to college I wanted to become a radio engineer.

B. E. Why did you switch to physics?

P. M. I liked physics and the open-minded physicists much more.

---

30. Both are available in book and video form. See Select Bibliography.

B. E.   You've got a reputation for having an unusual breadth and depth of knowledge. How did that come about?

P. M.   I was very bookish and very interested in making things, and I spent a lot of time doing that. Then recently, that is, in the last 30 years, I've been a book reviewer, which has this remarkable property of bringing me books on all subjects every month, and I have to read some of them. That's certainly been an easy way to maintain the wide interests I already had, and allow them to grow.

B. E.   When I was watching your program, "Ring of Truth," I was struck by your delight in, and amazement of, what's going on in the world around you.

P. M.   Well, I think it would be too bad to lose the sense of surprise and excitement, and coherence and question, all of which comes to you when you look at the real world.

B. E.   Perhaps nothing in science quite matches the surprise and excitement that many people experience when they realize that we can now look back virtually to the creation of the universe. When I talked to you 14 years ago, you were quite skeptical of the Big Bang theory. Are you still?

P. M.   That's a subtle question. I still believe that the general view of the public and the general view of the scientist are absolutely in contradiction on what is meant by the Big Bang, and that's where the difficulty has arisen. I think that owing to the mistaken views of the eighties, the Big Bang is interpreted as being the beginning of time and space and order, whatever that is. And in that sense I think it's gone. There's no evidence for it anymore. However, if instead, the Big Bang is interpreted as a tremendous expansionary phase of the universe, then the theory is still very strong.[31]

But the most likely thing now is that before inflation the universe was certainly not free of matter, space, and time. It was a straightforward little piece that obeyed Einstein's general relativity

---

31. In 1981, Alan Guth of MIT proposed that many of the problems raised by the Big Bang theory could be explained by assuming that the universe underwent an unimaginably large and rapid expansion. This "addendum" to the Big Bang theory of cosmic evolution is usually just referred to as "inflation." It's commonly taught that inflation occurred very early in the history of the universe, perhaps at 10^{-32} second. Morrison insists that we have absolutely no knowledge of how old the universe was—or what had happened previously—when inflation occurred.

equation exactly, and then it inflated as that equation allowed, but evidence of what happened was all wiped out by the inflationary stage. I would say there's certainly no evidence of the Big Bang happening before that. There might have been infinite numbers of inflations. There might have been no Big Bang, or there might have been a Big Bang, just as they say. It's an open question.

In that sense, the Big Bang is really over as a phenomenon in cosmology. It might be true, but its truth would depend only upon theoretical studies. I like to say the consequences of the Big Bang are still believable, and we have a lot of evidence for those. But we have no evidence for the event itself.

B. E.   In lay terms, is it fair to say that any data from before inflation has been "flattened out"?

P. M.   That's right. Very difficult to interpret. Stretched out to blandness!

B. E.   Is inflation a wall over which we're never going to get to see, back to the very beginning of everything?

P. M.   One doesn't like to say that, but it's certainly a big problem for us at the moment. Perhaps if we understood the forces and the particles involved we might be able to see beyond it. At present, we just don't know.

B. E.   You have said that Alan Guth's inflation proposal seemed bizarre when he proposed it 1981, yet now you are a dazzled enthusiast. Why is that?

P. M.   I think inflation is the most remarkable thing to come out of the past decade, and that even though we don't fully understand it, that understanding is within reach. The discovery of inflation was an absolutely extraordinary phenomenon. It's as though you were looking at a stream bed of beautiful pebbles—if you found one pebble that was a hundred times as large as all the others, perfectly transparent and perfectly round, you would have to be amazed. And people were!

When they saw that perfect symmetry, they had no answer save that it must have started that way from the beginning. In other words, a miracle had produced this simplest cosmos. That's what I think you would tend to say. Except that it became pretty clear around 1981 that the equation followed Einstein's equation. You just had to interpret it the right way: put the right term in, and it would give just what we saw.

I think that certainly is the most important thing in cosmology since the discovery of the redshifts, or perhaps the discovery of external galaxies.[32]

B. E.   In 1959, you and Giuseppe Cocconi published a scientific paper in which you proposed that interstellar communication at microwave radio frequencies was possible and plausible.[33] On Columbus Day [1992], NASA will begin a 10-year search for messages from intelligent life beyond Earth. What's the connection between the two events?

P. M.   NASA's search is a direct consequence. Our idea is, for the first time in 30 years, getting real systematic attention, and that's what it needed. The power of computing is so great now that it makes [a search] much more feasible than we could ever have imagined. We have a good chance to find something if we look hard for a considerable length of time.

B. E.   Are you daunted by the so-called "Fermi paradox," which says that if there are civilizations out there, some are going to be so far advanced that we should have had some indication that they're out there by now?

P. M.   I never understood that argument. If you look, which is what we're beginning to do, then maybe you'll find them. And that's what we're beginning to do. But if you don't even look, then it's pretty hard to know how you would find them. I don't believe they're going to build flying saucers or machines [multiplying] exponentially, polluting the whole universe with their progeny.

B. E.   You once wrote, "A characteristic of the human mind is to formulate models of the world, so as to predict what we will encounter in the next day, the next year. I think that science grew

---

32. In the 1920s, Edwin Hubble realized that most galaxies are moving away from us, that is, that the universe is expanding. Light from receding galaxies appears to move toward the red end of the spectrum, hence the term *redshift*.

33. Giuseppe Cocconi and Philip Morrison, "Searching for Interstellar Communications," *Nature*, September 19, 1959, page 844. The paper concluded: "Few will deny the profound importance, practical and philosophical, which the detection of interstellar communications would have. We therefore feel that a discriminating search for (interstellar) signals deserves a considerable effort. The probability of success is difficult to estimate; but if we never search, the chance of success is zero."

out of that curiosity." My reaction on reading that was, but isn't curiosity sufficient unto itself to ensure science? Do curiosity and intelligence have to go hand in hand?

P. M.   I don't know quite what you mean by intelligence. I put it in this rather hard-boiled way: If you make models of the future, it's very likely to imply curiosity. If you don't make models of the future, I don't think curiosity occurs. The curious cat or monkey has an idea that if it opens a box there'll be something good in there. A stick can't do that!

B. E.   Science seems to have two very different faces. Scientists think of science as an empirically testable process by which you converge on a model of the truth, while laypeople generally think of science as a black box full of content. Why are the scientist's and the layperson's views so far apart, and what can be done to bring them to some convergence?

P. M.   It's the problem with schools and writing and formalism. Packaged things are easier to deal with. The scientist knows that the packaged thing is only something to stand on. [The solution is to] let students answer their own questions about their own experiences, then encourage them to use this technique to gradually learn about things far away, no longer centered on themselves.

B. E.   Is science education too content-oriented?

P. M.   Yes, there's a tremendous penchant for mistaking names for ideas and things. If you learn the names of the planets, that's regarded as studying science. But it's not studying science at all. It's indeed interesting, and you should learn them, but it's a part of literature, not a part of science.

B. E.   Neil Postman said, "Children enter school as question marks and leave as periods." Is it getting worse?

P. M.   I don't know if it's getting worse. [Science education] has always been a struggle. I think it's gone through a bad time in the last 10 years, especially in the United States. There's been [a lot of pressure to institute] "back to basics" programs. That's naive.

B. E.   What direction should schools be following?

P. M.   Schools should be richer—that's the main thing. I don't mean richer in money, but richer in things and ideas and objects. Schools are getting impoverished in terms of the general view of American life, and that's a bad thing. They should be full of stuff that the kids make and bring in, like little treasure houses. Instead, schools tend to restrict themselves very much to words and simplicities.

I'm not saying those aren't important. Probably the best thing you can teach is reading, writing, and arithmetic, but it's not the only thing you can teach. Once it was more appropriate that these were the only things the schools taught, because the people knew everything about common everyday life. They knew about cows, the moon, the growth of animals. But now they don't know those. Instead, they know mainly the words and the images of TV, and now they come to school and get more of the same.

B. E.   What's the role of examinations?

P. M.   Largely negative—it's a credentializing procedure. I don't much approve of it. It's far too emphasized.

B. E.   Has your view of what science is changed over your career?

P. M.   I'd like to think I began with lots of enthusiasm and retained some of that, but now I've got a more mature understanding of what's involved. It's hard to say. I've certainly acquired a stronger impression of the importance of the relationship between experiment and theory.

The biggest change [for me] is that I'm beginning to realize science is a harder subject for many people than I thought, and that maybe the way of the scientist is quite an unusual way. Perhaps that's why we have so much trouble educating children in the ways of science.

B. E.   Can you identify a peak experience of your science career?

P. M.   Well, I don't know. You get a lot of hindsight with such things! I had several peak experiences that didn't pan out. I had a theory about the light curve of a supernova, which turned out to be entirely wrong. At the time it was wonderful, and it fit everything so well. It seemed such an ingenious solution, and I was very enthusiastic about it for years. It turns out it wasn't at all right. I suppose the best thing was my discussion over 30 years ago with Giuseppe Cocconi, which led to our proposal to search in the microwave spectrum for extraterrestrial intelligence. And who knows what we'll find?

Saturday's Puzzles

Quickies

The wise man solves the problem. The genius avoids it.

—Unknown author

Sometimes the simplest questions lead to the toughest answers. "Why am I alive?" a child might ask, and spend the next 80 years trying to find an answer. With luck, these 10 teasers should take a little less time to solve.

1. What is the opposite of "Not in"?[34]
2. How many months have 30 days?
3. Rearrange the letters of NEW DOOR to make one word.
4. Two princes, two horses, one race. The king says, "Whoever's horse comes in last gets the kingdom." They look puzzled until a wise old man whispers two words to them. They jump on the horses and race away. What were his words?
5. What word is mispelled on this page?
6. A sign writer always gets one letter wrong in his words. What did he mean to write on these signs? QUIST, PUAH, EFIT, EET PLINT

---

34. This and several other of these problems come from, or are adapted from, Martin Gardner's much-missed "Mathematical Games" column, which ran in *Scientific American* from 1956 to 1983.

7. What common word starts and ends with the letters "UND"? (Londoners might find this easier than, say, New Yorkers.)

8. What is this?

(Roger von Oech)

9. Starting with arrangement (a), what is the least number of glasses you have to move to obtain arrangement (b)?

(a)

(b)

10. What everyday four-letter word can be formed from four consecutive letters in the alphabet?

Puzzle answers are at the back of the book.

Saturday's Quotations

Informed Bewilderment

Part of the intellectual equipment of an educated person, however his or her time is to be spent, ought to be a feel for the queerness of nature, the inexplicable thing, the side of life for which informed bewilderment will be the best way of getting through the day.

—Lewis Thomas

Man errs so long as he is striving.

—Goethe

The most precious gift that you carry uniquely is your ignorance. This is heady stuff, this ignorance: far more seductive and amazing than knowledge. It's really the only tool you've got; fortunately, it's also the only tool you'll need. I do urge you to cherish your ignorance and husband it, because ignorance can quickly curdle into knowledge . . . That is the worst. If you know something, you stop asking questions, and once you stop asking questions it's all over. . . .

    At the center of every theory is an irreducible core of mystery, and it is always wise to keep your eye firmly on that mystery . . . It's what brings hope. When this particular compilation of fears and

*fads and guesses has long gone, the mystery will still be there.
That's the reason ignorance is such an effective strategy. It
concentrates on the one verity in life, which is that we don't know
what the verities of life are.*

**—Jon Carroll, speech, University of
California at Berkeley, May 1991**

*The most beautiful thing we can experience is the mysterious. It is
the fundamental emotion which stands at the cradle of true art and
true science. Whoever does not know it and can no longer wonder,
no longer marvel, is as good as dead, and his eyes are dimmed.*

—Albert Einstein

Doubt that which you would most believe.

—Robert Scott Root-Bernstein

Incredulity doesn't kill curiosity, it encourages it.

—Umberto Eco

*When you consider something like death, after which (there being
no news to the contrary) we may well go out like a candle flame,
then it probably doesn't matter if we try too hard, are awkward
sometimes, care for one another too deeply, are excessively curious
about nature, are too open to experience, enjoy a nonstop expense
of the senses in an effort to know life intimately and lovingly. It
probably doesn't matter if, while trying to be modest and eager
watchers of life's many spectacles, we sometimes look clumsy or
get dirty or ask stupid questions or reveal our ignorance or say
the wrong thing or light up with wonder like the children we all
are. . . .*

—Diane Ackerman, *A Natural History of the Senses*

Error defines new.

—John Dewey

The problem with most people isn't so much their ignorance; it's what they know that ain't so.

—Josh Billings

To be conscious that you are ignorant of the facts is a great step towards knowledge.

—Benjamin Disraeli

One thing I know and that is that I know nothing.

—Socrates

The mere formulation of a problem is often far more essential than its solution. To raise new questions, new possibilities, to regard old problems from a new angle, requires creative imagination and marks real advances in science.

—Albert Einstein

I used to think I was smart. Now I think I'm really lucky.

—Pam Stewart

It is impossible to dismiss mystery from life. Being is altogether mysterious. Mystery is all about us and in us, the Inconceivable permeates us, it is "closer than breathing and nearer than hands and feet." For all we know, that which we are may rise at death from living, as an intent player wakes up from his absorption when a game comes to an end, or as a spectator turns his eyes from the stage as the curtain falls, to look at the auditorium he has for a time forgotten. . . . Ultimately the mystery may be the only thing that matters, but within the rules and limits of the game of life, when you are catching trains or paying bills or earning a living, the mystery does not matter at all.

—H. G. Wells, *The Work, Wealth and Happiness of Mankind*

Sunday

Day of the Sun

Sunday, according to Biblical tradition, is the day God saw fit to take a breather after six hectic days of Creation. It's also traditionally a family day. Whatever our personal traditions, Sunday in the West is a day that inspires ritual: church, brunch, outings, taking a long walk with the dog, watching a sports event. For many of us, it's the best day of the week.

People who are quoted think so, anyway. Out of 13 entries for specific days of the week in *The Oxford Dictionary of Modern Quotations*, Monday got 1 (from Pooh Bear, no less), Tuesday to Friday weren't mentioned, Saturday got 3, and Sunday had a full 9 quotes.

Nineteen

Underground

Down, down to hell; and say I sent thee thither.

—William Shakespeare,
Henry VI, Part III

*Y*ou're lost, so you ask a local. "Drive six miles north then take Highway 84 two miles west," you're told. In your mind you might see a map with a road heading north, or up, and an intersecting road going west, or left. No problem. Most of us are at ease with the four primary directions north, south, east, and west. Even on the surface of the sphere we live on, those four directions are still self-evident: San Diego is 2,500 miles west and 500 miles south of New York. We just imagine that the part of the sphere on which the United States sits has been flattened out, that is, we think of a map: a two-dimensional model of the real world.

Moving from two dimensions to three, we're faced with up and down. We're familiar enough with up: that's where we find clouds and blue sky and stars. But what about down? Isn't it curious that we live inches away from a virtually secret world? Most of us know less about the realm beneath our feet than we do the stars in the sky, despite the fact that virtually all the planet we call home consists of the hidden inside. To visualize how little of the Earth we interact with, imagine wrapping a sheet of paper—as thick as this page—tightly round a golf ball. The ball represents the Earth, while the thickness of paper

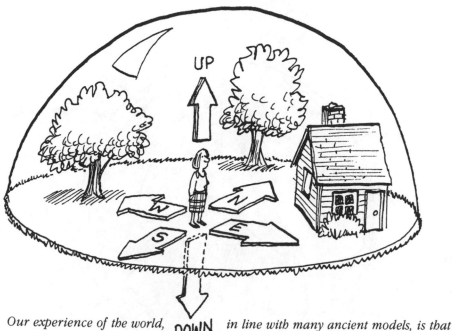

Our experience of the world, **DOWN** *in line with many ancient models, is that we live inside an upturned bowl. Our primary directions are north, south, east, west, and up. Rarely do we think of the sixth direction, "down," in the same way.*

A cosmologist of old doing what cosmologists are still engaged in: trying to figure out the universe from the little platform we call Earth. Despite its medieval look, this woodcut is only about 100 years old. It was probably created by Camille Flammarion, a French popularizer of astronomy.

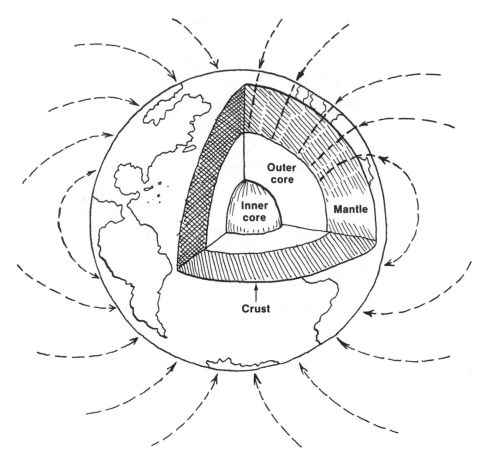

Earth's interior. About one-third of the total mass is in the comparatively small iron-nickel core. Rotation of the outer liquid core is responsible for Earth's magnetic field. Broken lines indicate lines of magnetic force. The continents "drift" around on plates that form the Earth's crust in a mechanism known as "continental drift" or "plate tectonics."

represents the entire biosphere, from eight-mile-deep ocean trenches to five-mile-high mountain peaks. Everything inside the paper is unknown to us.

Not totally unknown, perhaps. By analyzing waves from distant earthquakes and underground nuclear tests, seismologists have been able to visualize the general outlines of the composition of our planet. We know, for instance, that Earth's central core is hotter than the sun's surface.[1] The entire core is about 5,000 miles across, compared to Earth's

---

1. The inner core temperature is about 7,000 degrees Celsius, compared with about 5,600 degrees at the surface of the sun. The sun's core is much hotter, about 16 million degrees.

total diameter of about 8,000 miles. The core consists of the dense metals iron and nickel, in two distinct layers: a solid (perhaps partly molten) inner core and a liquid outer core. The slow rotation of the outer core is responsible for Earth's magnetic field.

Above the core, extending nearly to the surface, is the lighter rocky mantle. Literally floating on that lies the last few miles of solid planet, the crust. The boundary between crust and mantle is the "Mohorovicic discontinuity"—"moho" for short—named after the Yugoslav geologist who proposed its existence. The moho lies about 20 miles under the continents, but it is only about five miles beneath the floors of the oceans.

Geologists have long been fascinated with the moho. If only they could examine the boundary and the undisturbed mantle material[2] below, they reason, they could test theories of how continents move and how our planet was formed. In the early 1960s, a series of attempts, collectively known as the Mohole Project, were made to reach it. By 1966, when the project was cut short by Congress in the face of its escalating budget, drillers had obtained deep cores from several locations in the eastern Pacific Ocean. Their efforts advanced the technology of deep-water drilling to new levels, but the moho's depth had eluded them.

The world record for depth is currently held by (then) Soviet workers, who spent a decade drilling down about eight miles near Murmansk in the Kola Peninsula. That's still far short of the moho, but quite an achievement: eight miles is a little higher than passenger aircraft fly. Next time you're winging across the country on a 747, look down and imagine a drill pipe dangling from the plane all the way to the ground; now all you have to do is shift your vision vertically downward, so the pipe starts from the ground and drops the same distance through the rock beneath your feet. That's all there is to it: the world's deepest hole.

Earthquake High

Planet Earth is still in its formative adolescence. While other bodies in the solar system have reached states of relatively mature stability, Earth is

---

2. As opposed to disturbed mantle material, that is, volcanic lava. Volcanic processes have covered more than 80% of Earth's total surface with mantle material that originated from deeper than 50 miles below the surface. If you want to see disturbed mantle, take a trip to Hawaii, for instance, which is all lava.

still in the process of reaching equilibrium.[3] Our planet is geologically active because it's slowly cooling, releasing heat from the core by convection to the surface from where it's radiated away into space. This internal heat energy comes from two sources: that which is left over from Earth's formation, and that which is constantly generated by radioactive decay deep beneath our feet.

Today, it's no surprise that heavy elements such as radium and thorium generate heat as they decay into lighter elements, but 100 years ago all elements were thought to be unchangeable. Lacking the knowledge we now have, physicists and geologists locked horns in one of the longest and most bitter scientific debates ever fought. Taking the stand for the physicists was Britain's "grand old man" of science, Lord Kelvin. He was convinced, based on its present surface temperature and estimated rate of cooling, that Earth could not be more than about 25 million years old.[4] Geologists, meanwhile, looking at mile upon mile of deposition in such places as the Grand Canyon, knew it *had* to be older, even if they couldn't explain away Kelvin's calculations. The problem was resolved in 1903 when Pierre Curie announced that radium salts emit heat constantly, in a phenomenon he called radioactivity.[5] Here was the "missing" source of heat that keeps the Earth's surface much warmer than would otherwise be the case in its absence: the radioactive decay deep within the core of such heavy elements as radium and thorium.

The heat generated by this decay reaches the surface via the mantle, in a process analogous to water boiling in a pot on the stove. The water (mantle), heated by the element or flame (core) below, rises to the surface. As it flows out to the sides of the pot, it cools and begins to sink back down, where the cycle starts again. This roiling motion, in ultraslow motion, is what causes continental drift. Floating on the

---

3. More or less—Neptune's moon Triton, for example, has active nitrogen geysers. Earth is the only planet whose surface is constantly being rebuilt (although some doubt remains about Venus's vulcanism). Some solar system moons, notably Jupiter's Io, are geologically active.

4. For a popular account of Kelvin's arguments and geologists' reactions, see pages 128–138 of Stephen Jay Gould's *The Flamingo's Smile: Reflections in Natural History*. Note that Kelvin also used a model of our planet that was plausible in his time but is seen as erroneous today.

5. Antoine-Henri Becquerel discovered radioactivity in 1896. In this process, the nuclei of some atoms decay or disintegrate by spontaneous emission of particles called alpha, beta, and gamma rays. The phenomenon was further investigated by Pierre and Marie Curie. In 1903, the Curies and Becquerel were jointly awarded the 1903 Nobel Prize for physics. See also my *The Wrong-Way Comet and Other Mysteries of Our Solar System*.

mantle, comparatively thin "plates" of basalt, carrying the continents, move around the surface in response to the flowing mantle below.

New plates are constantly welling up from below in the middle of oceans, at the "mid-Atlantic ridge," for instance. Elsewhere, plates slide back down into the interior, usually at the edges of continents. The whole process, known as "plate tectonics," takes place at speeds of only

The San Andreas transform fault, looking south along Elkhorn Scarp. The Carrizo Plain on the right lies on the Pacific plate. It is moving north—toward the camera— about half an inch per year relative to the Elkhorn Plain (on the North American plate) on the left. Notice the offsets of the stream gulleys, signs of adjustment to the continuing slip. Over the last 29 million years, since the Pacific plate first started sliding past the North American plate, the total movement has been nearly 200 miles. (USGS, Wallace #116)

a few inches per year, so we're normally unaware of it except through indirect signs.[6]

The most obvious indication that the Earth's crust is in motion is the presence of earthquakes. Press your palms tightly together and move one hand up while moving the other down. Instead of moving smoothly apart, your palms will jerk apart in little jumps. That's a little how it is when two of the Earth's plates move past each other: tension builds up for a few years, then is suddenly released as the plates jerk by each other. We experience the jerk as an earthquake. So little do we know of the world beneath us that we can't predict with any accuracy where or when the next quake will occur.

About five miles west of where I'm sitting, the Pacific plate is moving jerkily northward relative to the North American plate along the San Andreas Fault. At 5:04 P.M. on October 17, 1989, decades of tension that had been building up between the plates was suddenly released. At the time, I was on the ground floor sitting in front of my computer. After a second or so of thinking, "Oh, just another tremor," I realized that this was a Big One and, forgetting advice about what one should do in such circumstances, ran outside. I remember standing in the back yard spellbound, grinning like a maniac, as trees swayed noisily and the whole world seemed to turn into plastic.

Later, knowledge of the death and destruction that happened in those few moments muted my excitement, of course. Yet, when I recently encountered philosopher William James's reaction to San Francisco's 1906 earthquake, I felt I'd met a kindred soul:

> *The emotion consisted wholly of glee and admiration; glee at the vividness which such an abstract idea or verbal term as "earthquake" could put on when translated into sensible reality and verified concretely; and admiration at the way in which the frail little wooden house could hold itself together in spite of such a shaking. I felt no trace whatever of fear; it was pure delight and welcome.*
>
> *"Go it," I almost cried aloud, "and go it stronger!"*[7]

---

6. As the floor of the Atlantic Ocean "spreads," Europe and Africa move away from North and South America at about two inches per year, the rate at which your fingernails grow. From at least the time of Francis Bacon in the early 1600s, scholars looked at maps and noted the uncanny similarity in the shapes of the shorelines of the Old and New Worlds.

7. Quoted in *The Magic Numbers of Dr. Matrix*, by Martin Gardner.

San Francisco's 1906 earthquake, courtesy of the San Andreas Fault, caused vast structural damage in the city. In seconds the plates shifted, on average, 13 feet past each other. (USGS, Brammer #118)

Most damage was caused by the subsequent fire after gas mains were broken. The photograph shows Nob Hill, San Francisco, from the corner of Van Ness and Washington. (USGS, W. C. Mendenhall #685)

A Brief History of Hell

Then I saw that there was a way to Hell, even from the gates of heaven.

                    —John Bunyan, *Pilgrim's Progress*

The invisibility and inaccessibility of the underground has led to wonderful and wild speculations, from ancient beliefs in a subterranean realm of the damned to "hollow Earth" theories that crop up from time to time.[8] (I'll pass over my first literary venture, at age 12, in which brilliant and dashing Sterling Blackstone burrowed his way deep into the Earth inside a cigar-shaped borer and found great caverns, lakes, and yes, good-natured monsters. If you remember an early "Star Trek" episode in which the mother monster called the Horta was only taking care of her eggs when she attacked the miners, you'll get the general gist.)

    Mythology has not dealt kindly with the direction of down. Starting with what is arguably the oldest legend known, the 5,000-year-old Babylonian epic of Gilgamesh, it's apparent that those who dwell in the underworld are not happy campers. In the epic, Gilgamesh's friend Enkidu has a terrifying dream (portending his own death) in which he is overpowered and taken down:

> *He seized me and led me down to the house of darkness, house of Irkalla,*
> *the house where one who goes in never comes out again,*
> *the road that, if one takes it, one never comes back,*
> *the house that, if one lives there, one never sees light,*
> *the place where they live on dust, their food is mud,*
> *their clothes are like birds' clothes, a garment of wings,*
> *and they see no light, living in blackness:*
> *on the floor and door-bolt, deeply settled dust.[9]*

    Hades, the predecessor of the Christian Hell, was originally the name given to the god who ruled the "infernal regions." That god later became Pluto, a tougher character, one suspects, than Disney's canine hero. Hades was a real place for the ancients, and Virgil even located its entrance near Mount Vesuvius, where "the whole country is cleft with

---

8. The original hollow Earth theory may have originated over 100 years ago with James Symmes of the United States Infantry. "In recent times it has even been suggested that there are great chasms at the Poles . . . and that you can get down through them into the interior of the earth," said Jules Verne's Doctor Clawbonny in *A Journey to the Centre of the Earth*, presumably referring to Symmes's ideas.
9. John Gardner and John Maier, *Gilgamesh*.

chasms, from which sulfurous flames arise, while the ground is shaken with pent-up vapors, and mysterious sounds issue from the bowels of the earth."[10]

Hades, unlike the Christian Hell into which it was to be transformed, was not so much a place of perpetual torment but rather one of boredom and frustration. Sisyphus, for instance, was condemned to eternally push a huge boulder to the top of a hill, watch it roll down, and immediately start again. Tantalus (from whom we get our word *tantalize*) was condemned to eternal thirst and hunger. Every time he bent down to drink water, it receded from his lips; every time he reached for fruit above him, it pulled away.

Where Hades had usually been cold and dark, Hell was hot and bright with flaming brimstone.[11] As portrayed in Christianity, Islam, Judaism, and Zoroastrianism, it's the final dwelling place of the dead after they've been condemned at the Last Judgment. The traditional Christian notion of Hell stems from Judaism, in which Jerusalem's real city dump, Ge (Valley of) Hinnom (once a site where children were burned as sacrifices to the god Moloch), was transformed into the fiery but mythical Gehenna.[12] From there it was but a short step to the blazing domain of Satan and his evil angels, portrayed glowingly by such artists as Hieronymus Bosch, William Blake, and Gustave Doré. Not too incidentally, 60 percent of Americans still believe in a literal hell according to a poll taken in 1990.[13]

Jules Verne thrilled his readers in 1864 with the publication of *A Journey to the Centre of the Earth*, in which his protagonists, while not getting all the way to the actual center, did have some wild adventures underground between Iceland's "Mount Sneffels" and Italy's still-active volcano, Mount Etna.[14] And the romance of the underground lives on. Not long ago, at least one inventive author discovered from where UFOs were coming: not from distant stars, he said, but from right under our feet—that's right, from inside the hollow Earth. They go home via a hole at the North Pole.

Which answers that problem.

10. Thomas Bulfinch, *Bulfinch's Mythology*, reprinted 1977.
11. For its location, at least according to Dante, see page 108.
12. Christ uses both "Gehenna" and "Hades" in early Greek Gospel texts.
13. Jeffery L. Sheler, "Hell's Sober Comeback," *U.S. News and World Report*, March 25, 1991, page 56.
14. Verne may have deliberately had them following in the footsteps of King Arthur. Early in the 1200s, Gervaise of Tilbury recounts the tale of an Italian bishop's groom who, searching for a lost horse on the slopes of Etna, stumbled across Arthur resting there in an earthly paradise.

Twenty

The Subtle Thief of Youth

How soon hath Time, the subtle thief of youth
Stol'n on its wing my three and twentieth year.

—John Milton, "Sonnet,"
on his 23rd birthday

In modern industrialized society the pace of our lives is determined
largely by economic considerations rather than by the rhythms of
human life or natural growing things. . . . The average human being
today seems to move from task to task with almost no time.

—Patricia Carrington

One crowded hour of glorious life
Is worth an age without a name.

—Sir Walter Scott

Time seems to stand quite still,
In a child's world it always will.

—The Moody Blues,
"Days of Future Passed"

I am an old man and have known a great many troubles,
but most of them never happened.

—Mark Twain

*I*t's been observed that all creatures on Earth live in the same moment but at different times. What time do you live in? Is it going by faster than it used to? In his book "The Innocent Assassins," the late Finnish paleontologist Björn Kurtén reflected on our changing perception of time from infancy to old age. The phenomenon, he said, is "what every human knows: in childhood the years are long; the older you get, the shorter they become. To a child, one day is an eternity; to the aged, the days pass all too quickly." A child can accomplish a new skill, such as speaking a foreign language or playing a musical instrument, in a short time compared with the painful aeons that most of us need as adults. A child's body, particularly when very young, heals much faster from wounds and fractures than does yours or mine. And a youngster's metabolism, as measured by rates of breathing and heartbeat, fairly races along. When we were in the womb, our fetal heart rate was a zippy 140, compared to our leisurely adult 60 beats per minute. Kurtén concluded that we spend one-half of our subjective lifetimes as children.

Here's the same point of view, in verse, from Guy Pentreath:

> *For when I was a babe and wept and slept, Time crept;*
> *When I was a boy and laughed and talked, Time walked;*
> *Then when the years saw me a man, Time ran,*
> *But as I older grew, Time flew.*[15]

"Tho' Much Is Taken . . ."

Well, yes and no. When you're five, a year represents 20 percent of your life. When you're 50, a year is 2 percent. But doesn't it work the other way, too? Why not consider time left rather than time passed? If you're 80 and you anticipate you've got five years left, one year is 20 percent of your remaining time on Earth! "Tho' much is taken, much abides," said Tennyson's aged Ulysses.[16] "Much" here doesn't mean much time, of course, but much potential greatness: "Some work of noble note may yet be done / Not unbecoming men that strove with Gods."

Yeah! Doesn't old age render each day more important and

---

15. Noted in *The Nature of Time*, G. J. Whitrow, page 39.
16. In his inspiring poem "Ulysses," which I plan to pin on my bathroom wall the day I decide my status has changed from young to old (I'm choosing to skip middle age).

significant, and therefore longer to us than when we were young? I know the older I get, the more invested I am in making each day feel like it counts for something.[17]

Does that mean today well-lived seems longer than a day when I was 20, say? I confess, I'm not sure, mainly because I forget how long it used to feel to me! How about you? Perhaps our perception of time has more to do with what we're actually doing at any particular period. In *The Magic Mountain*, Thomas Mann notes that time passes very fast when we're totally immersed in what we're doing, yet when we look back, the same period of "high-interest, full-content" activity appears to have been drawn out into a long span of time. I'm reminded of Alan Alda standing up in the punt, surrounded by his friends, in *The Four Seasons*. "I want us all to remember this day," he says, and promptly jumps fully clothed, champagne glass raised in a toast, into the pond.

Animal Time

Although small animals generally live shorter lives than large ones, they live life in the fast lane. From a human point of view, we can fantasize that nature has compensated them for their short lives with longer subjective times. To a mouse or a gnat, we must appear to be lumbering sleepwalkers.[18] Everyone has probably tried to catch a fly in flight: it's pretty tough, since the average human has a reaction time of a tenth of a second, while that of a fly is one-hundredth of a second. That's like pitting a Boeing 747 against an F16. Put it another way: our eyes process about 10 images per second at night (50 in daylight), so that a sequence of pictures projected in a darkened room at 24 frames per second appears to us as an unbroken sequence, that is, a movie. A bee, processing 300 images per second, would experience that movie as a series of still images.

Or consider the mayfly, whose "short, shimmering life" is reflected

17. How's this for a heroic deed in old age? On December 22, 1991, on his 80th birthday, renowned photographer Brett Weston followed through on a promise he had made to himself years previously and burned all his negatives. This was the only way he could satisfy himself that prints over which he didn't have full control could not be made. He died 13 months later.

18. A point graphically illustrated in the book *On Size and Life* by Thomas A. McMahon and John Tyler Bonner (New York: Scientific American Library, 1983), in which Gustave Doré's engraving of Sleeping Beauty is accompanied by the caption ". . . enchanted sleep. This may well be the view we present to animals smaller than ourselves. To them, we appear to lead sleepy, almost paralyzed lives."

in the name for its order, Ephemeroptera, derived from Greek *ephemeros*, or day (hence our word *ephemeral*). Taking its cue from the full moon, the mayfly sheds the "subimago" skin of its final nymphal stage. It then rests at the water's edge before taking off and joining thousands of its buddies for the nuptial flight. In its few hours of life as an adult, the only thing it has on its mind is the regeneration of the species. Nothing else matters (which is fortunate since the adult mayfly has no mouth and cannot feed). The males soon find and mate with the females, who promptly drop their load of fertilized eggs to the water and then themselves fall to the surface, prey to waiting fish. The morning after a nuptial flight, the shoreline is thick with dead mayflies. Truckloads of them are sometimes hauled from streets in cities on the Great Lakes, and bridges become too slippery for cars to drive on. Yet if we were to put an anthropomorphic spin on it, we could say that the adult mayfly "experiences" as much of a lifetime as we do in our many decades as adults.

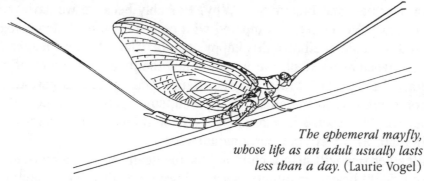

The ephemeral mayfly, whose life as an adult usually lasts less than a day. (Laurie Vogel)

One Billion Heartbeats

One way to measure life's passage with some objectivity is rate of heartbeat. Since the 1950s, it's been known that almost all mammals have a natural lifespan of between 600 and 1,200 million heartbeats, averaging out at nearly a billion. That's quite remarkable, considering the vast range of scales involved: an elephant weighs 25 million times as much as some shrews. The hearts of most species of shrew, with average lifespans of two years, canter along at 800 beats per minute, while an elephant, with its heart thumping at a steady 25 beats per minute, lives for 60-odd years.[19] Shrew or elephant, the heart of each creature beats about a billion times from birth to death.

---

19. The North American masked shrew's heart gallops along at an unbelievable 1,200 beats per minute!

Breathing is another measure of an animal's rate of living, or "metabolism" (from Greek *metabállein*, "to change"). Here again, the same kind of regularity applies: mammals all take about the same number of breaths in their lives, about one breath for every four heartbeats. In your case, for instance, your breath goes through 10–15 cycles while your heart beats about 60 times every minute.

Notice anything odd here? I said that almost all mammals live for about one billion heartbeats. If you were watching the numbers carefully, you'd have noticed that we're a fortunate exception to the rule, since the rule would put us in our graves by about age 30. Yet humans have had natural lifespans of 70-plus years for aeons. (Not too long ago, such factors as poor nutrition and saber-toothed tigers tipped the balance against such longevity, but there's no reason to believe that our ancient ancestors couldn't have lived that long. We know from skeletal remains that at least some did.)

In fact, we live nearly three times as long as we "should," given our rates of heartbeat and breathing.[20] Why? Probably because we have such long periods of adolescence compared with other creatures. Paleontologist Stephen Jay Gould attributes this happy state of affairs to our "neotenic" evolution, whereby as adults we have retained the juvenile features of our ancestors. We thus have much longer gestation and childhood periods than comparably sized mammals (or, indeed, any creature). Could members of other species reason, they might well envy our seeming eternal youth as we live out our long adolescences.

Whether this will help a child accept the death of its 12-year-old cat (whose 200 beats-per-minute heart endowed it with more "metabolic time" than a 60-year-old elephant), I don't know. I do know that each day lived is a day less, and I'd better get on with it if I'm going to meet my publisher's deadline!

Vladimir: *That passed the time.*
Estragon: *It would have passed in any case.*
Vladimir: *Yes, but not so rapidly.*

—Samuel Beckett, *Waiting for Godot*

---

20. The same applies to our mass. It's been shown that the rate of breathing and heartbeat in other mammals increases nearly 0.3 times as fast as body weight. Again, we're the exception.

Twenty-One

The Seven Wonders of the World

And on the pedestal these words appear
'My name is Ozymandias, king of kings:
Look on my works, ye Mighty, and despair!'
Nothing beside remains.

—Percy Bysshe Shelley,
"Ozymandias"[21]

*U*p until now, this book has focused mainly on wonders of nature. There's a group of man-made objects, however, that comes to mind whenever the word *wonder* is mentioned: "the seven wonders of the ancient world." What were they? And what was so wonderful about them?

Around 130 B.C., Antipater, a Greek poet, wrote a poem celebrating seven wonderful sights of his world: "I have gazed on the walls of impregnable Babylon, along which chariots may race, and on the Zeus by the banks of the Alphaeus. I have seen the Hanging Gardens and the Colossus of Helios, the great man-made mountains of the lofty pyramids, and the gigantic tomb of Mausolus. But when I saw the sacred house of Artemis that towers to the clouds, the others were placed in the shade, for the sun himself has never looked upon its equal outside Olympus."

His compilation is close enough to our "official" list that we can

---

21. Inspired by a fallen colossus of Ramses II near Luxor, Egypt.

safely date the seven wonders of the ancient world at least back to Antipater.[22] Later the walls of Babylon were dropped from the list in favor of the lighthouse at Alexandria. The final list includes three tombs, a palace, two statues, and a lighthouse. Only one of these survives— ironically, the first to be built. The wonders were, in order of creation and with approximate dates of construction:

- ◆ The Pyramid of Cheops at Giza, 2600 B.C.
- ◆ The Hanging Gardens of Babylon, 605–562 B.C.
- ◆ The Statue of Zeus at Olympia, 470–462 B.C.
- ◆ The Temple of Artemis at Ephesus, 360 B.C.
- ◆ The Mausoleum at Halicarnassus, 353 B.C.
- ◆ The Statue of Helios at Rhodes, 292–280 B.C.
- ◆ The Pharos (lighthouse) of Alexandria, 247 B.C.[23]

Antipater was from Sidon on the Lebanese coast. Today it's known as Saida, located at the westerly end of the Trans-Arabian oil pipeline. As you can see from the map, it's about at the center of the seven sites. The wonder farthest west is at Olympia (the Statue of Zeus) and the farthest east in Babylon (the Hanging Gardens): they're about 1,400 miles apart. The seven locations pretty well delineate that part of the known world then considered important by the Greeks.

Why seven? Why not four or five, or many more? After all, there are four points to the compass, and we have five fingers on each hand. As we've already seen in Chapter 8, "For the Week-Hearted," seven appears to have been a special, if not mystical, number since time immemorial. Consider, for instance, how often seven appears in classical literature and theological teachings:

- ◆ The Bible contains over 400 references to the number seven, starting with the seven days of creation.
- ◆ A menorah (Jewish ceremonial candle holder) has seven branches.[24]

---

22. An engineer, Philo of Byzantium (present day Istanbul), who lived about 100 years earlier than Antipater, is sometimes credited with the "original" list, entitled "the seven sights of the world." It's now thought the work in which this appears wasn't written until several centuries later, and was falsely attributed to Philo.
23. The Pharos was probably added to the list by Bishop (of Tours) Gregory around A.D. 580.
24. These days, it's usual to see nine-branched menorahs. The original seven-branched menorah was carefully specified in Exodus 37, "three branches of the candlestick out of the one side thereof, and three branches of the candlestick out of the other side thereof."

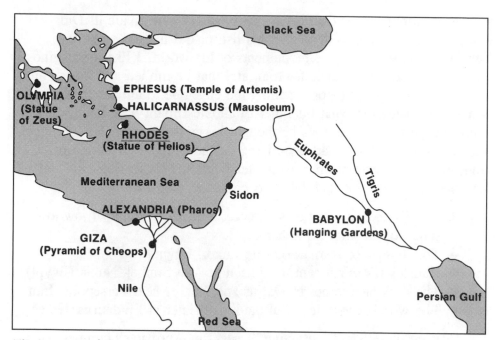

The locations of the "seven wonders of the ancient world."

♦ In both the Jewish (Kabbalah) and Muslim teachings, God dwells in the farthest of the spheres, the "seventh heaven."

♦ "The seven sisters," daughters of Atlas, are immortalized in the Pleiades star cluster.

♦ "The seven against Thebes" were seven heroes who made war on the king of Thebes, according to Aeschylus's play of that name.

♦ "The seven sleepers of Ephesus" were legendary martyrs immured in a cave near Ephesus. Upon awakening 200 years later, they convinced the emperor Theodosius II to embrace Christianity.

♦ In oriental tradition, there are "seven gods of luck" (not to mention *The Seven Samurai*, a movie remade in the U.S. as *The Magnificent Seven*).

♦ Rome was founded on seven hills.

♦ We have seven of each: virtues, sages, purple passions, deadly sins, pillars of wisdom, and bodily orifices (I have, anyway).

♦ Of the 11 possible sums from a pair of rolled dice, seven is more likely than any other number to be the sum of the spots. Ask anyone who's played Monopoly or craps.[25]

---

25. Of 36 possible combinations, six (1-6, 2-5, 3-4, 4-3, 5-2, and 6-1) give a sum of seven.

Any number other than seven just wouldn't have made it! Did Antipater find it easy to decide on his list, or did he find seven too limiting to do justice to the monuments of his world? I like to imagine that it wasn't an easy choice for him, and that he mulled and mused and fretted for a few years before opening the envelope to announce the winners. Considering what his other candidates might have been, we can appreciate just how wondrous he thought his winners were. For instance, the Colossus of Rhodes had been lying on the beach, half-buried by sand, for over a century when Antipater made his choices, yet it—and the other six—beat out such fabulous contenders as:

- The Parthenon of Athens, Greece, with its legendary (now lost) statue of the goddess Athena
- The Temple of Karnak outside Luxor, Egypt
- Ramses II's monument to himself at Abu Simbel, Nubia (Egypt)
- The rock-face tombs of Darius and Xerxes near Persepolis, Iran
- The world's most beautiful outdoor theater at Epidaurus, Greece

Visiting these largely surviving "losers" in Antipater's competition for the seven wonders, I'm saddened. Apparently, even greater beauty and grandeur than what has survived has been lost in the Mausoleum at Halicarnassus and the Colossus of Rhodes, for instance. Other than Cheops's pyramid, which is largely intact today, few (or no) fragments of the others remain. Here's a summary of what we know about the other six. I discuss the Pyramid of Cheops, which is in a league of its own, in the sidebar to this chapter.

Hanging Gardens of Babylon, c. 600 B.C.

"Babylon shall become ruins, a haunt of wolves. Her cities shall become waste places, a land dried up and desert," prophesied Jeremiah. Preaching in the decades immediately before Jerusalem's capture by Babylon (586 B.C.), he viewed the latter as sinful but luxurious: "Oh opulent city standing beside the waters." The waters he refers to are but a side channel of one of the world's great rivers, the Euphrates. And the psalmist's refrain, "By the waters of Babylon, there we sat down, yea, we wept when we remembered Zion," serves as a reminder that there are many today who suffer the agony of not being able to live in their homeland.

The king largely responsible for Babylon's opulence, Nebuchadnezzar (c. 605–562 B.C.) was a little younger than Jeremiah. He probably

Little remains at the supposed site of the Hanging Gardens of Babylon, save a few million crumbling bricks. (Barry Evans)

ordered the Hanging Gardens to be built, too, although so little is known about them that it's impossible to be sure.[26] The gardens were hanging, that is, they were terraced, in the same way geologists refer to a "hanging valley." The popular story is that Nebuchadnezzar married Amytis, daughter of the king of the Median empire, Cyaxares, in a politically motivated match. He brought her back to Babylon as one of his wives, but she pined for the green grass and valley of her homeland, so her husband ordered his builders to create a huge terraced garden, full of lush vegetation, to lift her spirits. It's a good legend, but, since our source[27] lived 400 years later, it's fair to ask, "Does it fly?"

When excavations started at Babylon a century ago, the tale of the Hanging Gardens seemed to be just that, a tale—until German archaeologist Robert Koldewey found a building near the remains of Nebuchadnezzar's palace that seemed to fit the bill. On each side of a long central corridor, Koldewey found seven vaulted chambers with

26. Another version of the story is that the gardens were built 200 years earlier for the semimythical Assyrian queen Sammu-ramat (Semiramus).
27. Berossus, a Babylonian priest. He refers to gardens laid out on a brick terrace 75 feet (in our units) above ground.

foundations made of stone, a rarity in clay-brick Babylon. Why would
the builders have imported costly stone for foundation material?
Presumably, reasoned Koldewey, because the building was multistoried.
In the western walls, he found a well. "It has three shafts placed close to
each other, a square one in the center, and oblong ones on each side, an
arrangement for which I can see no other explanation than that a
mechanical hydraulic machine stood here, which worked on the same
principle as our chain pump. . . . This contrivance would provide a
continuous flow of water."[28]

We can only imagine gangs of captive slaves working day and night
to turn screws that lifted water from the muddy Euphrates to the fragrant
gardens above. What little remains of Babylon—enough bricks to reach
the moon if placed end to end, a moat where once stood the ziggurat
that inspired the story of the Tower of Babel, and a few gorgeously glazed
tiles—may seem hardly enough to warrant the dusty 50-mile drive from
Baghdad. Yet the ghosts remain.

Try to see it by moonlight.

Statue of Zeus at Olympia, c. 470 B.C.

You can walk around what, at least according to some archaeologists, are
the remains of the Hanging Gardens. No such luck with this wonder.
Decades of excavation, starting in 1876 with German archaeologist Ernst
Curtius, have revealed nothing to suggest a large statue. It wasn't until
1955 that the first meager evidence appeared: a few terra-cotta molds
that were probably used in its manufacture and, best of all, a black cup
(you can see it today in the Olympia Museum) inscribed *I belong to
Pheidias.*

That may not sound like much, but it confirmed what had been
long suspected, that Pheidias, c. 500–432 B.C., one of the greatest
sculptors of ancient Greece, and perhaps of all time, created the statue of
Zeus. He was definitely responsible for another famous, and now lost,
sculpture. His Athena in the Parthenon, commissioned by Pericles, was
the main reason to visit Athens in those days.

After leaving (or, according to some sources, getting kicked out of)
Athens, he is thought to have moved to the sacred city of Olympia, inside
whose walls the Olympiads had been held every four years since 776
B.C.[29] There, according to Pausanius, a Greek writer of the second

---

28. Robert Koldewey, *The Excavations at Babylon.*
29. The date is year 1 in the ancient Greek calendar.

century A.D., Pheidias created a statue, "tall as a three story house . . . on his head lies a wreath of olive sprigs, in his right hand he holds a figure of victory, in his left a scepter upon which an eagle is perched. His flesh is of ivory [on a wooden frame], and his robe and sandals are of gold. His gold throne is studded with precious jewels, ebony and ivory. . . ." We're not sure what happened to it. One story is that it was destroyed by fire in its original site, another that it was first moved to a palace in Constantinople (now Istanbul) where it was destroyed by fire in A.D. 462.

It's logical that the king of the gods, Zeus (Roman Jupiter), would be honored with a statue at Olympia since, after Mount Olympus, the city was considered to be his second home. Again, we can only guess at the size and beauty of the work, aided in our imagination by the exhortation given to his disciples by the Stoic philosopher Epictetus: "Go see it, for it would be a misfortune to have died without doing so!"

Temple of Artemis at Ephesus, c. 360 B.C.

The temple of the great goddess Diana should be despised, and her magnificence should be destroyed, whom all Asia and the world worshippeth.

—Acts 19:27

Who was this goddess who so upset Paul? Zeus's daughter Artemis, identified by the Romans with Diana, has suffered several transformations in mythology. Originally an earth goddess, she's probably best known today as the virgin huntress, although she later became associated with the moon under the name Selene.[30] She was certainly a major force to the Ephesians, citizens of one of the major cities of the ancient world. The first temple dedicated to her at Ephesus was built by the Lydian king Croesus about 550 B.C. It seems her temples were fated to burn down. The one referred to by Antipater, completed in about 323 B.C., was probably the fifth to be built on the same site. The previous temple was apparently set on fire in 356 B.C. by one Herostratus, who wanted to be sure his name was immortalized. Legend says Alexander the Great was born the night of the fire.

---

30. Hence our word *selenography*, the science of mapping the moon; and the element selenium.

What was the "new" temple like? For one thing, it was huge: about 400 feet by 250 feet by 60 feet high. Possibly as many as 127 (or as few as 36, depending on whom you believe) painted columns held the roof up. It was also magnificent, and remained so long after it was built. Over 300 years after it was built, Philon of Alexandria (c. 30 B.C.–A.D. 45) echoed Antipater, writing: "He who has laid eyes on it once will be convinced that the world of the immortal gods has moved from the heaven to earth."

The importance of Ephesus peaked after Diocletian split the Roman Empire up into western and eastern portions in A.D. 285, but it declined when the river, on which the city depended for trade and access to the outside world, silted up. You can still walk down the road that once led to the bustling harbor, only to be stopped by water lapping at flagstones that were once far above water level. Today, only marshes lie beyond. The temple, which may have already been in bad shape, was probably destroyed by raiding Goths in A.D. 262.

Fifteen centuries later, British archaeologist John T. Wood began digging at Ephesus and found the remains of two huge amphitheaters, dozens of buildings, and miles of streets. His goal, however, was to find the legendary temple. On New Year's Day in 1870, after seven years of effort, his search ended. He wrote in his diary, "The excitement caused by this discovery and the hard work to which I was then subjected were too much for my health. By a note in my journal on the 3rd of January, I find that I had been working that day from 9 A.M. to 10:45 P.M., and that I had suffered from fever every night for three weeks. I did not, however, give in, but continued my work without relaxation."[31]

Coin minted at Ephesus circa A.D. 237 showing the facade of the temple of Artemis.
(Barry Evans)

Other than a single reconstructed column, the waterlogged site (outside the city walls and a 15-minute walk from downtown Ephesus) gives little indication of what Philon had enthused over. A few bits have ended up in the British Museum, where they share two rooms with

31. Edgar J. Banks, *The Seven Wonders of the Ancient World.*

Column drum recovered from the site of the Temple of Artemis, now in the British Museum. The center figure is Alcestis, wife of Admetus, king of Pherae, who so loved him that she was willing to die for him. She stands between the figures of Death and Hermes, guide of the Underworld (later Roman Mercury). (Copyright © British Museum, XIV D9)

fragments from the Mausoleum of Halicarnassus, and for these we should be grateful. But I wish photography had been invented 2,000 years ago.

Mausoleum at Halicarnassus, c. 353 B.C.

We derive two words in the English language, *mausoleum* and *colossal*, directly from the seven wonders. The first comes from Mausolus, governor of Caria, an autonomous state within the Persian empire, whose tomb was *the* Mausoleum. He lived from 377 to 353 B.C., and when he died his wife (and sister, in accordance with Carian dynastic tradition) Artemesia so missed him that she drank some of his ground-up ashes in wine. She topped that by commissioning the most beautiful memorial ever.

At least that's how one version of the story goes. Or did Mausolus himself commission the tomb in his own lifetime? We're not sure. According to Pliny (who referred to Mausolus as "a petty king of Caria"), the tomb structure was unfinished when Artemesia died in 351, but the sculptors remained, "considering that it was at once a memorial of their own fame and of the sculptor's art; and to this day, it is undecided which of them has excelled."

Pliny (A.D. 23–79) also tells us that four master sculptors were brought over from Athens for the job, each of whom was responsible for a side. Most archaeologists now believe that the tomb was probably started much earlier than Mausolus's death, perhaps in A.D. 367, and that the whole project took about 70 man-years. It was an astonishing 140 feet high, with a massive rectangular base surmounted by 36 columns and a pyramidical roof, and it lasted a long time. In the twelfth century A.D., a traveler named Eustathius wrote, "It was and is a wonder." The structure probably fell soon afterward during an earthquake. All you can see on the site today is a rectangular cutting in the rock with a tomb chamber below. What happened to the remains?

When the Knights of Saint John came to Halicarnassus,[32] now Bodrum, in 1402, they used steps of white marble, which they had found in the middle of a field, in the building of their Castle of Saint Peter. Much later, in 1852, a member of the staff of the British Museum arrived

"I was a handsome man. . . ."
Figure recovered from the site of the Mausoleum of Halicarnassus, now in the British Museum. It's generally believed to be that of Mausolus himself.
(Copyright © British Museum, B 5060)

---

32. Birthplace, incidentally, of the "Father of History," Herodotus, in 484 B.C.

Part of a frieze of 17 slabs spanning 85 feet in the British Museum. The frieze depicts a combat between Greeks and Amazons. Some participants are naked, some clothed; some young, some old; some on horseback, others on foot. In all, it's an animated, energetic struggle in which we can, perhaps, glimpse something of the psyches of the sculptors, who lived over 2,300 years ago. (Barry Evans)

Detail from the frieze. (Barry Evans)

at the Bodrum castle and was astonished to find six white marble lions
built into the walls. It seems the tattered remnants of one of the world's
seven wonders had been looted as quarry stone for a fortification. Some
were salvaged, fortunately, and today you can visit the British Museum in
London and see the capital of a column, a lion, a huge horse, and part of
an evocative (and, for me, deeply moving) frieze showing Greeks in
frenzied battle against Amazon warriors. Two larger-than-life statues of a
man and a woman were recovered and now stand side by side in the
Museum. He is almost certainly Mausolus, and she may be Artemesia.
(But probably isn't. They make an impressive couple, just the same.) His
rendering is terrific, with long hair and a tough, forceful gaze. If you get
to see it, note the Greek himation, which he wears on top of a tunic. In
a touch of realism, the marble carving shows storage creases below the
left knee! Let Mausolus himself have the last word: "I was a handsome
man, and formidable in war."[33]

Statue of Helios at Rhodes, c. 280 B.C.

Why, man, he doth bestride the narrow world
Like a Colossus; and we petty men
Walk under his huge legs, and peep about
To find ourselves dishonourable graves.
>   —Cassius, speaking of Julius Caesar
>   in Shakespeare's play of that name

Did the Colossus really "bestride" anything? Legends of the Middle Ages
said that the statue, one of the largest ever built then or now, had one
foot on each side of the entrance to the Rhodes harbor, in the
Mediterranean. It's a good, but utterly unbelievable, tale. (Much more
likely, it was situated a little way inland, on the site of an old Turkish
school.) We know less about the Colossus of Rhodes than we do about
the other six wonders.

The island of Rhodes was unsuccessfully besieged by the
Macedonian king Demetrius Poliocetes in 305 B.C. To commemorate the
raising of the siege a year later, the triumphant Rhodians decided to erect
a huge statue of Helios, the sun god. It took 12 years to complete and

---

33. From Lucian's *Dialogues*.

Traditionally, the Statue of Helios bestrode the entrance to Rhodes harbor right here, between the two (modern) pillars surmounted by deer. This would have been quite impossible: cast bronze (then or now) won't span the 1,300-foot width. In fact, the huge statue probably stood a little way inland, on the site of an old Turkish school. (Gaynor Barber)

was about 110 feet high and 60 feet around the chest. It was made of hollow bronze, and one arm was raised, perhaps to shield the eyes from the sun (according to a surviving relief). Sadly, it was toppled by an earthquake in about 225 B.C. and probably lay disintegrating on the ground until about A.D. 660, when it was sold for scrap to a Jew, who is said to have needed 900 camels to take it all away.

Pliny tells us,

> *Most worthy of admiration is the colossal statue of the sun which stood formerly at Rhodes, and was the work of Chares the Lindian, no less than seventy cubits in height. The statue, 56 years after it was erected, was thrown down by an earthquake, yet even as it is, it excites our wonder and imagination. Few men can clasp the thumb with their arms, and the fingers are larger than most statues. Where the limbs are broken asunder, vast caverns are seen yawning in the interior. Within, too, are to be seen large masses of rocks, by the aid of which the artist steadied while erecting it.*

I wonder whether Philon was exaggerating when he wrote of it, "The artist expended as much bronze on it as seemed likely to create a dearth at the foundries; for the casting of this statue was the world's [triumph] in metal working."[34]

Pharos of Alexandria, c. 250 B.C.

The Pharos, which probably wasn't on Antipater's "seven wonders" list, is the only one that had a function, that is, to help navigators in the Mediterranean make it home safely to the port of Alexandria.[35]

Alexandria, which was founded by Alexander the Great on the site of an old fishing village, is today one of the largest cities on the Mediterranean. The lighthouse was built on a limestone outcrop called Pharos that used to be separated by the sea from the mainland. Today, you can walk along a road to the old fort built on the site of the Pharos lighthouse. Pay your dollar (or whatever it is these days) to go inside and inspect what appears to be a reasonable model of the old lighthouse. It has a square base, with an octagonal section near the top, and a cylindrical top. Take a look at the walls of the fort, too—they were probably built from the remains of the lighthouse.

The architect of the Pharos was Sostratus of Cnidus, and it was built for Ptolemy II, the son of Ptolemy I, Soter, one of Alexander's generals, who ruled Egypt after his leader's death in 323 B.C. According to sketchy reports, a wide ramp, with a gentle-enough grade for horse-drawn wagons, spiraled up the outside of the lighthouse almost to the top. There, perhaps 500 feet above the sea, the light from fires was reflected in polished brass plates so it could be seen far out to sea at night. The whole edifice may have been topped by a statue of Alexander or Ptolemy I. It was the highest man-made structure of ancient times, as high as a 40-story skyscraper.

According to his *Commentaries*, Julius Caesar used the lighthouse as a fortress while awaiting reinforcements before conquering the city of Alexandria. In all, the structure lasted for nearly 900 years, although it only functioned as a lighthouse until the Arab conquest of A.D. 641. After that, it was probably damaged in a series of earthquakes, and

---

34. Quotations from *The Colossus of Rhodes* by H. Maryon, translated by R. J. H. Jenkinds, in the *Journal of Hellenic Studies*, Volume LXXVI.

35. Despite rather wooly claims that the Pyramid of Cheops was really an astronomical observatory (or even a spacecraft landing beacon).

finally fell in the fourteenth century. In 1477, Memluk Sultan Quait-Bay built his fort, at least partly, out of limestone blocks from the toppled lighthouse. Little else remains except an odd linguistic legacy: *faro*, *phare*, and *pharos* are respectively the Spanish, French, and Greek words for lighthouse.

——————————— Cheops Pyramid, c. 2600 B.C. ———————————

*F*rom my journal, November 16th, 1981:

> *Last day of my trip. I got up at 5 and took the first bus out to Giza for my planned ascent of Cheops' Pyramid, since I'd heard it was illegal to climb the pyramid after an American woman had fallen to her death two years earlier. Not early enough. It was light when I started, and I'd made it to about one-quarter of the way up when a car stopped below me and a guy in a uniform yelled in English to get on down. Said he was the local Chief of Police. I believed him. So I climbed down (Trickier than getting up: the easiest way is up the edge, where two faces join, but you have to step up about three feet at a time, and the old blocks are crumbling, so everything is very loose and scary. I can easily see how, if you slip, you wouldn't stop falling until you got to the bottom.). At another corner of the pyramid, a guy invited me into a tent. "You want to climb the pyramid?" he asked. "I tried, but someone stopped me. He said he was the Chief of Police," I said. "No problem, you give me $5 and it'll be OK." "What about that guy?" "It's OK. He's my uncle."*
>
> *I shot up to the top in six minutes flat, must have been a world record. I didn't want to be stopped again; in fact once I'd got halfway up, I decided I'd carry on, no matter what. And yes and yes and yes. At the top, a flat area a few feet across (the topmost stone had been removed, I suppose it was polished marble, too good to leave there!). Cheops, the wind and me. . . .*

Of the 94 pyramids in Egypt, not to mention hundreds more in South and Central America, Cyprus, the Sudan, Thailand, and Burma, there's only one *Great* Pyramid. That's simply because the pyramid of

Khufu (Greek Cheops) is the biggest. At six-and-a-half-million tons, Cheops is simply the single greatest building ever erected by humankind. Volumes, literally, have been written about it, so I'll just pick a couple of items from my "pyramid lore" file.

◆ How long did the tomb take to build? The pyramid consists of about 2,300,000 blocks, not counting the original polished-marble outer sheath, long since used for buildings in nearby Cairo. According to Roman historian Herodotus (who was farther removed in time from Cheops's builders than we are from him), it took 20 years to build, using 100,000 men who worked on the pyramid during the Nile's annual flood. More recent estimates, based on the length of Khufu's reign, put the time of building at no more than 23 years. Is that feasible? Suppose they all worked 14 hours a day 100 days a year, for a total of about 3 billion man-hours. That gave them 1,400 man-hours per block to quarry and rough-cut it, skid it (no wheels[36]) up to the working area, cut it to

The Great Pyramid of Cheops (or Khufu), built c. 2600 B.C., and two modes of transport from different periods. (Peter Hamilton)

---

36. We have many Egyptian frescoes showing blocks being skidded. It's also been proposed that four pieces of stone, round on one side, flat on the other, were tied around each end of a block. The flat sides pressed against the block, which could then be rolled.

To get some sense of scale, compare the figures at the base of the Great Pyramid with its height. (Peter Hamilton)

precise size (with copper tools, no diamond saws), skid it up and around the spiral construction ramp that they had presumably built around the pyramid (no block and tackle), and lever it into place. Each finished "it" in the preceding sentence weighs about the same as a Honda Civic. Fourteen hundred man-hours per item? Just for quarrying it in the first place, without modern tools, that sounds tight. A typical worker today puts in about 1,800 hours per year. What do you think? Could *you* manage one block in a year?

Looking at it from another way, using the above assumptions, one block would have to be placed every 50 seconds. I tend to think they were using more men than Herodotus reported. If you don't believe me, try walking around it, and perhaps climbing it. Nothing else really gives a sense of its overwhelming size.

◆ Second, did they slope the faces of it with a particular ratio in mind? Herodotus suggested that the area of a face equals the height squared. If that was deliberate, then another "magic" number, sometimes referred to as "phi," or the golden number, might have been in the architect's mind. The number crops up in geometry (pentagons), nature

*A few of the two-million plus
limestone blocks from which the
pyramid is built.*
(Peter Hamilton)

(the Fibonacci series), architecture (the Parthenon), and art (aspect ratios of many classical paintings).[37] A "phi pyramid" would have a slope of 51 degrees, 49 minutes, and 38 seconds.

However, it's also suggested that Cheops is a "pi" pyramid, that is, that the ratio of the base area to its height is equal to pi, giving a side slope of 51 degrees, 51 minutes, and 14 seconds. Yet another possibility is simpler yet: maybe they just sloped the faces using the ratio of 11 horizontally to 14 vertically. That would give a side slope of 51 degrees, 51 minutes, and 34 seconds.

Do you see the problem? The angles are so nearly identical, it's impossible to test which one is correct. Even if the missing marble sheathing was in place, you still couldn't measure a difference of one minute with any confidence. So we can speculate that the architect,

37. Phi (ϕ) = 1.61803398 . . . Phi's extraordinary properties all derive from the fact that its reciprocal is this number without the initial "1," i.e., $\phi = 1 + \frac{1}{\phi}$. For more, read Chapter 8 of Martin Gardner's *More Mathematical Puzzles and Diversions* (London: Penguin Books, 1966).

Is the Great Pyramid built according to phi or pi? Herodotus suggested that the area of a face equals the square of the height, $x = h^2$. But in the shaded triangle, $x^2 = 1^2 + h^2$. From these two relationships, you can show that $x = \frac{(1 + \sqrt{5})}{2} = phi$. Then the cosine of angle A is the reciprocal of phi, and A = about 51 degrees, 50 minutes. On the other hand, suppose it's a pi pyramid, that is, the area of the base equals the square of its height. Then the height $= \frac{4}{\pi}$ and the cosine of angle A is $\frac{\pi}{4}$ and A is about 51 degrees, 51 minutes. All we can say with certainty is that the faces are sloped at approximately 52 degrees.

Imhotep, who was probably aware of all three ratios, designed the pyramid according to one. We'll never know for sure which one.

We can be certain, however, that that ugly unfinished pyramid surmounted by the divine eye in the "Great Seal" engraved on the reverse of your dollar bill bears no relationship to pi or phi. The slope, despite its masonic origins, is a rather impractical 70 degrees. Incidentally, notice the ubiquitous presence of the number 13 in the seal (for the 13 founding states): rows in the pyramid, stars, stripes, clouds, arrows, laurel leaves, berries, feathers in each wing and tail, and letters in the motto at the top. Speaking of which, what does *Annuit coeptis* mean? And what's its origin? (See Puzzle Answers at the back of the book.)

The Great Seal. You can find the masonic "unfinished pyramid" on the back of every dollar bill, with "1776" in Roman numerals at the base, and surmounted by the eye of God. Many of the Founding Fathers were masons.

A Letter from
Diane Ackerman

---

*Because I write at length about little-known animals in curious
landscapes, people often ask, for example, Do you prefer whales to
bats? I prefer life. Each of the animals I write about I find
beguiling in and of itself; but in all honesty there is no animal that
isn't fascinating if viewed up close and in detail.*

—Diane Ackerman,
The Moon by Whale Light

*I*n response to my inquiry about her science writing, "What excites you
about science in your day-to-day work, and what roles do curiosity and
wonder play?" Ms. Ackerman wrote:

*People sometimes ask me about all of the Science in my work,
thinking it odd that I should wish to combine Science and Art, and
assuming that I must have some inner pledge or outer maxim I follow. But
the hardest job for me is trying to keep Science out of my writing. We live
in a world where amino acids, viruses, airfoils, and such are common
ingredients in our daily sense of Nature. Not to write about Nature in its
widest sense, because quasars or corpuscles are not "the proper realm of*

Diane Ackerman (James McGoon)

poetry," as a critic once said to me, is not only irresponsible and philistine, it bankrupts the experience of living, it ignores much of life's fascination and variety. I'm a great fan of the Universe, which I take literally: as one. All of it interests me, and it interests me in detail.

Writing is my form of celebration and prayer, but it is also the way in which I enquire about the world. I seem to be driven by an intense, nomadic curiosity; my feeling of ignorance is often overwhelming. As a result, prompted by unconscious obbligatos, I frequently find myself in a state of complete rapture about a discipline or field, and rapidly coming down with a poem or a book. For as little as six months, perhaps, or as long as three years, I will be obsessed with aviation, or astronomy, bats, the senses, or the oceans, and eagerly learn everything I can about the field. Any raw facts I might acquire about the workings of Nature fuel my creative work and are secondary to my rage to learn about the human condition, which I don't think we can see whole from any one vantage point. If I hadn't spent a year as a soccer journalist many years ago, to get atmosphere for a novel set in the soccer world which I was writing, I would never have learned as much as I did about the history of play, and certainly would never have written the four soccer poems at the end of Lady Faustus, *which have nothing at all to do with soccer, but are really about the rhythm of the mind and what it means to know something.*

I try to give myself passionately, totally, to whatever I'm observing, with as much affectionate curiosity as I can muster, as a means to understanding a little better what being human is, and what it was like to have once been alive on the planet, how it felt in one's senses, passions and contemplations. I appear to have a lot of science in my work, I suppose, but I think of myself as a Nature writer, if what we mean by Nature is, as I've said, the full sum of Creation.

Sunday's Puzzles

Words

The question to ask is not whether you are a success or a failure, but whether you are a learner or a non-learner.

—Benjamin Barber

*A*re you a Sunday crossword or acrostic solver? Puzzles and a few plain curiosities follow, in the spirit of the last page of the magazine section of many Sunday papers.

Palindromes

Palindromes, words or sentences that read the same backward and forward, have intrigued people for centuries. Here are some well-known ones:

- ◆ A man, a plan, a canal, Panama! (Around the time of the U.S. invasion of Panama, when Presidents Bush and Noriega clashed, the following emerged: A man, a pain, a mania, Panama!)
- ◆ Yreka Bakery. (Yreka is a small town in northern California.)
- ◆ Never odd or even.
- ◆ Step on no pets.
- ◆ Now Sir, a war is won!
- ◆ Was it a can on a cat I saw?
- ◆ Sums are not set as a test on Erasmus.

Anagrams

Rearrange the letters of the word "cat" and you get "act." Anagrams
sometimes attempt to define the original word, for example, "William
Shakespeare" becomes both "We all make his praise" and "I ask me:
Has Will a peer?" (You might try to make a neat anagram out of your
name.)

See if you can find appropriate anagrams from:

- ◆ The Mona Lisa
- ◆ Punishment
- ◆ The nudist colony

Inversions

I first met Scott Kim in a Palo Alto copy shop just halfway between
where he works (in the computer science department of Stanford
University) and our house in Palo Alto. Scott is best known for his book
Inversions, which contains dozens of names and phrases that remain the
same when reflected or inverted. Here's his business card, unfolded.

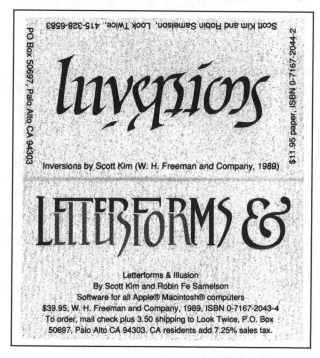

Notice, too, two words from the title of his book secreted into one.
I asked him if he could do anything with my name. "Spell it for

me," he said. I did. "Great! Five letters each. Easy." I watched bemused as, with barely a pause, he wrote the following on the back of his card. He must have taken all of 30 seconds between hearing my name and reproducing it.

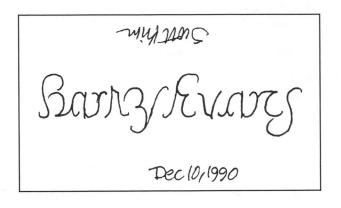

Exercise: Once again try doing the same with your name. No time limit!

Word Puzzles

The answers to the following puzzles are right here, in front of you.

◆ What everyday 10-letter word can be formed with letters found on the top row of a typewriter keyboard, "QWERTYUIOP"? (You can use each letter more than once or not at all.)

   Hint: Note I didn't say a word processor keyboard.

◆ Cross out six letters to make a common word:
   B S A I N X L E A T N T E A R S

   Hint: There's more than one way of interpreting "six letters."

◆ How about a common word with three pairs of double letters? "Keeper" (a word you can find in any book) has one pair, for instance.

   Hint: My "for instance" isn't exactly meaningless.

The Numbers Game

"7 D I A W" stands for "seven days in a week"; "4ever Y" means Forever Young. What do the following stand for? (When you're done, you can create some of your own.)

- ◆ 3 C I A F
- ◆ A 4 1, 1 4 A
- ◆ 10der I T N
- ◆ G 4th A M
- ◆ A T O 2 C
- ◆ 7 D S
- ◆ 8een12 O
- ◆ T 7th S
- ◆ T 19th H
- ◆ E 1ders

Puzzle answers are at the back of the book.

Sunday's Quotations
Potpourri

Human knowledge will be erased from the world's archives before we possess the last word that a gnat has to say to us.

—Jean Henri Fabre

The universe: a device contrived for the perpetual astonishment of astronomers.

—Arthur C. Clarke

The universe is not only queerer than we suppose but queerer than we can suppose.

—J. B. S. Haldane

The universe is simply one of those things that happen from time to time.

—Edward Tyron

The Earth from the frontiers of the solar system is a pale, blue dot. That's here. That's home. That's us. And on that dot everyone you love, everyone you know, everyone you ever heard about, every human being who ever was, lived out their lives. Every act of human

heroism or betrayal, the sum total of human joy and suffering,
thousands of confident religions, ideologies, and economic
doctrines, every hunter and forager, every creator and destroyer of
civilization, every king and peasant, mother and father, hopeful
child, every inventor and explorer, moral teacher and corrupt
politician, every saint and sinner in the history of our species lives
there, on a mote of dust suspended in a sunbeam.

—**Carl Sagan**

I have never heard of anyone stumbling on something sitting down.

—**Charles Kettering**

He who would, may reach the utmost height—but he must be
anxious to learn.

—**Buddha**

If you don't make mistakes, you aren't really trying.

—**Coleman Hawkins**

There is a distance incomparable between the things men imagine
by natural reason and those which illuminated men behold by
contemplation.

—**Thomas à Kempis**

All other creatures look down toward the earth, but man was given
a face so he might turn his eyes towards the stars and his gaze upon
the sky.

—**Ovid**

Pain will come, just like pleasure. Hate will come, just like love.
And when both are accepted, unaffected by the mind, then there will
be peace.

—**Baba Hari Das**

People don't notice whether it's winter or summer when they're happy.

—**Anton Chekhov**

So many of us fail: We divorce our wives and husbands, we leave the roofs of our lovers, go once again into the lonely march, mustering our courage with work, friends, half-pleasures which are not whole because they are not shared. Yet I still believe in love's possibility, in its presence on earth.

—**Andre Dubus**

We are born princes and the civilizing process makes us frogs.

—**Eric Bern**

Happiness is a state of mind where pleasure and pain caused by attachment do not exist.

—**Baba Hari Das**

The happiest person is the person who thinks the most interesting thoughts.

—**Timothy Dwight**

Ours is not a caravan of despair. Come, even if you have broken your vow a thousand times, come.

—**Jalal ed-Din Rumi**

. . . laughter is surely
The surest touch of genius in creation
Would you have ever thought of it . . .
If you had been making man?

—**Christopher Fry**

I needed a new land, a new race, a new language; and although I couldn't have put it into words then, I needed a new mystery.

—**John Fowles**

Endpiece

———

The Banquet Is Laid

Enough of science and of art;
Close up these barren leaves;
Come forth and bring with you a heart
That watches and receives.

—William Wordsworth,
"The Tables Turned"

*M*ost of the chapters in this book ask something of the reader: I ask you to notice. Behind the obvious meaning of the word, I believe there's a deeper significance that I'd like to explore in this final section.

Dewitt Jones is a talented photographer for *National Geographic*. In a speech he gave about a year ago, he used a wonderful phrase that's haunted me since. He told us about how he was standing at dawn by the side of a lonely road near Glacier Bay in Alaska, waiting impatiently for a helicopter that was scheduled to transport him to a mountain where he planned to take some nature photographs. The chopper was late, the morning was cold and overcast, and Dewitt's mood was dark. On the far side of a roadside fence, a quarter of a mile away across a meadow, stood an old farmhouse. As he looked vacantly at the scene, he was suddenly struck with the realization that in front of him was the most sublime landscape he'd ever seen in his life. In a few minutes he was able to capture, on film, the image that he nearly missed seeing. It made the magazine in an essay on John Muir in April 1973. Dewitt added that a teacher of his had said something to him that summed up his experience that morning: "The banquet is laid yet nobody comes."

Black and white doesn't do Dewitt Jones's photograph justice. You can see it in color in the April 1973 issue of National Geographic. (Dewitt Jones)

The phrase hit me like a sledgehammer. All around me, every moment of my life, lies a banquet, a feast of wonder, whether it's my hands typing on this keyboard, the sun in its routine journey across the sky, water gushing from a faucet, the sound of wind in trees, or the fantastic world I can create simply by closing my eyes. Yet most of the time, I don't notice it. I don't bother to come to the banquet.

I recently remembered Dewitt's line. I had driven up to Skyline Boulevard early one morning to try to figure out, yet again, what I was doing with my life. Skyline, as it's usually called, is a little-traveled road that runs down the San Francisco peninsula, straddling the 2,000-foot ridge that separates the bay from the Pacific. I parked and walked up to the top of Windy Hill, a fine viewpoint. It was a wild and crisp April morning, achingly beautiful, and I imagined as I stood there that nature had laid on a banquet just for me: grass, clouds, wind, birds, rabbits, smells, my own breath, life, and I thought, "This is as good as it gets."

I even had this fantasy of a BBC-accented voice booming down from the clouds, "I say, you down there! Come in Evans! Your time is up!" And I'd look up and say, "Ma'am, what perfect timing. I'm ready to leave right now with no regrets and nothing but gratitude." It was one of those moments.

Later, as I drove back down the hill to Palo Alto, I knew exactly why I had felt so good up there: because, at that moment, I knew I had everything I really wanted. And I thought wistfully how much of my life is just the opposite, wanting what I haven't got, and not wanting what I have got. I remembered what Michel, an old buddy, used to ask me. Years ago, when I worked as a civil engineer, he'd sometimes drop by the office, stick his head round my door, and say, "Still struggling?" And if I was honest, I'd answer, "Yes, Michel, still struggling."

Down from the Hill

And I am, still, today. Not as painfully, not as often as I used to, but yes, when I'm honest, I'd have to say that at some level, I'm still struggling. Talking to friends, I find that they, too, are still struggling, in the sense I think Michel meant. That is, for many of us, there are precious few moments when we can honestly say, "This is as good as it gets."

Why is that so? I buy the Buddha's point of view, that the struggle centers around expectations. We're brought up on fairy tales that end "And they all lived happily ever after," and some of us are still waiting to get to the land of happyeverafters. Instead of appreciating what we have got, we're still waiting to get what we haven't: When I graduate . . . when I get a job . . . when I get a nice house . . . when I lose weight . . . when I find the perfect relationship . . . when I've got enough money . . . everything will be all right.

I love that last one. "When I've got so much money, everything will be all right and I'll be happy." Now, is it money I really want? I look at actual money and think, "Green paper." No, I don't think it's that. If it's not money, is it the things money will buy? No, I don't think it's that either; rather, I think it's the feelings I imagine I'll have when I've got the things money will buy. Not the things themselves, but the feelings: the intangible stuff like security, self-esteem, self-respect, and, mainly, freedom.

At about this point in this internal dialogue of mine, I start feeling pretty silly, because I know I can have all that stuff without the hassle of money. The truth is, money sometimes just gets in the way. As Kris wrote, and Janis sang, "Freedom's just another word for nothing left to lose."

Man with Many Keys

Years ago, I gave a guy from the Middle East a ride in my car at a time when I had about 20 keys on my key ring. I saw him looking at them, dangling from the ignition, and I asked him what he was thinking. He replied, "I was remembering an old Persian saying: Man with many keys, many worries; man with few keys, few worries." His words rang as true back then as now. Does money, or even the things money can buy, bring happiness? I don't think so. I do think the pursuit of it can get in the way.

So thinking about all this, trying to make some sense of it all, I made a list of moments when I've experienced a great deal of happiness recently:

- ◆ Standing up on Windy Hill early that morning, of course
- ◆ Listening—with all my being—to Sibelius's Fifth Symphony
- ◆ Falling asleep listening to the sound of heavy rain
- ◆ Getting into a hot bath after a hard cycle ride
- ◆ Noticing a small act of kindness at the library, a little girl holding the door open for an elderly man

I often do this, listing my happiness "triggers." Most of the items usually have one thing in common: they're free! They're there for the taking, just waiting to be noticed. The banquet is laid yet nobody comes. It seems to me that the banquet is always laid, waiting for us to come. There's no admission fee, nothing to do really other than show up and notice. That morning on Windy Hill, and during those other special moments, I did come and I did notice. And I wonder if all I really did was to stop struggling.

It's so ironic that I spend so much of my life in an often painful chase, struggling to get something I haven't got. And yet, as I remind myself time after time after time after time again, the banquet is already laid, waiting. All I have to do is show up and notice the wonder all around.

Appendixes

Appendix One

─────

Newton's Law of Universal Gravitation

*I*n showing that terrestrial gravity (an apple falling from a tree) and celestial gravity (the moon in orbit around the Earth), are the same, Isaac Newton showed that the force attributable to gravity, *F*, is given by

$$G\frac{m_1 m_2}{d^2}$$

where m_1 and m_2 are the masses of the two bodies being attracted (e.g., you and the Earth) and d is the distance between the centers of their masses (about 4,000 miles for you or the apple at the Earth's surface). G is Newton's "universal constant of gravitation," a number whose value depends only on the units being used.

To get a feel for why the force is inversely proportional to d^2, visualize the cone of light from a flashlight shining on a sheet of paper one foot away. Note the area of the cone of light as it falls on the paper. Move the paper two feet away. Now the cone of light has an area four times what it was when the paper was only a foot away. At three feet, the cone's area is nine times what it was. Since the same amount of light is available each time, we can say that the intensity of light falls off according to the square of the distance, that is, it follows the *inverse square law*.

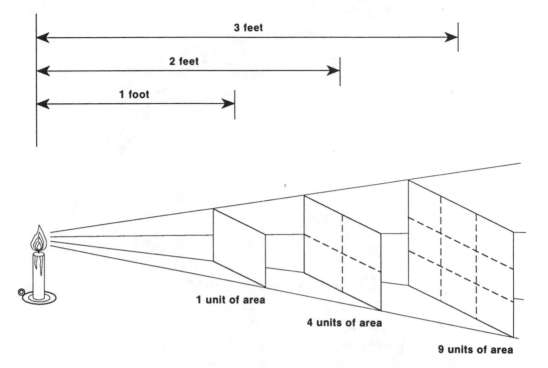

Demonstrating the inverse square law. Light from a candle falls off proportionally to the square of the distance. Does the force of gravity fall off similarly?

Newton, in trying to formulate a universal law of gravity, thought gravity might also follow an inverse square law. Was the force that caused an apple to fall to the ground the same as that keeping the moon in its orbit around the Earth? He reasoned thus: 4,000 miles from Earth's center, that is, at the surface, an apple falls about 16 feet in one second. The center of the moon is about 240,000 miles from Earth's center, 60 times farther than the apple. Now, he said, if the force of gravity falls off in the same way the intensity of light does, then Earth's force on the moon should be $\frac{1}{60^2}$ what it is on the apple, and thus the moon should fall $\frac{16}{60^2}$, or 0.0044 feet, in one second. Sure enough, that's exactly what's needed to keep the moon in its orbit around the Earth. He concluded that terrestrial gravity (force on the apple) and celestial gravity (force on the moon) were one and the same thing: gravity was a *universal* force.

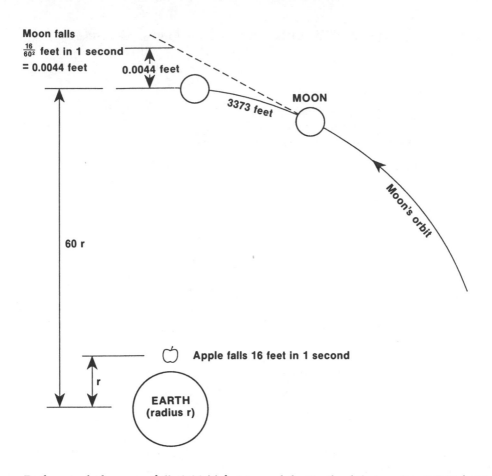

Moon falls
$\frac{16}{60^2}$ **feet in 1 second**
= 0.0044 feet

0.0044 feet

3373 feet

MOON

Moon's orbit

60 r

Apple falls 16 feet in 1 second

r

**EARTH
(radius r)**

Each second, the moon falls 0.0044 feet toward the Earth while traveling 3,373 feet in its orbit. This can be explained by assuming the Earth's gravitational force on the moon is $\frac{1}{60^2}$ what it is on an apple at the surface. Since the moon is 60 times farther from the center of the Earth than the apple, it seems that the inverse square law works for gravity as well as light.

Appendix Two

Time to Fall Through the Earth

The Easy Way

First, simplify matters by making some major (and wrong!) assumptions:

- Bodies fall anywhere within the Earth with the same acceleration they fall at the surface.
- The Earth is spherical and of uniform density.
- All travel is friction-free (including air resistance).
- The Earth isn't spinning.

According to Newton, the time a body takes to move while in uniform acceleration is

$$\sqrt{\frac{2 \times \text{distance}}{\text{acceleration}}} \; .$$

Therefore, the time to fall from the Earth's surface to the center is given by Newton as

$$\sqrt{\frac{2 \times 6{,}371{,}004\text{m}}{9.80665\text{ms}^{-2}}} \; ,$$

(substituting the Earth's mean radius and acceleration of gravity) = 1,140 seconds or 19 minutes. You'd take twice this time, 38 minutes, to reach the other side, since your deceleration from the center to the far side is symmetrical with your initial acceleration to the center.

Note that this is the time you'd take to fall from anywhere on the Earth to anywhere else in a straight line, because the effects of your reduced distance and reduced acceleration cancel each other out. That is, your travel time straight through the Earth from one point on the surface to another is always 38 minutes.

As it turns out, this isn't a bad approximation for travel from pole to pole in a vacuum (so that only the first assumption is badly wrong, we ignore the second, the vacuum takes care of the third, and the pole-to-pole axis route makes the fourth irrelevant). The following calculation makes allowance for the fact that the closer you get to the center, the less your acceleration, so the longer your trip will be.

Pole-to-Pole Travel: A Better Approximation

Wherever you are inside the Earth (falsely assuming it's perfectly spherical and homogenous), the gravitational attraction is the same as if the entire shell external to you had been stripped away. This beautiful simplification, as Newton realized, results from the fact that the mass of the external shell above you, pulling you away from the center, is exactly counteracted by the mass of the external shell below you, tugging you toward the center.

Assume you (mass m) are distance r from Earth's center. The mass of the Earth inside a sphere of radius r is $\rho(\frac{4\pi r^3}{3})$ (where $\rho =$ density), so, using the formula in Appendix 1, the force F on the particle at radius r is

$$F = G\frac{(4\pi\rho r^3)m}{3r^2} = (G\rho\frac{4\pi m}{3})r = kr \text{ where } k \text{ is a constant.}$$

Now $F = kr$ is the formula for simple harmonic motion.
The period of simple harmonic motion,

$$T = 2\pi\sqrt{\tfrac{m}{k}},$$

giving in this case

$$T = \pi\sqrt{\frac{3m}{G\rho 4\pi m}} = \tfrac{1}{2}\sqrt{\frac{3\pi}{\rho G}}$$

for half a complete to and fro swing

$$G = 6.67 \times 10^{-11} \text{ Nm}^2\text{kg}^{-2} \text{ and } \rho = 5.52 \times 10^3 \text{ kg/m}^3,$$

yielding $T = 2{,}529$ seconds $= 42$ minutes, 9 seconds. Thus it takes about 42 minutes to free-fall from pole to pole.

Period of an Orbital Satellite

Equating gravitational and "centrifugal"[1] forces:

$$\frac{mv^2}{R} = \frac{GMm}{R^2}, \text{ therefore, } v = \sqrt{\frac{GM}{R}}.$$

(Where m and v are the mass and velocity, respectively, of the satellite, M is the Earth's mass, R is the radius of the satellite's orbit, approximately equal to the Earth's radius in low orbit, and G is as before.)

The time for a satellite to go halfway around the Earth is

$$t = \frac{\frac{1}{2} \text{ Earth's circumference}}{v} = \frac{\pi R}{\sqrt{\frac{GM}{R}}} = \pi \sqrt{\frac{R^3}{GM}}$$

But $M = \frac{4}{3}\pi R^3 \rho$ so (substituting for M), $t = \sqrt{\frac{3\pi}{4G\rho}}$

With G and r as above,

$$t = \sqrt{\frac{3\pi}{4(6.67 \times 10^{-11})(5.52 \times 10^3)}} = 2{,}529 \text{ seconds, as before.}$$

Therefore, an orbital satellite takes the same time, about 42 minutes, to travel halfway around the Earth as it takes someone to fall from pole to pole.

---

1. Again, so-called centrifugal forces don't exist. The force of gravity on a satellite in a circular orbit around the Earth is just the force necessary to constantly change the satellite's forward motion into a curved path.

Appendix Three

───

The Irrationality of the Square Root of Two

Suppose that the square root of two is rational (i.e., the opposite of what we expect to prove), and that it's the ratio $\frac{p}{q}$, where p and q are whole numbers having no common factor.

If $\sqrt{2} = \frac{p}{q}$, it follows that $2 = \frac{p^2}{q^2}$, so $p^2 = 2q^2$, meaning that p^2 is an even number, so p is even (if p were odd, p^2 would also be odd, since odd times odd equals odd).

Therefore, p can then be written as $2r$, where r is an integer having half the value of p.

Substituting, we have $(2r)^2 = 2q^2$, or $4r^2 = 2q^2$, or $q^2 = 2r^2$.

So (reasoning as before) q is even.

If p and q are both even, they have a common factor (2).

But we previously defined p and q as having no common factor, so our original assumption that the square root of two can be expressed as the ratio $\frac{p}{q}$ (where p and q are whole numbers having no common factor) must be false.

Therefore, the square root of two is irrational.

Appendix Four

Area of a Circle and
Volume of a Sphere

Area of a Circle _____

We define pi, or π, as the ratio of a circle's circumference to its diameter. Since the diameter is twice the radius, we can write

$$\text{Circumference} = 2\pi r \text{ (where } r \text{ is the radius)}$$

One way (used by the Greeks, and probably by the Babylonians previously) to show that the area of a circle equals πr^2 follows:

(a) Take a circle, diameter d, circumference (by definition of π) πd. Cut the circle like a pie into eight equal slices.

(a)

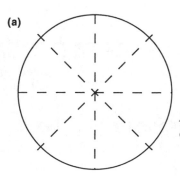

Demonstration that the area of a circle equals πr^2.

(b) Arrange them like this.

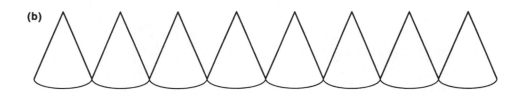

(c) Rearrange them like this. You've got an approximately rectangular shape, length $\frac{\pi d}{2}$, height $\frac{d}{2}$.

(d) Note that if you'd started off with 16 slices, your approximation would have been better.

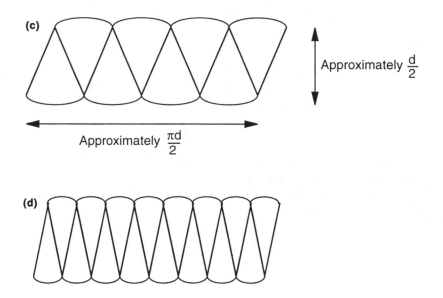

The leap of faith now is to assume that if the circle were cut into an *infinite* number of pieces, they could be rearranged into a perfect rectangle with an area of

$$\frac{\pi d}{2} \times \frac{d}{2}, \text{ i.e., } \frac{\pi d^2}{4} \text{ or } \pi r^2.$$

Volume of a Sphere

Archimedes showed that if a cone and hemisphere are exactly enclosed by a cylinder, then the sum of the volumes of the cone and hemisphere equals that of the cylinder. Knowing the volumes of the cone and cylinder, it was thus possible for him to calculate the volume of the hemisphere, and thus of the sphere. His proof is simple and beautiful, well worth following through:

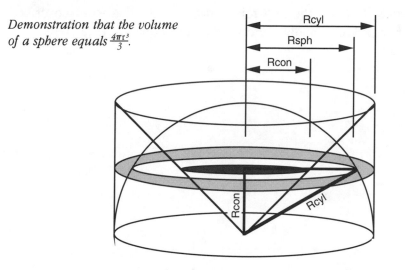

Demonstration that the volume of a sphere equals $\frac{4\pi r^3}{3}$.

Any plane parallel to the cylinder ends cuts through the cylinder, hemisphere, and cone. Let the radii of the three circles so formed be R_{cyl}, R_{sph}, and R_{con}. Note that in the right-angled triangle (heavy lines):

$$R_{cyl}{}^2 = R_{sph}{}^2 \times R_{con}{}^2$$

Since a circle's area is proportional to the square of its radius, for any such plane:

area of the cylinder's circle = area of hemisphere's circle
+ area of cone's circle

Archimedes, anticipating integral calculus by nearly 2,000 years, reasoned that the plane was equivalent to a thin (infinitely thin!) slice, so that:

volume of cylinder's slice = volume of hemisphere's slice
+ volume of cone's slice

By imagining the summation of an infinite number of infinitely thin slices, Archimedes concluded that

volume of cylinder = volume of hemisphere + volume of cone

That is, $\pi r^2 \cdot r$ = volume of hemisphere + $\frac{\pi r^2 \cdot r}{3}$

Hence the volume of a sphere = $\frac{4}{3}\pi r^3$.

From which it's apparent, as Archimedes was thrilled to discover, that the volumes of the cylinder, hemisphere, and cone are in a 3 to 2 to 1 ratio.

Puzzle Answers

Monday

1. Three. If you first pick one of each color, the third must match one of them.
2. The number 7 mated to its mirror image. If you cover up the left side of each symbol, you'll see the numbers 1 through 6. The left side is their mirror reflection.
3. *E*. The letters are the first letters of the words *one*, *two*, *three*, etc.
4. My son. (I am "my father's son.")
5. They're two of triplets.

Tuesday

1. See Figure 133.

(Barry Evans)

2. Part (1). No. The board consists of 32 black and 30 white squares. Since you cover up one black and white square with each domino, you'll end up with two black squares uncovered.

Part (2). No. Each move takes you to a square of a different color, so you have to end on a white square for an odd number (25) of moves. But there is one more black square than white on the board, so you'll be stuck with one black square uncovered, similar to Part (1).

3. Thirty-five. Did you find them all? (If you peeked at the hint, you might have guessed the correct answer, since the answer must be a multiple of five, given the five symmetry of the figure.)

4. See Figure 134.

(Barry Evans)

5. It will cost you three dollars. Have the jeweler cut all three links of one chain and use them to join the other three chains.

Wednesday

1. Here's how to make a hypercard:

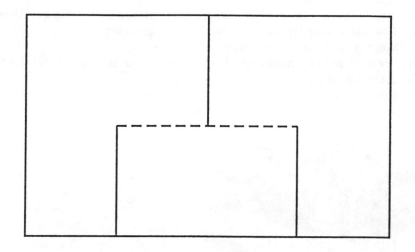

2. $\frac{4}{3}\pi$, a little over four cubic inches. The long way to the answer (without using calculus!) is to deduct the volume of the cylinder and two spherical caps from the volume of the sphere, after deducing that the radius of the cylinder is $\sqrt{(r^2 - 1)}$. All terms containing r cancel out, so the radius of the sphere is immaterial.

   The shortcut, as I said in the hint, is to trust it works for any size diameter hole, including one of zero diameter. In that case, the diameter of the sphere is two inches. The volume of such a sphere (radius one inch) is $\frac{4}{3}\pi(1)^3 = \frac{4}{3}\pi$.

3. No. The center cube will have to be cut on all six of its faces, no matter how you rearrange the rest of the block.

4. Ten inches. This is a "3-4-5" triangle. The other diameter is a radius of the circle.

5. So it doesn't fall down the manhole.

6. $9^{(9^9)}$. 9^9 is 387,420,489. That number to the ninth power is a 77 digit number. But 9 to the 387,420,489th power has about 300 million digits! That's a number 300 miles long, at the size of this text.

Thursday

1. The amount of wine in the water glass must equal the amount of water in the wine glass, since each is replacing the other.
2. One hundred twenty-four matches were played. Each match eliminates a player. After 124 players have lost, only 1 player remains unbeaten.
3. The chance is one in six. Dice don't have memories.
4. The lines meet at a 60-degree angle. If you draw the connecting line, you'll see you have an equilateral triangle.
5. See Figure 135.

Friday

1. Bahia Blanca, southwest of Buenos Aires, Argentina. Bahia Blanca and Beijing are antipodal to each other, so you can stop anywhere on the globe en route without incurring additional mileage.
2. Columbus placed the first egg in the dead center of the table. Wherever his opponent then placed an egg, Columbus placed one diagonally opposite it, so the pattern was symmetrical. So long as his opponent could place an egg, Columbus could do the same.
3. Accept two-to-three odds. Either the bag contains two white balls or one white and one black ball. In the first case, you might draw out either of the two white balls (for two possibilities). In the second case, you could draw out either a white or a black ball (for two possibilities). Since your friend has drawn a white ball, one possibility is eliminated. Out of the remaining three, two will leave you with a white ball in the bag.
4. She removed one pebble and immediately dropped it on the ground, where it was indistinguishable from the other pebbles on the beach. Since the remaining pebble in the bag was black, she could claim that she must have picked the white one. (In another version, beads are used, and she swallows one.)
5. The time and place that the monk and his brother monk meet on Monday is the spot that the first monk occupied at the same time and in the same place on Sunday. Alternatively, two lines, no matter how wiggly, have to intersect *somewhere* on a graph of time and distance.

Saturday

1. In.
2. Eleven, all except February. A 31-day month still contains 30 days.
3. ONE WORD.
4. "Swap horses!"
5. Misspelled.
6. QUIET, PUSH, EXIT, WET PAINT.
7. Underground.
8. Lincoln, upside down. Squint a bit!
9. One. Pick up the second glass and fill the fifth.
10. Rust or ruts.

Sunday

Anagrams: No hat, a smile; *OR* Not a "ha" smile. Nine thumps. No untidy clothes.
Word Puzzles: TYPEWRITER, BANANA, BOOKKEEPER
The Numbers Game: Three Coins in a Fountain, All for one, one for all, Tender Is the Night, Go forth and multiply, A Tale of Two Cities, Seven Deadly Sins, 1812 Overture, The Seventh Seal, The nineteenth hole, Everyday Wonders.

Chapter 16

What are the three misteaks in thi sentence? Two typos, obviously. The third mistake is that there are only two mistakes. But if there are only two, then there aren't three mistakes, so there *are* three . . . *ad infinitum.*

Chapter 18

Vase puzzle: 100 square inches. The three parts as shown can be rearranged to form a square 10 inches by 10 inches.

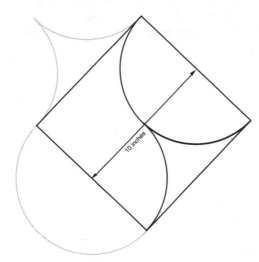

Chapter 21

Annuit Coeptis = "He (i.e., God) has favored our undertakings." William Barton, designer of the Great Seal, took this and *Novus Ordo Seclorum* ("a new order of the ages") from Virgil's *Eclogues.* Virgil (or Vergil), full name Publius Vergilius Maro (70–19 B.C.), was perhaps the greatest—and certainly the most sensitive—Latin poet.

Glossary

air resistance—drag caused by friction of a body interacting with molecules of air.

amino acid—organic compound containing at least one amino group and one carboxyl group. Just 20 (of over 80 naturally occurring) amino acids form "chains" from which proteins are formed.

antipode—point diametrically opposite another on a globe.

aphelion—point in its orbit at which a planet or comet is farthest from the sun.

asteroid—one of thousands of small (compared to planets) rocky objects in orbit around the sun. Also known as "minor planet."

astrology—the study of the supposed influence of celestial bodies on human affairs.

astronomy—the study of celestial bodies.

atom—traditionally, the smallest possible particle, literally, "that which can't be cut." The atom is now routinely "split" in particle accelerators. Most of the mass of an atom is concentrated in the central nucleus, comprised of protons and neutrons. Negatively charged electrons are perhaps infinitesimally small particles "in orbit" around the nucleus. (The quotation marks around "in orbit" refer to the quantum vagueness of their statistically defined positions.)

atomic nucleus—central part of an atom, consisting of protons and neutrons, in which nearly all the mass of an atom resides.

atomic number—number of protons in the nucleus of an atom.

bacteria—tiny, simple prokaryotic (i.e., containing an unconfined nucleus) microorganism.

Big Bang—originally a term of derision coined by "steady state" theorist Fred Hoyle (who didn't and still doesn't believe in it), the Big Bang cosmological model states that all matter and energy originated in an explosion (the "primordial fireball") some 15 billion years ago. It's been generally accepted by most cosmologists, who point to the many lines of evidence (e.g., the "background radiation" and the relative abundances of elements in the universe) that support it; however a significant minority of scientists, in particular astrophysicist Halton Arp, contest the basic assumptions of the model.

bilateral symmetry—property whereby an object can be divided down the middle into mirror-image right and left halves. Most animal bodies are bilaterally symmetrical.

billion—1,000,000,000. In scientific notation, 10^9.

biosphere—Earth's life-containing zone. It includes the lower part of the atmosphere, soil, and bodies of water.

Bode's law—arithmetical relationship concerning planetary distances from the sun. It works quite well for planets out to Uranus, if the asteroids are counted as one planet. It may be a fluke, or it may represent some hidden requirement in the formation of the solar system.

butterfly effect—corollary of chaos theory by which immeasurably small changes in initial conditions can cause major changes in the outcome, e.g., whether or not a butterfly flaps its wings in Tokyo could conceivably determine whether Florida is or isn't hit by a hurricane.

carbon—C, element with atomic number 6. It occurs naturally as diamond, graphite, and coal.

carbon dioxide—CO_2, compound whose molecules each consist of one carbon and two oxygen atoms. It normally occurs as a colorless, odorless gas.

centrifugal force—apparent force acting on a rotating body away from the center of rotation. It's really the inertial force of the body that "wants" to move in a straight line, i.e., tangential to its curved path.

CERN—particle accelerator, the European Center for Nuclear Research, located near Geneva. Its 19-mile-diameter ring straddles the French-Swiss border.

Cleopatra—last of the Ptolemy dynasty, daughter of Macedonian king Ptolemy Auletes of Egypt. She lived from about 70 to 30 B.C., becoming queen in 48 B.C. Shakespeare's portrayal of her suicide by snakebite is probably accurate.

cognate—linguistically, words having a common root.

comet—minor member of the solar system, a small body generally thought to resemble a dirty snowball. Most comets are thought to reside in the Oort Cloud, at great distances from the sun. Short-period comets are those that are in an elliptical orbit around the sun with a period of less than 150 years, e.g., Halley's Comet, which has a period of about 76 years.

compass—magnetized pivoted needle. When allowed to rotate in a horizontal plane, it aligns with the horizontal component of the Earth's lines of magnetic force.

compound—substance consisting of molecules of unlike atoms that cannot be separated by physical means.

core (Earth's)—spherical center of our planet, about 5,000 miles in diameter. The inner core is solid, while the outer core is liquid. The core consists primarily of nickel and iron. The temperature at the core may reach 7,000 degrees C.

Coriolis Force—tendency for a body not fixed to the surface to drift sideways due to Earth's rotation. In the Northern Hemisphere the drift is to the right, and vice versa.

crust (Earth's)—outer surface of the Earth on which we live. It's about 20 miles thick under the continents and about five miles thick under the oceans.

dinosaur—name given (by English anatomist Sir Richard Owen in 1841) to extinct reptiles of the orders Saurischia ("lizard-hipped") and Ornithischia ("bird-hipped"). The word *dinosaur* means "terrible lizard."

ecliptic—imaginary line on the celestial sphere along which the sun appears to move through the year.

electromagnetic force—one of the four fundamental natural forces, acting on all electrically charged particles.

electromagnetic radiation—flow of energy produced by the acceleration of charged bodies (e.g., electrons). Light is the most familiar form of electromagnetic radiation.

electron—elementary atomic particle possessing a negative charge, little or possibly no size, and a mass about one two-thousandth that of the other "basic" elementary particles, the proton and the neutron.

element—substance consisting of similar (i.e., with the same atomic number) atoms.

entropy—measure of disorder or randomness of a system; equivalent to measure of the amount of energy not available for work.

equator—imaginary circle around the Earth exactly halfway between the poles.

evolution—biological theory that holds that complex living things developed from simpler ones. The primary mechanism by which this occurs is termed natural selection.

Foucault pendulum—pendulum allowed to swing freely, thus demonstrating the rotation of the Earth beneath it.

free-fall—motion under the influence of gravity alone.

friction—surface resistance to movement in which energy of motion is converted into heat, sound, etc.

fundamental particle—indivisible "ultimate" particle. According to modern physics, there are just three "families" of fundamental particles in the universe, each family having four members, for a total of 12. Each has an oppositely charged antiparticle. Of those 12, only 3 fundamental particles are found in "ordinary matter." (These 12 particles are fermions. A second class of fundamental particles, bosons, "mediate" forces between fermions.)

galaxy—conglomeration of stars (and gas and dust) held together by mutual gravitational attraction. Our galaxy is known as the Milky Way.

gamma rays—very short-wavelength, high-energy electromagnetic energy.

gas—state of matter in which a substance readily expands to fill its containing vessel. Gas molecules do not interact with one another.

genome—entire genetic code of a living animal or plant. In humans, the code is carried by 23 pairs of chromosomes. It totals about 3 billion nucleotide base pairs.

gestation period—period from conception to birth.

globe—spherical object, e.g., the Earth; three-dimensional model of the Earth.

gravity—one of the four known forces in the universe, and the only one to have an appreciable effect over large distances. In Newtonian terms, any body is attracted to any other body by an invisible force proportional to the product of the masses of the two bodies divided by the square of their distance apart.

greenhouse effect—mechanism whereby atmosphere of a planet (or moon) can trap heat energy from the sun. An atmosphere containing, for example, carbon dioxide and water vapor, is transparent to visible light from the sun but partially opaque to resulting infrared radiation from the planet's surface.

helium—He, chemical element, atomic number 2, which occurs naturally in our environment as a colorless gas.

hydrogen—H, the lightest and most common element, atomic number 1, which occurs naturally in our environment as a colorless gas. In its most abundant form, an atom consists of a proton orbited by an electron.

hydrogen bond—relatively strong connection between hydrogen atoms and atoms belonging to other molecules.

infrared—electromagnetic radiation in the band between radio and visible light. Infrared radiation has a wavelength of between 1,000,000 and 800 nanometers.

inverse square law—natural law by which the effects of gravity and light, for example, diminish in accordance with the square of the distance from the source.

iron—Fe, metallic element, atomic number 26. Iron is the most stable of all elements.

isotopes—forms of an element having different numbers of neutrons in each nucleus. For instance, an atom of helium is defined as having two protons in its nucleus. In its most common form, helium-4, those two protons are joined by two neutrons in its nucleus. The nucleus of a less common form, helium-3, comprises one neutron and two protons. The chemical properties of isotopes are virtually identical.

Large Magellanic Cloud—one of two irregular "satellite" galaxies (the other is the Small Magellanic Cloud) near to our own, each about 100,000 light-years away. They are only visible from the Southern Hemisphere and were first noted by navigator Ferdinand Magellan in 1519.

latent heat of vaporization—energy required to convert a boiling liquid into gas.

latitude—angular distance of a point on the Earth's surface measured due north or south from the equator.

light—form of electromagnetic radiation. See *visible light*.

lines of magnetic force—imaginary lines whose tangent at any point give the direction of the magnetic field at that point.

liquid—state of matter intermediate between solid and gas in which a substance conforms to the shape of the confining vessel, has a free surface, and is relatively incompressible. Liquid molecules interact loosely with each other.

longitude—angular distance of a point on the Earth's surface measured due east or west from a line passing through the poles and Greenwich, England.

magnet—object, usually of iron or steel, which attracts iron or similar material.

magnetic field—natural force found in the vicinity of any magnetic body or varying electric current.

magnetite—a black oxide of iron, Fe_3O_4.

mammal—vertebrate, usually hairy, animal that feeds its young with milk from female mammary glands. Other than monotremes (which are born from eggs), mammals are born live.

mantle—vast layer of the Earth lying between the top of the core and underside of the crust.

mass—amount of matter in a body, roughly equivalent to the number of nucleons present.

meteor—streak of light resulting from a small interplanetary particle, usually the size of a grain of sand, which burns itself out in Earth's upper atmosphere.

micron—one millionth of a meter, that is, 10^{-6} meters.

Milky Way—(1) broad, pale swath of light, resolved into individual stars by binoculars or a telescope, visible on moonless nights from a dark location. This is our view of our own galaxy, seen edge-on to us. (2) Our galaxy, a conglomeration of between 100 and 400 billion stars held together by mutual gravitational attraction. Most hot, bright stars are found in spiral arms in the Milky Way's disk. "Globular clusters," consisting mainly of older stars, lie in a roughly spherical "halo" centered on the central nucleus. The Milky Way is about 100,000 light-years across. Our sun lies about 30,000 light-years from the nucleus, on the inner edge of one of the spiral arms. In addition to the visible portion, it's believed 90 percent (or even 99 percent) of our galaxy is not only invisible, but is composed of "dark matter" of (at present) unknown material.

moho—see *Mohorovicic discontinuity*.

Mohorovicic Discontinuity—interface between Earth's crust and mantle (after Andrija Mohorovicic, Yugoslavian geologist, 1857–1936).

molecule—smallest unit of a chemical compound, consisting of two or more atoms.

moon—body in orbit around a planet. Our moon is Earth's natural satellite, a body having about one-eightieth the mass, and one-quarter the diameter, of Earth. It orbits us at a distance of about one-quarter of a million miles, with the same hemisphere always facing Earth.

nanometer—one billionth of a meter, that is 10^{-9} meters.

natural selection—natural process in which those plant and animal species best adapted to a specific environment tend to survive and perpetuate themselves more efficiently than those less well adapted.

neutrino—fundamental particle with zero charge and a spin of $\frac{1}{2}$.

neutron—atomic particle found in atom's nucleus, approximately equal in mass to the proton. It has no charge.

neutron star—a massive star that has collapsed to such a degree that it consists essentially of neutrons.

nuclear fusion—atomic interaction in which nuclei, i.e., protons and neutrons, are forced together, creating new nuclei and releasing energy in the process. In a hydrogen bomb and the core of the sun, four nuclei of hydrogen are fused into one of helium.

oxygen—O, colorless, odorless element, atomic number 8, which comprises about 20 percent of Earth's atmosphere.

paleontologist—scientist who studies forms of ancient life using fossil evidence.

particle accelerator—machine (e.g., CERN, SLAC) in which electrons and/or protons are accelerated to speeds near that of light, then targeted into collisions with protons or nuclei. Debris from these collisions offer clues about the fundamental structure of matter.

perihelion—point in its orbit at which a planet or comet is closest to the sun.

periodic table of elements—table in which chemical elements are arranged according to their atomic number. Elements sharing the same column have similar properties.

photosynthesis—process in which plants convert carbon dioxide and water into carbohydrates and oxygen using sunlight for energy and chlorophyll as a catalyst.

physicist—scientist who studies physics, i.e., matter, energy, motion, and force.

planet—one of nine large (compared with the asteroids) bodies in orbit around the sun. In order from the sun, they are: Mercury, Venus, Earth, Mars, Jupiter, Saturn, Uranus, Neptune, and Pluto (Pluto periodically comes inside Neptune's orbit). Other stars are presumed to have planets, but none have so far been directly detected. The word *planet* comes from the ancient Greek for "wanderer."

plate tectonics—model of the Earth in which "plates" of brittle crust material move relative to each other. The plates literally float on mobile mantle material beneath, whose movement is driven by convection currents.

Platonic solid—see *regular polyhedron.*

Polaris—relatively bright star about 700 light-years away from us. Polaris lies about half a degree from true north, that is, from the Earth's axis extended from the South Pole to the North Pole and out into space.

Poles, North and South—northernmost and southernmost points on the Earth. The points at which the Earth's axis of rotation intersects with its surface.

polyhedron—solid figure having plane (flat) faces.

primate—order of mammals, including apes, monkeys, lemurs, and humans.

Principal of Equivalence—postulate that inertial forces and gravitational forces are one and the same.

proton—atomic particle found in an atom's nucleus. It is positively charged, with a mass approximately equal to that of the neutron and almost 2,000 times that of the electron.

quantum mechanics—application of quantum theory to the motions of particles. Quantum theory states, essentially, that (1) everything comes in discrete units and (2) any measurement affects what it is you're measuring.

radio—electromagnetic radiation having a long wavelength and therefore low energy.

radioactivity—radioactive decay, in which particles are emitted by certain unstable elements.

regular polyhedron—polyhedron having congruent (i.e., all the same) faces, each of which is a regular polygon. (A polygon is a straight-sided plane figure; a regular polygon has sides of equal length meeting at equal angles.) Also known as *Platonic Solid.*

reptile—cold-blooded, usually scaly, vertebrate animal.

seismograph—instrument that measures movement of the Earth's crust.

sidereal day—time it takes for the Earth to rotate once on its axis relative to the fixed stars, about 23 hours and 56 minutes.

SLAC—Stanford Linear Accelerator Center. Particle accelerator located 30 miles south of San Francisco, California.

solar day—average period of Earth's rotation relative to the sun, about 24 hours.

solar eclipse—celestial event when the (new) moon passes between the sun and Earth. If the moon is close enough and directly in line, the sun's disk is completely cut off from Earth's surface and a total eclipse results. If it's not in line, we see a partial eclipse. If it's in line, but too far from Earth, we experience an annular (ring) eclipse.

solar system—set of celestial bodies bound to (and including) the sun by gravitational attraction.

solid—state of matter in which a substance has a definite volume and shape. Solid molecules bind to each other.

sonar—detection by echolocation, in which sound waves are bounced off objects and the resultant echoes are analyzed. From *so*(und) *na*(vigation) *r*(anging).

specific heat—capacity of a material to retain heat.

star—massive gaseous body which generates energy through thermonuclear fusion. All that's needed is sufficient mass: a mass equivalent to about 80 Jupiters automatically creates a sufficiently high density, hence temperature, at a star's core for nuclear fusion to start.

sun—name we give to our star.

sundial—instrument for measuring time of day from the position of the sun's shadow cast by a gnomon.

supercool—to cool a liquid below its freezing point without it becoming solid.

supernova—violent "death" of a massive star in which gravitational forces overcome internal gas forces, resulting in the collapse and subsequent "bounce back" of stellar material. A supernova can temporarily outshine the entire galaxy of which it is a part.

surface tension—elastic force in the surface of a liquid.

tetrahedron—solid bounded by four plane (flat) faces; a triangular pyramid.

trillion—1,000,000,000,000. In scientific notation, 10^{12}.

ultraviolet—electromagnetic radiation in the band between visible light and x-rays. Ultraviolet radiation has a wavelength of between 800 and 91 nanometers (x-rays start at 12 nanometers: the gap between 91 and 12 nanometers is filled by XUV radiation).

universe—everything. Usually applied to the visible universe, that part of the entire universe about which we can possibly have any knowledge (light from beyond the visible universe will never reach us due to the universe's expansion).

visible light—electromagnetic radiation in the band between infrared and ultraviolet radiation. Visible light radiation "officially" has a wavelength of between 320 and 800 nanometers, but most of us see between 380 (red) and 750 (violet) nanometers.

water—colorless, odorless liquid, a compound consisting of two parts of hydrogen and one of oxygen, H_2O. It freezes and boils at 0 and 100 degrees C, respectively.

weight—force experienced by a body as a result of the gravitational attraction of another.

x-rays—high-energy electromagnetic waves with a wavelength between 12 and .0024 nanometers.

Z^0 boson—("zee-naught") mediator, or carrier, of one of the four fundamental forces, the electroweak nuclear force.

zodiac—imaginary band in the sky through which the sun, moon, and planets (other than Pluto) appear to move. It is centered on the ecliptic and extends about five degrees on each side.

Select Bibliography

(The asterisks indicate my personal favorites, for what it's worth!)

Introduction ⎯⎯⎯⎯⎯⎯⎯⎯⎯⎯⎯⎯⎯⎯⎯⎯⎯⎯

Carson, Rachel. *The Sense of Wonder*. New York, NY: Harper & Row, 1965.

Fowles, John. *The Collector*. New York, NY: Little, 1963.

Khayyam, Omar. *The Original Rubaiyat of Omar Khayyam*. Trans. Robert Graves and Omar Ali-Shah. Garden City, New York, NY: Doubleday, 1967.

*Zerubavel, Eviatar. *The Seven Day Circle: The History and Meaning of the Week*. New York, NY: Free Press, 1985.

Chapter 1 ⎯⎯⎯⎯⎯⎯⎯⎯⎯⎯⎯⎯⎯⎯⎯⎯⎯⎯⎯

Barrow, John D., and Frank J. Tipler. *The Anthropic Cosmological Principle*. New York, NY: Oxford University Press, 1986.

Evans, Barry. *The Wrong-Way Comet and Other Mysteries of Our Solar System*. Blue Ridge Summit, PA: Tab/McGraw-Hill, 1992.

Judson, Horace F. *The Eighth Day of Creation*. New York, NY: Simon & Schuster, 1979.

*Lee, Laurie. *As I Walked Out One Midsummer Morning*. New York, NY: Atheneum, 1969.

Chapter 2

Bakker, Robert T. *The Dinosaur Heresies: New Theories Unlocking the Mystery of the Dinosaurs and Their Extinction.* New York, NY: Morrow, 1985.

Colbert, Edwin H. *Dinosaurs, An Illustrated History.* Maplewood, NJ: Hammond, 1983.

Dixon, Dougal. *The New Dinosaurs: An Alternative Evolution.* Topsfield, MA: Salem House, 1988.

Lambert, David. *A Field Guide to Dinosaurs.* New York, NY: Avon Books, 1983.

Lampton, Christopher. *Mass Extinctions: One Theory of Why the Dinosaurs Vanished.* New York, NY: F. Watts, 1986.

Muller, Richard. *Nemesis: The Death Star.* New York, NY: Weidenfeld & Nicholson, 1988.

Raup, David M. *The Nemesis Affair: A Story of the Death of Dinosaurs and the Ways of Science.* New York, NY: Norton, 1986.

Simpson, George G. *Fossils and the History of Life.* New York, NY: Scientific American Books, 1983.

Stanley, Steven M. *Extinction.* New York, NY: Scientific American Library, 1987.

*Thomas, Lewis. *The Lives of a Cell: Notes of a Biology Watcher.* New York, NY: Viking Press, 1974.

Wilford, John N. *The Riddle of the Dinosaur.* New York, NY: Knopf, 1985.

Chapter 3

Keyes, Ken. *The Hundredth Monkey.* St. Mary, KY: Vision Books, 1981.

Chapter 4

Gould, Stephen J. *The Panda's Thumb: More Reflections in Natural History.* New York, NY: Norton, 1980.

Kurtén, Björn. *The Innocent Assassins: Biological Essays on Life in the Present and Distant Past.* New York, NY: Columbia University Press, 1991.

Thompson, D'Arcy. *On Growth and Form.* Cambridge, U.K.: Cambridge University Press, 1917.

Waterman, Talbot H. *Animal Navigation.* New York, NY: Scientific American Library, 1989.

Chapter 5

Lucretius Carus, Titus. *The Nature of Things.* New York, NY: Norton, 1977.

*Wheeler, John A. *A Journey into Gravity and Spacetime.* New York, NY: Scientific American Library, 1990.

Chapter 6

Wilford, John N. *The Mysterious History of Columbus: An Exploration of the Man, the Myth, the Legacy.* New York, NY: Knopf, 1991.

Chapter 7

Barth, Friedrich G. *Insects and Flowers: The Biology of a Partnership.* Princeton, NJ: Princeton University Press, 1985.

Cloudsley-Thompson, John, et al. *Nightwatch: The Natural World From Dusk to Dawn.* New York, NY: Facts on File, 1983.

Downer, John. *Supersense: Perception in the Animal World.* New York, NY: Holt, 1989.

The Guinness Book of Records. U.S. ed., New York, NY: Facts on File.

Gaskin, Ina May. *Spiritual Midwifery.* Summertown, TN: Book Publishing, 1975.

Klauber, Laurence M. *Rattlesnakes: Their Habits, Life Histories and Influence on Mankind.* Berkeley, CA: University of California Press, 1982.

Lorus, Johnson. *The Secret Life of Animals: Pioneering Discoveries in Animal Behavior.* New York, NY: E. P. Dutton, 1975.

Schmidt-Nielsen, Knut. *Animal Physiology: Adaptation and Environment.* New York, NY: Cambridge University Press, 1975.

Sinclair, Sandra. *How Animals See: Other Visions of Our World.* New York, NY: Facts on File Publications, 1985.

Chapter 8

Balsdon, John Percy and Vyvian Dacre. *Life and Leisure in Ancient Rome*. New York, NY: McGraw-Hill, 1969.

Bliss, Corinne D. *The Same River Twice*. New York, NY: Atheneum, 1982.

Irwin, Keith G. *The 365 Days*. New York, NY: Crowell, 1963.

Petronius, Arbiter. *The Satyricon of Petronius*. New York, NY: Limited Editions Club, 1964.

Smullyan, Raymond. *5000 B.C. and Other Philosophical Fantasies*. New York, NY: St. Martin's Press, 1983.

Zerubavel, Eviatar. *The Seven Day Circle: The History and Meaning of the Week*. New York, NY: Free Press, 1985.

Chapter 9

*Ferris, Timothy. *Coming of Age in the Milky Way*. New York, NY: Morrow, 1988.

Trefil, James S. *Meditations at 10,000 Feet: A Scientist in the Mountains*. New York, NY: Scribner, 1986.

Chapter 11

Atkins, Peter W. *The Second Law*. New York, NY: Scientific American Library, 1984.

Dyson, Freeman, J. *Infinite in All Directions: Gifford Lectures Given at Aberdeen, Scotland*. New York, NY: Harper & Row, 1988.

*Penrose, Roger. *The Emperor's New Mind: Concerning Computers, Minds, and the Laws of Physics*. New York, NY: Oxford University Press, 1989.

Chapter 12

Gardner, Martin. *More Mathematical Puzzles and Diversions*. London, U.K.: Penguin Books, 1966.

*Tolkien, J. R. R. *The Hobbit, or There and Back Again*. Boston, MA: Houghton Mifflin, 1984.

Chapter 13 _____

Calder, Nigel. *Einstein's Universe.* New York, NY: Viking Press, 1979.

Eco, Umberto. *Foucault's Pendulum.* San Diego, CA: Harcourt, Brace Jovanovich, 1989.

*Schwartz, Joseph. *Einstein for Beginners.* New York, NY: Pantheon Books, 1979.

*Schwinger, Julian S. *Einstein's Legacy: The Unity of Space and Time.* New York, NY: Scientific American Library, 1986.

Wheeler, John A. *A Journey into Gravity and Spacetime.* New York, NY: Scientific American Library, 1990.

Chapter 14 _____

Casti, John L. *Searching for Certainty: What Scientists Can Know About the Future.* New York, NY: Morrow, 1990.

*Sagan, Carl. *Cosmos.* New York, NY: Random House, 1980.

Chapter 15 _____

Corballis, Michael C. *The Lopsided Ape: The Evolution of the Generative Mind.* New York, NY: Oxford University Press, 1991.

Gardner, Martin. *The Ambidextrous Universe.* New York, NY: Penguin Books, 1970.

Chapter 16 _____

Gardner, Martin. *Order and Surprise.* Buffalo, NY: Prometheus Books, 1983.

*Hofstadter, Douglas R. *Gödel, Escher, Bach: An Eternal Golden Braid.* New York, NY: Basic Books, 1979.

Von Oech, Roger. *A Whack on the Side of the Head: How to Unlock Your Mind for Innovation.* Menlo Park, CA: Creative Think, 1983.

Chapter 17 _____

Pilar, Frank L. *Chemistry, the Universal Science.* Reading, MA: Addison-Wesley Pub. Co., 1979.

Chapter 18 ————————————————————————

Beckman, Petr. *A History of Pi.* Boulder, CO: Golem Press, 1971.

Davis, Philip J., and Reuben Hersh. *The Mathematical Experience.* Boston, MA: Birkhauser, 1981.

Dorrie, Heinrich. *100 Great Problems of Elementary Mathematics: Their History and Solution.* New York, NY: Dover Publications, 1965.

Gardner, Martin. *New Mathematical Diversions from Scientific American.* New York, NY: Simon and Schuster, 1966.

Gould, Stephen J. *The Flamingo's Smile: Reflections in Natural History.* New York, NY: Norton, 1985.

Hildebrandt, Stefan. *Mathematics and Optimal Form.* New York, NY: Scientific American Library, 1985.

Kasner, Edward, and James J. Newman. *Mathematics and the Imagination.* Redmond, WA: Microsoft, 1989.

Sagan, Carl. *Contact: A Novel.* New York, NY: Simon & Schuster, 1985.

Chapter 19 ————————————————————————

Bulfinch, Thomas. *Bulfinch's Mythology.* New York, NY: Modern Library, 1934.

Gardner, Martin. *The Magic Numbers of Dr. Matrix.* Buffalo, NY: Prometheus Books, 1985.

Gilgamesh: Translated from the Sin-leqi-unninni. John Gardner and John Maier, trans. New York, NY: Knopf, 1984.

Verne, Jules. *A Journey to the Centre of the Earth.* 1864.

Chapter 20 ————————————————————————

Benford, Gregory. *Timescape.* New York, NY: Simon & Schuster, 1980.

Coveney, Peter. *The Arrow of Time: A Voyage Through Science to Solve Time's Greatest Mystery.* New York, NY: Fawcett Columbine, 1991.

Cowan, Harrison J. *Time and Its Measurement: From the Stone Age to the Nuclear Age.* Cleveland, OH: World Publishing Co., 1958.

Fraser, Julius T. *The Genesis and Evolution of Time: A Critique of Interpretation in Physics.* Amherst, MA: University of Massachusetts Press, 1982.

*Fraser, Julius T. *Time, the Familiar Stranger*. Amherst, MA: University of Massachusetts Press, 1987.

Gould, Stephen J. *Time's Arrow, Time's Cycle: Myth and Metaphor in the Discovery of Geological Time*. Cambridge, MA: Harvard University Press, 1987.

Kurtén, Björn. *The Innocent Assassins: Biological Essays on Life in the Present and Distant Past*. New York, NY: Columbia University Press, 1991.

McMahon, Thomas A. *On Size and Life*. New York, NY: Scientific American Library, 1983.

Niven, Larry. *A World Out of Time*. New York, NY: Holt, Rinehart and Winston, 1976.

Pohl, Frederik. *Gateway*. New York, NY: St. Martin's Press, 1977.

Sandow, Stuart A. *Durations: The Encyclopedia of How Long Things Take*. New York, NY: Times Book, 1977.

*Whitrow, G. J. *The Nature of Time*. New York, NY: Holt, Rinehart and Winston, 1973.

Chapter 21

Banks, Edgar J. *The Seven Wonders of the Ancient World*. London, U.K.: G. P. Putnam, 1916.

Clayton, Peter, and Martin Price, eds. *The Seven Wonders of the Ancient World*. New York, NY: Dorset Press, 1989.

Foss, C. *Ephesus After Antiquity*. Cambridge, U.K.: Cambridge University Press, 1979.

Fraser, P. M. *Ptolemaic Alexandria*. Oxford, U.K.: Oxford University Press, 1972.

Koldeway, Robert. *The Excavations at Babylon*. Agnes S. Johns, trans. London, U.K.: Macmillan & Company, 1914.

Mendelssohn, K. *The Riddle of the Pyramids*. London, U.K.: Praeger, 1974.

Smith, A. H. *A Catalogue of Sculpture in the Department of Greek and Roman Antiquities in the British Museum*. London, U.K.: British Museum, 1900.

Conversations (and Letter) ─────────────────────

Ackerman, Diane. *The Moon by Whale Light and Other Adventures Among Bats, Penguins, Crocodilians, and Whales.* New York, NY: Random House, 1991.

*Ackerman, Diane. *A Natural History of the Senses.* New York, NY: Random House, 1990.

Crick, Francis. *Life Itself: Its Origin and Nature.* New York, NY: Simon & Schuster, 1981.

*Crick, Francis. *What Mad Pursuit: A Personal View of Scientific Discovery.* New York, NY: Basic Books, 1988.

*Gould, Stephen J. *Wonderful Life: The Burgess Shale and Nature of History.* New York, NY: W. W. Norton, 1989.

Judson, Horace F. *The Eighth Day of Creation.* New York, NY: Simon & Schuster, 1979.

*Morrison, Philip, *Powers of Ten: A Book About the Relative Size of Things in the Universe and the Effect of Adding Another Zero.* Redding, CN: Scientific American Library, 1982.

*Morrison, Philip. *The Ring of Truth: An Inquiry into How We Know What We Know.* New York, NY: Times Books, 1987.

Pauling, Linus. *How to Live Longer and Feel Better.* New York, NY: W. H. Freeman, 1986.

*Schwartz, Joseph. *The Creative Moment: How Science Made Itself Alien to Modern Culture.* New York, NY: HarperCollins Publishers, 1992.

Schwartz, Joseph. *Einstein for Beginners.* New York, NY: Pantheon Books, 1979.

Snow, Charles P. *The Two Cultures: And a Second Look.* Cambridge, U.K.: University Press, 1963.

Teller, Edward. *The Pursuit of Simplicity.* Malibu, CA: Pepperdine University Press, 1981.

Watson, James D. *The Double Helix: A Personal Account of the Discovery of the Structure of DNA.* New York, NY: Atheneum, 1968.

Puzzles

De Bono, Edward. *Lateral Thinking: Creativity Step by Step*. New York, NY: Harper & Row, 1970.

Gardner, Martin. *Aha! Gotcha: Paradoxes to Puzzle and Delight*. San Francisco, CA: W. H. Freeman, 1982.

Gardner, Martin. *Aha! Insight*. New York, NY: Scientific American Books, 1978.

Gardner, Martin. *Mathematical Carnival*. New York, NY: Knopf, 1975.

Scott, Kim. *Inversions: A Catalog of Calligraphic Cartwheels*. Peterborough, NH: Byte Publications, 1981.

*Smullyan, Raymond M. *What Is the Name of this Book?: The Riddle of Dracula and Other Logical Puzzles*. Englewood Cliffs, NJ: Prentice-Hall, 1978.

Von Oech, Roger. *A Kick in the Seat of the Pants: Using Your Explorer, Artist, Judge and Warrior to Be More Creative*. New York, NY: Harper & Row, 1986.

General Reading

Barrow, John D. *The World Within the World*. Oxford, U.K.: Clarendon Press, 1988.

*Bodanis, David. *The Secret House*. New York, NY: Simon & Schuster, 1986.

Casti, J. L. *Alternate Realities: Mathematical Models of Nature and Man*. New York, NY: Wiley, 1989.

Davies, P. C. W. *The Mind of God: The Scientific Basis for a Rational World*. New York, NY: Simon & Schuster, 1992.

Diagram Group. *Comparisons of Distance, Size, Area, Volume, Mass, Weight, Density, Energy, Temperature, Time, Speed, and Number Throughout the Universe*. New York, NY: St. Martin's Press, 1980.

*Hazen, Robert M., and James Trefil. *Science Matters: Achieving Scientific Literacy*. New York, NY: Doubleday, 1991.

Lederman, Leon M. *From Quarks to the Cosmos: Tools of Discovery.* New York, NY: Scientific American Library, 1989.

McAleer, Neil. *The Cosmic Mind-Boggling Book.* New York, NY: Warner Books, 1982.

Morris, Richard. *The Edges of Science: Crossing the Boundary from Physics to Metaphysics.* New York, NY: Prentice-Hall Press, 1990.

Paulos, John A. *Beyond Numeracy: Ruminations of a Numbers Man.* New York, NY: Alfred A. Knopf, 1991.

Paulos, John A. *Innumeracy: Mathematical Illiteracy and Its Consequences.* New York, NY: Hill and Wang, 1988.

Rogers, Eric M. *Physics for the Inquiring Mind.* Princeton, NJ: Princeton University Press, 1960.

Rothman, Tony. *Science à la Mode: Physical Fashions and Fictions.* Princeton, NJ: Princeton University Press, 1989.

Trefil, James S. *Reading the Mind of God: In Search of the Principal of Universality.* New York, NY: Scribner's, 1989.

The World Treasury of Physics, Astronomy, and Mathematics, Timothy Ferris, ed. Boston, MA: Little, Brown, 1991.

Index

*I*f you have any comments for the author, write him at 1001 Forest Avenue, Palo Alto, CA 94301. Fax: (415) 324-1206.